ORATORS OF THE AGE:

COMPRISING

PORTRAITS,

CRITICAL, BIOGRAPHICAL, AND DESCRIPTIVE.

BY G. H. FRANCIS, ESQ.,

EDITOR OF

"THE MAXIMS AND OPINIONS OF THE DUKE OF WELLINGTON."

NEW YORK:

HARPER & BROTHERS, PUBLISHERS,

1854.

ADVERTISEMENT.

The interest felt by every British subject in those public men whose conduct and personal character so much influence the affairs of this country, may be held to be a reason for the publication of the sketches contained in the following pages. The author is conscious that on no other plea can he hope to escape an obvious imputation of presumption, in that he should have arrogated to himself the function of pronouncing judgment on some of our most distinguished cotemporaries. He further urges, that he has striven, however unsuccessfully, to study his various subjects in the spirit of strict impartiality; and that his impressions are the result of constant observation and a long personal experience. Believing that public men are, in at least a large majority of cases, actuated by honorable motives and objects, he has rather sought to discover the good that is in them, than to dwell upon errors for which party is generally more responsible than the individual.

A considerable number of the following pages consists of reprints of articles that have already been published in Fraser's Magazine; but those parts which are not new have been subjected to careful revision. Many of the sketches have been rewritten or remodeled, and some of them have not appeared before.

LONDON, *December*, 1846.

CONTENTS.

ORATORS OF THE AGE.

SIR ROBERT PEEL.

Sir Robert Peel is, and for many years has been, the most prominent and influential politician in this country. In office, he has made his will the law of his fellow-countrymen; out of office, he has cast the shadow of his power on his rivals. In his social rank, not so advantageously placed as most of those with whom he has struggled in the course of his career, he had to contend against aristocratic prejudice on the one hand, and the want of popular sympathy on the other. He has conquered the former by constituting himself its organ and leader; he has, however late, secured the latter by his bold adoption of a popular policy. But in the mean while, though his position as a statesman has often been anomalous, he has always maintained a high, if not the highest, place in the favor of the House of Commons, notwithstanding that there are in that assembly speakers who far transcend him in the loftier attributes of oratory. It is worth while to inquire into the causes of this preference.

Eloquence, in this empire, is power. Give a man nerve, a presence, sway over language, and, above all, enthusiasm, or the skill to simulate it; start him in the public arena with these requisites; and ere many years, perhaps many months, have passed, you will either see him in high station, or in a fair way of rising to it. Party politics, social grievances, "humanity-mongering," and the like, are to him so many newly discovered worlds wherein he may, with the orator's sword—his tongue—carve out his fortune and his fame. Station—the prior possession, by rank or wealth, of the public ear—is, no doubt, a great advantage. It is much for a man to be asked as a favor to speak to a cause, for that his position and name will influence the people; or to have secured to him by his birth a seat in the senate: these things, doubtless, give one man a start before another in the race. But, without the gift of eloquence, all these special favors of Fortune are of no avail in securing you influence over your countrymen. Unless you have the art of clothing your ideas in clear and captivating diction, of identifying yourself with the feelings of your hearers, and uttering them in language more forcible, or terse, or brilliant, than they can themselves command; or unless you have the power—still more rare—of originating, —of commanding their intellects, their hearts,—of drawing them in your train by the irresistible magic of sympathy,—of making their thoughts your thoughts, or your thoughts theirs; unless you have stumbled on the shell that shall make you the possessor of this lyre, never hope to rule your fellow-men in these modern days. Write books rather; be a patient and admiring listener; make other men puppets if you can, and hold the strings; but rest content with a private station, and make it as influential as you may. Publicly and ostensibly powerful you never will be unless you have mastered the art of oratory.

We are so accustomed to the influence of this talking power in the state, that we have ceased to wonder at its successes. Yet the triumphs of the tongue have in our own days almost equaled those of the sword. England is generally accounted an aristocratic country, and her aristocracy have the credit (undeservedly, perhaps) of being peculiarly tenacious of their privileges,—jealous of the intrusion of adventurers into their ranks. The career of one man among our cotemporaries, however, has shown that eloquence has a potency as great as parchment pedigrees; that the owner of that talisman may storm the very strong-hold of the exclusives; appropriate their rank, titles, dignities, and turn their power against themselves; while, by the agency of their own legalized formularies, he sways the supreme, and rules even the rulers. Emerging from the comparative obscurity of a provincial capital, as an advocate he talks himself into the distinction of being talked about; thence he talks himself into the popular branch of the legislature; where again he talks to such purpose as to become the mouthpiece of the most exclusive section of an exclusive aristocracy: arrived at this point, he reappears on his old scene of action, and talks to the people with the new sanctions and powers which his parliamentary talking has obtained for him; he talks at meetings, he talks at dinners, he talks at mechanics' institutes; he talks to the men of the south, he talks to the men of the north; he talks to every one of every thing, till the whole land is filled with the echo of his voice—till, with all England, nay, with all the world, for his listeners, men wonder where next he will find an audience: when, lo! suddenly, incomprehensibly, as if by magical power, at a few more waggings of that ever-vibrating organ of his, the doors of the senate itself fly open, and peers of ancient lineage crowd down to welcome him to this sanctuary of noble blood, to usher him up even to the judgment-seat itself, to make him lord paramount over themselves and their proceedings, the licenser of their thoughts, and the originator of their laws! Could the greatest triumphs in arms achieve much more? The hero who has served and saved his country in the field secures a higher and more lasting fame, and a reward in the gratitude of his countrymen; but in all the external and ostensible marks of honor, such as constituted authorities can bestow, the heaped titles of the victorious warrior exceed the simple nobility of the successful orator only in degree; while the influence of the one culminates where that of the other declines—with the ascendency of peace.

But if we look to Lord Brougham as a great and glaring instance of the success that may be achieved by the aid of oratory—if we select him because he is, and has been throughout his active career, the type of the talking power, let us not, therefore, overlook the innumerable minor instances which go to prove the vast influence exercised over modern society by those who have acquired the habit of addressing with confidence and skill assembled numbers of their fellow-countrymen. The events of every day tend to increase their numbers and their influence. That the people are the source of all power has long been a maxim of a large and growing political sect. The domestic history of the last fifteen years goes far to elevate it to the dignity of an admitted truth. The "pressure from without" is now looked to as the ready solution of all political difficulties and dilemmas. Never, even in the days of the Commonwealth, were appeals to the popular will made so systematically as now; never was it more the fashion to look to the constituencies of the country, rather than to the legislature, for the agencies which are necessary to work out political changes. "The Agitator" was at one time a term of reproach applied to a particular individual: now, there are so many agitators that all opprobrium is removed from the epithet. Even those who coined it are themselves among the foremost in the race for popular favor; and no better means can be found to oppose the efforts of the popular or democratic party, than counter-appeals to the people by those who formerly scouted their interference. The highest and gravest in the land are not exempt from the same prevailing necessity. For every Plebeian Demagogue you will find a match in some Aristocratic Tribune; for every open conspiracy against the laws or the constitution, you will find an equally open combination in their favor. Anti-Corn Law Leagues, and Agricultural Protection Societies; Exeter Hall enthusiasts, and Crown and Anchor brawlers; holders of "monster meetings," and Protestant Operative Associations; ministerial speeches at anniversary dinners, and Chartist harangues to the dregs of the populace; each and all, though opposed as the poles in the principles they propound, and the objects they seek to attain, agree, with a marvelous unanimity, only paralleled by the instinct of self-preservation, in submitting their cause to the suffrage of the people, and in seeking to import into the discussions of the legislature an influence in their favor derived from public opinion out of doors. The whole empire is from time to time under the influence of public speakers. Look at Ireland. At any given time, one man, with a half-a-dozen or so of his satellites, can, within a week, so influence the willing and infatuated people, that they adopt his views and objects, and become imbued with his opinions, even although the solemn annunciation of to-day may be a contradiction of the declarations of years. Scotland has not yet recovered from a convulsion which shook society to its foundations, produced by the eloquence of a few determined men. And in England, the question which, during the last year or so, most agitated the public mind has been brought to a triumphant issue, solely through the indomitable energy of one man, —a man not bred to oratory, yet who has learned, from contact with the masses, the art of appealing to their passions, and making their prejudices subservient to the accomplishment of his darling projects. O'Connell, Candleish, Cobden,—each is powerful in his own sphere; each has worked, or is working, great changes for evil or for good. To what do they owe their power? To their eloquence.

It is, of course, needless to ascribe this influence of public speakers to the popular constitution of the country. Although the privilege of voting for members of parliament is, comparatively speaking, confined, the influence of public opinion on those who enjoy that privilege is illimitable. Although at any given public meeting there may be a very small minority of registered electors present, the excited feelings of the non-electors communicate themselves to the privileged few; and thus a public opinion is created and propagated. The deliberations of parliament, particularly in the lower house, are insensibly affected by similar causes. Although the then members may have been elected but a few months, and may reasonably look forward to a tenure of a few years, yet the fear of a dissolution, and a desire to stand well with future constituencies, will operate on them, so that the proceedings of a very numerous public meeting, even though composed for the most part of non-electors, may, by the enthusiasm communicated through the press, influence the opinions and votes of the legislators of the country. Again, of late years a practice has grown up of endeavoring to force great political changes, contrary to the avowed determination of the legislature, against even the fundamental laws of the constitution, by appeals from the privileged and representative bodies, not to the constituent body merely, but, beyond them, to the masses of the people, whether taking part in elections or not. This is a practice altogether different from the constitutional form of holding legally convened meetings for the purpose of petitioning. These popular assemblies do not profess to express the wishes or the opinions of the people, but their absolute will. Where they are successful, they invariably resort to the system of pledges from representatives, and end by degrading the House of Commons from the high position of a deliberative assembly to that of a mere monster deputation of delegates. The eloquent, enthusiastic, and impassioned opponents of slavery, blinded by the holiness of their cause to the evil effect of their courses, first introduced this baneful practice, which has since been perpetuated, for very different objects, by the Irish Catholic leaders, and by the Anti-Corn-Law League.

What a field, and what a temptation, does this state of things open to public speakers! The germs of great events, the first motive-springs of change have their origin, no doubt, in the closet, in the minds of men of deep thought and extensive observation, who are not, perhaps, actually engaged in the arena. But the people are the great lever by which the movement is carried out. Therefore, the people must be acted upon; therefore there must be orators to act upon the people, to imbue them with the ideas of the men of the closet. The same necessity which calls up the men has also taught them the art by which they act. The public mind is not always to be influenced by straightforward appeals to reason, or explanations of the desired object. Prejudices have to be worked upon, or, as the case may be, avoided. A very roundabout, or a very tortuous course must in many, unhappily in most cases, be resorted to. A plain, blunt enthusiast, or an honest thinker, above guile or reserve of his opinions, might sometimes mar the best laid scheme of a public meeting (ay, or even of a debate in the senate), by letting the real objects peep out too soon. Hence, to speak in public, it is not merely required that you shall know how to string words gracefully together, learn exordiums and perorations by rote, and practice inflections and intonations; you must also learn to feel the pulse of the public, to form a diagnosis of the popular fever, command your own enthusiasm or your own passion, in order the better to arouse those of your hearers. To a dispassionate observer, it is most amusing to see the arts and tricks that are resorted to for the attainment of these desired objects. Little do the deluded audiences of Exeter Hall, or the Corn Exchange, ay, or even the great House of Commons itself, suspect the sly manœuvers of a practiced speaker. The highest in rank and the greatest in talent are not exempt from the necessity of employing these arts. Like love, politics level all distinctions; and you may see the philanthropic peer, the ubiquitous ex-chancellor, the hireling lecturer on free-trade, the fiery Chartist, the clerical advocate of the wrongs of the poor, and the master of debate in the House of Commons, all employing the same arts, and stooping to the same artifices, according to the greater or less degree of pliability there is in the assembly they address.

The greater the art, the greater, too often, is the insincerity. Indeed, it would not be difficult, though it would be invidious, to point out a few glaring instances where the least honest men are the most successful speakers both in parliament and in public. The reason is obvious: careless about the truth, and thinking only of the immediate expediency or effect of what they utter, they are the more free to study the character of their audience, to pamper their appetite, season their intellectual food, and thus, by pandering and flattery, to gain the ascendency over them. On the other hand, it may fairly be urged, that insincerity in public speakers is almost a matter of necessity, as public opinion is now constituted. It may appear a hazardous assertion, but it is true, as applied to the great majority of distinguished public men, that they have two characters and two sets of opinions; one for the initiated, and another for the public. By the latter, affairs are supposed to be under the influence of moral agencies; the others know too well that the real power is of a much more material nature. Too often, while a minister is laying down principles, he is all the while counting votes, and how they are to be obtained. But put all sinister influence out of the question, and still the double face is too often resorted to. Public leaders are often in advance of those whom they lead, yet they dare not always let this be known. Too often they are compelled to enunciate, not their own real opinions, but the opinions which they know will find favor with those whom they address. They have one opinion for themselves, and another for their party.

The leaders of party in both Houses of Parliament are judged by the public according to a standard totally different from that by which they judge each other. In the one case, the measure of merit is political opinion; in the other, it is talent. If you go into private society, or among the people in the country, nothing is more common than to find my Lord This or Sir James That depreciated on the score of his being a Tory, Whig, Radical, or Chartist; or to hear him denounced as being politically ruined, because of some apostasy—some avowed or suspected change of party. Yet place these very detractors in the gallery of one of the Houses of Parliament, and they would see the object of their criticism ruling paramount over the one or the other assembly, listened to with deference and attention, and treated with respect, even by the persons supposed to be injured by their tergiversation. Without stopping to inquire into the morality of these apparent contradictions, they may be at once ascribed to a species of necessity. The parliament is an arena for the free discussion of principles.

The House of Commons has often been called a giant debating-club; and very often, at the time of great party struggles, it deserves that name. But ordinarily it takes a higher ground. It is not a mere battle-field for gladiatorial combats, the aim of which is personal distinction and public honor alone, but an assembly in which the opinions and interests of rival classes are set forth and judged by the master-spirits of the time, who are the real legislators, in order that they may be as far as possible equalized, and mutually satisfied, without too great several sacrifice. For this purpose it is necessary that those views and interests should be set forth clearly to either House; and the men who can do this the most effectually, pointedly, or truly, are those who become eminent. If they can superadd the charms of eloquence to its more essential requisites, their power is the greater; but the fact remains the same, that it is to the ability with which the individual expounds his opinions, not to the supposed honesty of his convictions, that respect is paid. If this be disputed, let the reader run over the names of the most distinguished orators now in parliament, and he will find that, with a few exceptions (and those the men of the less talent), they are all now engaged successfully in defending opinions which during their former lives they had attacked. The power of exposition, then, not the tendency of the opinions, is the standard of merit in our parliament.

To be a successful public speaker and to be a first-rate orator, are two very different things. The country swarms with the one class; the others might almost be counted on one's fingers. Of the former, some of the requisites and characteristics have already been pointed out; the latter stand in a far higher position, and require far higher powers. It has now become almost trite to remark on the decline of British eloquence. All readers of the cotemporary gossip of the latter part of the last century, and all who are old enough to have heard the great speakers who figured in the early part of the present, are ready to draw an unfavorable contrast between the parliamentary orators of our own day and their predecessors. It is true that, from the insufficient records we have of the speeches of the latter, we are not able ourselves to institute a comparison altogether satisfactory to the critical judgment. It is true, also, that we are somewhat at the mercy of the common desire of men to exalt the past,—of that senile querulousness which leads us to magnify the merits of dead actors, or the charms of those reigning beauties who were the toasts of our youth. But, on the other hand, the orators who shone so brilliantly during the last seventy or eighty years passed a severe ordeal of criticism; those who pronounced them great were themselves great men, and on other subjects we have always been content to bow to their opinions. Our records of the speeches of those distinguished statesmen and orators, although imperfect, are still sufficiently clear and copious to indicate their lofty tone of thought, and the pure, nervous language they used. They even justify, to a great extent, the high eulogium passed upon the speeches by those who heard them delivered.

In our own day there are no such obstacles in the way of a judgment. The wonderful progress recently made in the art of reporting has removed that difficulty. We now have the speeches of the first orators of the day with all the advantage which the taste and appreciation of highly educated men can superadd to mere literal and mechanical accuracy. There are the full means of forming an opinion. Still, the most biased admirer of the present must admit a deficiency of power and eloquence as compared with the past. Yet we are not deficient in men of first-rate talent—men of, perhaps, more general information and greater knowledge of the science of statesmanship, than even those idols of their country, the parliamentary orators of the Georgian era. Lyndhurst, Brougham, Peel, Stanley! they are men of first-rate ability. In what may be termed the mechanics of oratory, in all that part of the art of the speaker which does not directly depend upon the animating spirit, they are certainly not inferior to any of those great men. Mr. Macaulay, too, as a talking essayist, has produced effects which, for brilliancy and polish of language, will vie even with some of their master-pieces. It is in the *animus* that vivified the speeches of the elder orators—their concentration of soul—their indifference to all external modifying influences, to all but the full development of the spontaneous creations of their intellects, that modern speeches are deficient. What have been the causes of the decline of what, in a popular country, must ever be one of the most powerful agencies of change?

The speeches of the past had two sources of high and concentrated interest: the one arose where the speakers were engaged in direct personal contest. Prominent as they were before the world, their combat aroused a high dramatic interest. The other was when the subjects before the senate involved considerations so important as to compel the speakers to probe to the very first principles on which human society is based, and where their oracular effusions presented us with that noblest and most enlarged kind of virtue, Philosophy, animated by enthusiasm for the public welfare.

Again, the speeches of Chatham, Pitt, Fox, Sheridan, Grey, Plunket, and the earlier speeches of Brougham, were delivered to an assembly, the *élite* of whom were the choice spirits of the age. The greater part of the members of those parliaments were men to whom politics were a profession—with too many a trade. At that time, under the influence of the nomination system, the House of Commons was the high-road, if not the sole road to political power. A man could not then so readily ride into office on the shoulders of the multitude. To sway the House of Commons was then much more essential even than it is now. A great proportion of the members were undergoing their training for parliamentary speaking, to whom a rigid observation of those who were to form their models was a part of their duty as being a part of their political education. The majority of the remainder were men of education and long political experience, grown old in the habit of weighing the relative value of different speakers. Thus a critical tribunal of a severe character, not unassisted in the rigidity of its scrutiny by the mutual asperities of party, was established within the walls of parliament; and the constitution of the thinking, critical public of that day presented scarcely more than a reflex of it. Then, parties were dependent for their combinations upon men of a high genius for politics; now, those men of genius are obliged to shape their course in accordance with the movements of parties.

Many causes combine to lessen the interest of cotemporary speeches. In the first place, the strong excitement of personal contest on personal grounds is wanting to them. The decencies of debate, as regards indulgence in personality, are more observed in the modern House of Commons than in the old one. Measures are attacked, not men. If a man like Lord Stanley secedes from his old political associates, they do not make it a personal, but a political difference. No criminations or recriminations take place, beyond those which the difference of political opinions gives rise to and justifies. The House has become the property of the public ; and deference is paid to the public, by public men merging their private quarrels in the more important contests of the class interests which they represent. If, indeed, a man like Mr. O'Connell, for instance, contrives to unite in his own person the suffrages of his countrymen, he then becomes an object of attack because of his influence ; still, we have none of that direct personality which characterized the contests of old, but all is carried on under a thin veil of irony, or indirect allusion.

Another and a more influential cause of the altered tone of cotemporary eloquence is the altered character of the House of Commons. The extension of the elective principle, which dates from the Reform Bill, has much augmented the numbers and increased the importance of a class of members for whom orators half-a-century ago would have entertained the most profound contempt—the *bona fide* representatives of borough constituencies. Public men find it necessary to conciliate them; and a particular style of speaking has grown into favor in consequence. Parliamentary orators now find it necessary to do something more than merely display their own talents. The commercial calculating spirit of the *bourgeoisie*—though these borough members will very likely reject the term—jeers at fine speaking. It comes to transact business, not to be amused; for that it has the theater, or the last new novel. It has railway bills, local government bills, and free-trade dogmas to uphold or oppose; and its time is too precious to be wasted on prepared perorations or magnificent exordiums. It requires something practical; prefers figures of arithmetic to figures of rhetoric, and pounds, shillings, and pence, to poetry. Great questions it treats to a *cui bono?* It knows nothing about first principles, nor can it calculate remote consequences; but it can tell to a shilling how much it will lose or gain within a month by a proposed change. There is a shrewd common sense—the commonest sense, that of self-interest—about it, which makes the art of the orator a dangerous one, if he be bent on dazzling or astonishing. Insensibly the quality of cotemporary eloquence has become deteriorated in order to meet the taste of these influential men.

Again, this country, during the last twenty years, has been undergoing a revolution, silent, slow, and gradual, but still emphatically a revolution. It has been an age of compromises, and the greatest compromises of all are still in progress. To speak in the language of the popular philosophy, we are in a state of transition, a condition of things favorable to the development of the wisdom of the statesman or the philosopher, but not to the genius of the poet or the orator. Experience has shown that the more remote the prospect of change, the less an orator hopes for the immediate accomplishment of that for which he is striving, the more earnest and enthusiastic is his advocacy; the more fearless his declaration of principles; the more brilliant and fascinating the picture he draws of the good to be attained—a picture, the coarse and glaring elements of which are the more discovered, the more near it is brought to the mind's eye by the test of immediate practicability. Finer speeches are made on behalf of any given object fifty years before it is near accomplishment, than when the subject is worn threadbare, and the edge of enthusiasm dulled by the probable termination of the conflict. It was so with the Slavery question; it was so with Reform. The rule applies to the present hour. The legislature is working out in detail the changes which it was the object of the people to effect when they carried the Reform Bill. Great principles are almost entirely in abeyance. If they are referred to at all, it is chiefly to disavow them; for our public men are so surrounded by the men of figures and mechanical patchwork statesmanship, that they are compelled to affect a holy horror of all lofty political aspiration, lest they should be set down as theorists or philosophers, and so be ruined for life. Contests in either House are now no longer the inspiring scenes they were in the days of the elder orators; they are mere squabbles of detail, tooth-and-nail fights about degrees of concession. Occasionally, but rarely, a great theme will arise, and then it is we find that not the orators but the audience are in fault. It is cheering to see the avidity with which the chief men of the day will then rush to slake their thirst at the old fountains. The "practical" men look on in utter astonishment at their delirious joy in being thus able to indulge the daydreams of their youth, and fructify the study of their manhood. Perhaps their confidence is just beginning to shake, and they are looking out for some steady mediocrity in whom to put their political faith; when the inebriated sinners, having run the full riot of their intellectual debauch, catch a faint glimpse of the mischief they are doing, and rush hastily back to the old steady ways, which they know from experience are strewn with votes, to them more precious in their sober moments than all the flowers of poetry or eloquence. Their dogged, determined dullness after one of these escapades it is edifying to behold.

Such are some of the disadvantages under which cotemporary orators are struggling. It was necessary to state them briefly, because in estimating the merits and describing the peculiarities of the leading public speakers of this country, they will not so much be judged by comparison with any ideal standard of what the orator should be, as considered in reference to those modifying influences which so much impair their brilliancy.

When Sir Robert Peel made his emphatic declaration, on resigning the government in April, 1835, that his future life would be spent in the House of Commons, he was, perhaps unconsciously, establishing one of the landmarks by which the present age will be distinguished from its predecessors. His prophetic promise embodied the conviction of a statesman preëminent in the wisdom which studies the signs of the times, that hereafter the popular or representative branch of the legislature, regulated no doubt, to a great degree, by the will of the monarch and the theoretical right of veto of the peers, will be the really influential power in the state.

But Sir Robert, at the same time, exhibited no slight amount of self-knowledge. Looked at inferentially, that declaration showed that he had formed a correct estimate of his own position and powers. Sir Robert is an ambitious man, but his ambition is of a high and honorable character. He covets fame, and a page in the history of his country, more than personal rank or dignities. His ambition is not that which would be satisfied, though it has been flattered, by having two queens as his voluntary guests, with an earl's coronet glittering in the distance. Yet to one who, with a manly independence, points continually to the origin of his family, such distinctions might count as something. Sir Robert Peel's ambition grasps at what is emphatically *the* power of modern times, influence over the opinions of his fellow-men. He wishes to leave the impress of his own mind upon the character of his countrymen. He hopes to be regarded, if not as the pilot who weathered the storm, at least as having held the helm amid the eddies and whirlpools of exasperated rival interests. Represented as they are in the House of Commons, which is the scene of their action, he who would influence them must learn the art of commanding the ear and swaying the passions or prejudices of that assembly. Of that art Sir Robert Peel has obtained the mastery. Therefore he acts wisely, with the examples of Pulteney and Chatham before him, in not quitting a sphere where his triumphs are certain, and where the amount he may store up of good for his country, and fame for himself, is incalculable.

Sir Robert Peel is indeed the master-spirit of the House of Commons. Sheil or Macaulay may be more brilliant, may approach more nearly to the ideal standard of oratory; Lord John Russell may excel in delicate tact, in the skillful appointing of party allusions, or the unpedantic infusion among them of philosophical deductions; Lord Stanley may have brought the keenest intellectual powers more ably to the service of political passion; Mr. D'Israeli may have used the weapons of sarcasm and invective with more recklessness and effect: each of these may, in some separate quality, excel Sir Robert Peel; but no public speaker, be his eloquence, his tact, his logical power, or his moral energy or political earnestness, what it may, surpasses him in the one great art, the constant object of his efforts, of exercising influence over the House of Commons.

To gain this power he sacrifices much. Glimpses of a subdued enthusiasm, of an unsatisfied imagination, of ambitious aspirations, of enlarged views of the destiny of man, have been given, at intervals long distant, in his speeches, enough to show that, had he chosen to persevere in the more ornamental and flowery paths of oratory, his ascendency might have been of a different kind. But as it is, looking to his reported speeches only, while you admit their comprehensiveness, their verbal copiousness and accuracy, their information, their fertility of illustration, and the sustained self-possession which they indicate, you are still at a loss to account for his high reputation as an orator. That concentrated thought and vigorous expression, those passages of rhetoric prepared and inlaid, those sudden turns of humor, those quick flashes of imagination, upon which the fame of great orators, past and present, has been so mainly founded, you look for in vain in the speeches of Sir Robert Peel. In their place you have a steady, persevering pursuit of the object in view, a constant reproduction of the opinions it is desired to inculcate on the auditory, an adroitness in pressing their known prejudices into the service, and a general plasticity of sentiment and tone, which render it less surprising that one so indifferent to the charms of oratory should have at least secured its solid advantages. His object is not so much to be deemed a great orator as to preserve his character as a practical statesman. If the two are incompatible in the opinion of the great mass of commonplace minds, he gives up the attempt to attain the one reputation, in order to secure the other. He never, or at least very seldom, leaves the level of the average understanding of the House. He chooses his subjects from those which most occupy the minds of the mercantile and agricultural members. His illustrations are for the most part utilitarian. They point to positive certain advantages, or warn of equally certain mischiefs. He will sometimes remind you of the constitutional fiction that each member is the representative of the whole people, but he well knows the truth is otherwise—that, in fact, all the rival interests in the country are arrayed against each other in the House of Commons, and that they are now so nearly equal in power that preponderance of concession would be fatal to some, while it would unduly exalt others and make them too powerful. Hence the vagueness (except at some great and rare crisis) of Sir Robert's annunciations of policy, the empty pomposity of his declarations of principle, the verbose inconclusiveness of his whole speeches. How can a man even strive at high eloquence, whose political fate condemns him to play such a part? You can not get rid of the difficulty by a general charge of mediocrity. Used in this case, mediocrity is a term of comparison —disparagement. But where there is no aim at any thing higher—on the contrary, a studious avoidance—the term appears misapplied if it means an inherent mediocrity. To be equal to your position, in whatever sphere, is a sign of greatness of mind. To shape out your own means and accomplish your end with them entitles you to choose your own measure of praise. Sir Robert knows his men, and speaks to them in the language they understand. The Commons are to him a large jury, and he manages them in the spirit of an advocate.

This rejection of all objects save that of obtaining influence over the House of Commons has necessitated a constant sacrifice of consistency in opinion. Sir Robert has been the leader and mouthpiece of his party through singularly checkered and changing events. He led their opposition to Emancipation; he led a great portion of them in their support of that measure. He was again at the head of their reunited forces in the struggle against Reform; he was the expounder, if not the originator, of their conforming and conserving policy when the Reform-bill had become law. In the long and glorious campaign of the Conservative minority against Whig ascendency, who more eloquent or more apparently sincere in denouncing the policy of the administration than Sir Robert Peel? He comes into office with an overpowering majority, in which there is a large infusion of the mercantile interest, and his first act in power is to adopt those portions of the Whig measures which would rally the mercantile influence round him, without utterly compromising the avowed principles and interests of his own party. These are historical facts, but they would not be introduced in this sketch, which is not intended to be political, did they not distinctly bear upon the character of Sir Robert Peel's public speaking. His speeches when in opposition, and those made while he has been in power, differ in tone. The former are full of that ardor of assault which is natural in a man leading his party on to victory, and whose only duty is to destroy; the latter breathe a spirit of moderation, a determination to check and curb, which are equally natural in one who has to build up. All party men do the same. Sir Robert only does it with more power and art; with the addition, that it was he who set the example of defending this species of inconsistency on the plea of necessity. Studying his career, one might almost decide that he has been preparing the House of Commons for his ascendency. To keep his station as a leader of a party which, though shaken in 1829, and again in 1830, had within itself the elements of permanency, it was necessary that he should stand forth as the uncompromising advocate of their then opinions. When, as their leader, he seceded from some of those opinions, he strengthened his own position by transferring their faith from the opinion to the man. Having thus acquired power, having spread his fame far and wide for practical statesmanship, he turns round and says, Henceforth I will be free to propose my plans. You may support them or not, as you choose. Meanwhile, the same disorganization of party was, by the same causes, effected among his opponents, many of whom learned to adopt the cry, "Measures, not men," and, at the same time, to look for those measures to the man whom they had been used to denounce. When "HB." published his print of Sir Robert Peel, with pickax in hand, macadamizing his own road by breaking up parties into fragments, he hit out a great truth.

Sir Robert Peel's speeches are an index to his career, not merely in the opinions they convey, but in their quality and tone. In the whole of his early parliamentary life, indeed, up to within the last fifteen years, they took, chameleon-like, the hue that prevailed among his party. They were arguments, sometimes elaborate and founded on logical deduction (for Sir

Robert, with all his mystification, can be logical when he likes), sometimes temporary and founded on utilitarian considerations, sometimes the sudden growth of his dexterity in debate, but always arguments in support of a certain set of principles marked out, not by him, but for him. Yet, even in his most uncompromising harangues, if he could gain his object without directly pledging himself, he would. For instance, on Mr. Plunket's motion for a committee on the Roman Catholic claims, that gentleman had asked, "What has the State to do with religion?" Sir Robert undertook to answer the question. How did he do it? By an appeal to the highest principles for the recognition of the divine authority in the direction of human affairs? No; but he reminded Mr. Plunket that he had himself felt it necessary, in deference to the feelings of the people, to preface his motion by a proclamation of his attachment to the Church of England. "If," said he, "Mr. Plunket felt how important would such a declaration be, on account of the influence which religion has over the minds of the people of England, was not that reason enough why religion should not be left out of the question?" Thus the duty of the Church in the spiritual government of man was made to depend, first on Mr. Plunket's declaration, and secondly on the feelings of the people of England. Had those feelings been the other way, there was an end of the obligation. Such *ad captandum* arguments abound in the early speeches of Sir Robert; they are also to be found in his late ones. It is a common trick with him, and his supporters are so pleased at the temporary triumph it yields, that they overlook the lurking weakness of principle.

Now it was while engaged in this species of advocacy that Sir Robert Peel's style as a speaker was formed, and he has never wholly discarded the habits he then acquired. Without going the length of doubting the sincerity of Sir Robert Peel in his early character of Protestant champion, one may be permitted to estimate the degree of his fervor. We are not sitting in judgment on his political character, but inquiring into the causes of his style of oratory; and, of all eloquence which is not mere scholastic exercise, a degree of enthusiasm is a necessary condition. Now it is not easy to associate the idea of sincere earnestness with the speeches made by Sir Robert Peel in his character of advocate of the Conservative party, although they by no means encourage the suspicion of deliberate insincerity. It is not necessary that you should remind yourself, that when the future champion first entered parliament he refused to pledge himself to oppose Emancipation, or that he took up the cause when it afforded a ladder for ambition. No imputation of motives is necessary. The speeches rather suggest the picture of a man of cold temperament, who had, by some process or other, brought himself to the conviction that he ought to pursue a certain course, and whose ingenuity was at work to find good reasons for it, and arguments in its defense. They are like a elaborate address spoken from a brief. They are very ingenious, very convincing, very powerful: could only have been delivered by a man of first-rate talents, and who could command any subject he touched upon: but they are deficient in true eloquence. There is none of that lofty thought which follows a reliance on high principle. On the contrary, they eschew principles, and fight the battle on details. There is a want of "heart" in them. There are none of those sudden touches which stir the soul. They appeal to the thinking faculty, not to the moral nature or the passions. The language is correct, nay, faultless, without being powerful. The illustrations are apt and serviceable, but dry. There is a want of that warm coloring which an ardent spirit infuses into a favorable theme.

Sir Robert's speeches against the Reform-bill, though falling very far short of the high eloquence so imposing a theme might have inspired, were more concentrated and vigorous because there he was more in earnest. He had already made himself the most distinguished man in the old House of Commons. His ideas, his illustrations, were all associated with a state of things very different from that which was threatened while that great struggle was proceeding. It was, therefore, natural that he should view with real alarm the prospect of so utter a subversion of those established habits of thought on which his influence was founded. At that time all was fear or despair in the minds of the friends of constitutional government. Hope—the first prompting of that statesmanship which has since shaped out the art of ruling the new as formerly the old—had not yet dawned on the Conservative leader. He, therefore, spoke in earnest; and his speeches on the Reform-bill may be pointed to as being the best he ever made. In fact, he was there speaking for himself as well as for his party.

But his later speeches during the last two years of his leadership of opposition, when the victory was won but the leader delayed the triumph, and since he has assumed power almost on his own personal responsibility—these reflect all the defects ascribed to the earlier ones, but much increased: in consequence of the greater personal restraint imposing on him, and the more extended political insincerity required, as he seems to think, by a statesman whose position amid rival parties obliges him, in order to gain his objects, to be on good terms with all.

If posterity shall decide to rank Sir Robert Peel among great men, he will rather be classed among the statesmen than among the orators. He may be talked of with Walpole, but not with Pitt or Fox. Oratory is a severe and exacting art. Its object is not merely to excite the passions or sway the judgment, but also to produce models for the delight or admiration of mankind. It is a study which will not brook a divided attention. The orator speaks rarely, at long intervals, during which he saturates his mind with his subject, while casting it in the mold to which his taste guides him, as being the most calculated to enhance by its charm the intrinsic worth or beauty of his thoughts. Like the poet, he works either from love of his theme, or in the anticipation of triumph. But the exigencies of modern political warfare have called into being a class of public speakers, whose effusions fall as far short of those of the professed orator in permanent beauty as they excel them in immediate utility. As the character of the House of Commons, remodeled under the Reform-bill, has become more business-like, so the most popular and powerful speakers there are those who, rejecting the beautiful, apply themselves to the practical. Eloquence has become a positive element of power. A party leader is compelled to enter with almost equal energy into the most trifling as into the most important affairs. He must be always ready with facts, with arguments, with simulated enthusiasm; he must identify himself with all the interests of those whom he would lead. Even were there time for that preparation which a great orator needs, there is no scope for his display.

At the head of this class of public speakers—of those who either do not aim at, or fall short of acquiring, the divine art which, harmonizing language till it becomes a music, and shaping thought into a talisman, gives a man the right to be called an orator—stands forth conspicuously, Sir Robert Peel. We have already said that he sacrifices much possible fame as an orator, in order to secure substantial influence as a statesman. Some may be prepared to combat this; to say that Sir Robert Peel's inherent mediocrity is such that he could not, if he would, have rivaled even the most distinguished of living orators, much less the mighty dead. But it is difficult to suppose that a man of such high and such varied attainments, one in whom the scholastic fervor has survived amid the uncongenial pursuits of a stormy political life—one who, as for instance in his speech at Glasgow, and in some few of his speeches in parliament, or at public places, has breathed the purer atmosphere of poetry and philosophy; it is scarcely possible to believe that, had he early devoted himself to the study and imitation of the greatest models, to the perfection of style, to the discriminating choice of language, he could not have elevated himself as an orator to the highest rank. No; Sir Robert Peel's aim is different. His political weight depends on his power of charming or influencing the House of Commons. He has studied political opinion until even its minutest shades are made palpable to him. They are all more or less represented in the popular assembly, and there he displays his knowledge of all their wants, and avails himself, concealing his purpose, of all their rivalries and prejudices. Not one but finds, from time to time, an echo in the speeches of Sir Robert Peel. His caution, and, at the same time, his determination, are so well known, that the slightest hint he lets fall as to his purposes is instantly caught up. One cause of the breathless attention with which he is heard is, that each section of the House is anxious to penetrate the mystery of his future policy, knowing well that he will not utter any direct promise as a mere flourish, or unless he means to fulfill it. If he be oracular in his mystery, he is often equally so in his studied mystification. As no man can more clearly explain himself when he pleases, so no man can more adroitly wrap up his real meaning in an unintelligible involvement of words. Look at him while in power from 1841 to 1846, while still he was concealing his intentions with respect to the commercial policy of the country: Sometimes a sturdy Radical or an indignant Agriculturist determines to catch the eel by the tail and electrify him. He puts some plain, direct question, and demands an answer. You think Sir Robert must now be fairly posed; his veil must be rent; parties must soon resume their old habits; for he must say something positive on which a war-cry can be raised. He rises, leans forward on the table, playing with his glasses, or puts his hands under the tails of his blue frock-coat; and, in the most open and candid way, declares his determination to answer frankly the question that has been put to him. This is satisfactory, it propitiates. All are on the *qui vive*. There is hushed silence; all heads are stretched forward in expectation of the announcement of policy. Perhaps Lord John Russell and Lord Palmerston exchange a glance or smile of incredulity, for they know their man. Meanwhile the soft, bland voice has poured itself forth, its faintest tone heard in the most remote corner; the bearing bespeaks a full consciousness of the responsibility of the duty of the moment; the face wears the placid expression of innocence. You are fairly prepossessed for such a man. But what is he saying? By that cheer from Mr. Cobden and his Sancho, Mr. Bright, he appears to have said something pleasant to the manufacturers. But that roar of delight from the other side? Oh, he has convulsed the country gentlemen by some well timed compliment to agriculture, not as yet the object of his ridicule. And now another cheer, more general, is the reward of some pompous maxim of the public good. It is clear the House has warmed to him. The more kindly they entertain, the more candid grow the speaker's tones, the more earnest is he to do the best which the state of things allows. An elaborate statement follows of the different courses open to him, of their several advantages and disadvantages, in all of which he adroitly rouses the prejudices slumbering for the moment around him, and establishes a sympathy with each; centering hopes in himself, and setting old hatreds anew against each other: until, having thus led the various parties into a mental *mêlée*, he winds up with an "upon the whole," leading, with pompous affectation of resolve, to a declaration of what he means to do, which, in fact, comprises—in an artful woof of phrases, sounding but bodiless—almost every thing that he does not mean to do. Meanwhile he has skillfully diverted the attention of all from the real point at issue, to their mutual jealousies and asperities. Ten to one he sits down "amid loud cheers," having uttered much, but avowed nothing. It may be asked, How can such a body be so transparently cajoled? The answer is, It is done—done every day, in almost every speech; and the more it is done, the more they seem to like it.

This, however, is but one phase of Sir Robert Peel's parliamentary character. There are occasions—and they have multiplied during the last year or two—when he boldly throws aside all these arts of finesse, and assumes a much more lofty position. Patient, painstaking, a dissembler, even politically speaking a hypocrite, in order to obtain power, he no sooner felt the scepter firm in his grasp, than his mind seemed to expand; he grew in moral stature; he disdained to look back at the tortuous path by which he had ascended, but pressed with proud confidence forward. A magical change came over Sir Robert Peel from the hour that he finally resolved to make the attempt to obtain a pure majority of the House of Commons without the aid of the agricultural members: to be the minister, not of a party, but of the nation. Whether it was that the desperate nature of the game, and the magnitude of the stake (nothing less than the fealty of a party and the reputation of a life) inspired an unwonted magnanimity; or that, a long sought opportunity having arrived for throwing off a mask of hateful subservience, Sir Robert Peel now for the first time displayed his real character; assuredly there was in his speeches during the last two years, and especially the last six months of his official life, a tone to which his cotemporaries were wholly unaccustomed. With a sense of power, and a consciousness of self-sacrifice, he assumed the air, now of a dictator, now of a martyr. Defiance to the agriculturists, and threats to the legitimate opposition, were backed by a kind of covert appeal to the public out of doors. Occasional flashes of spirit, rare but emphatic and decisive instances of plain-speaking, induced a momentary doubt whether this man, so metamorphosed by a great peril and an unparalleled responsibility, could really be the same Sir Robert Peel whose name had long been a by-word for plausibility and slipperiness in statesmanship, whom you had so often seen shivering with ludicrous indecision, on the very brink of a positive declaration. But it is a singular fact, illustrating the real character of Sir Robert Peel, that at every great crisis of his public life,—on bringing in the Emancipation-bill, on assuming office in 1834, and finally, on introducing the measure for repeal of the Corn-law,—he has thus flung aside his disguise, and has spoken out plainly and boldly his real mind, regardless of personal consequences. This may have been magnanimity; it may have been moral hardihood: political passions will always usurp in such cases the decision of a calm judgment.

If Sir Robert has acquired, by long study and practice, the art of leading and molding to his will a body of several hundred intelligent men, he may be pardoned if the matter of his speeches be not first-rate. Excepting occasional passages of the kind just referred to, the character given already of his earlier speeches applies to his later ones. Neither the thoughts nor the language ever rise above the level of common sense. They are political manœuvers and purposes put into language, because a free constitution requires that the people shall at least seem to be parties to the policy of statesmen. The difference between Sir Robert Peel and other statesmen is, that he does not think in public, does not invite the public to think with him. He forms his plans out of the elements of thought he finds in the House of Commons, and trusts to each party liking the ingredient it has separately contributed to the hash.

A stranger to the House of Commons, who, having heard of Sir Robert Peel's influence there, had conceived some ideal portrait of a great orator, would assuredly be disappointed. He would observe in his speeches a want of strong reasoning on fixed principles, a lax, loose, many-sided mode of viewing the most vital questions, and a great command of that sort of logic which takes in common minds by clever fallacies. He would look in vain for vivid imagination, or profound thought. He would find no outline of a complete scheme of policy, nor any one ruling idea with which his own views and political sympathies could associate. The style he would pronounce inartificial; not that there is no attempt at construction, but that the speech is so crowded with extraneous matter, and so many ends have to be gained by it, that a perfect plan would be impossible. He would complain of verbosity; of repetition of ideas, nay, whole arguments, in different words, and then imperfectly expressed; of a pervading pretension to something very profound which constantly falls short of accomplishment. Of the action used by the speaker he would be tempted to say that it was neither modest as becomes an unassuming reasoner, nor imposing as ought to be the action of a great orator. He would see at one time a pompous solemnity leading to nothing; at another, the most trivial postures of everyday, after-dinner conversation ushering in the most important topics. He would notice with surprise the orator's elbow resting on the table before him, while his pointed finger shakes ominously at his opponents, and one leg is crossed over the other, the posture of a man laying down an argument to a familiar friend; or, his thumbs buried in the pockets of his capacious waistcoat, while his coat is thrown back ostentatiously, as some foreigners do to show their fine velvet linings; or, as is more commonly the case, his hands hidden under his coat-tails, while he stands much as he might with his back to a fire—these are not exactly the positions or gestures of a great orator.

But, on the other hand, whatever the defects of Sir Robert Peel, when his speeches or his actions are looked at critically, you can not fail to admire his ease and self-possession, the thorough knowledge he has, even to the minutest details, of every subject he undertakes; the adroitness with which he enters into all the different feelings, prejudices, and interests which surround him; and the art he evinces in wielding them so as to produce all the appearance of enthusiasm, and in molding them to his purpose of subduing their varieties to one harmonious course of action. In the art of managing the House of Commons he is, indeed, unrivaled.

LORD JOHN RUSSELL.

Lord John Russell, like his great rival, Sir Robert Peel, depends for his parliamentary influence upon his proficiency in the art of managing his audience. He does not aspire to, or at all events does not attain, those high flights of rhetoric, or declamation, or poetical embellishment, which, with the aid of other commanding qualities, go to form the characteristics of the professed orator. In these departments of the art of public speaking he is excelled by many of his own supporters,—by Mr. Macaulay, by Mr. Sheil, and even by Lord Palmerston; but there is no man on the Liberal side of the House who exercises so much general influence over the opinions or conduct of his party, no man on that side whose views on all questions are listened to with more respect and expectation by the House generally, than are those of Lord John Russell. In this kind of popularity he certainly ranks next to Sir Robert Peel.

The traits and characteristics of Lord John Russell are not so marked to a superficial observer as are those of Sir Robert Peel. The tenor of his political life has been more uniform, and he has not filled so large a space in the public eye. Yet when we look along the "Liberal" benches, and observe how many men of a high order of parliamentary talent are ranged there, it must be confessed that the man who, by general consent, has been elevated to the leadership of the party, must have, on some score or other, some very strong and decided claims on our attention.

Lord John Russell, in fact, is almost as great a proficient in the tactics of parliamentary management as Sir Robert Peel himself. He is the rival of that right honorable baronet in more senses than one. He is not merely his rival for place, and for popularity out of doors, but he also competes with him, and successfully, for the favor of the House of Commons as a speaker. The same, or nearly the same arts which secure to Sir Robert Peel his attentive and willing auditory, also work out the same results, although in a modified degree, for Lord John Russell. But the sphere of his influence is more confined. What Sir Robert Peel is to the whole House, Lord John Russell is to his party. Formed as it is of the most discordant elements, and difficult as it is for the representatives of interests and opinions so various to act in harmony; yet such is the skill with which the noble lord humors their foibles, adapts himself to their prejudices, selects their points of agreement as the ground of common coöperation, and echoes all their favorite views and opinions, that his persuasion and address induce them to acquiesce in courses of action the most contradictory, the most opposed to their avowed and pledged principles.

As the mover of the Reform-bill, Lord John Russell has secured for himself a page in history. Up to that period his parliamentary position may be traced to the historical career of his family. His selection by the Whig government of 1830 to introduce the bill, was a tribute to the party services of the house of Russell; but from the date of the passing of that measure, or at least from a time very shortly after it, his influence in the House of Commons grew to be personal. He was at first a sort of pet of the Whig party; and while the men who occupied the most prominent position in the Grey government were on the arena, he was, with almost the single exception of his being allowed to introduce the Reform-bill, kept in what was comparatively the background. Always a sincere politician, consistent as far as the necessities of his party would allow, he used at this time to occupy himself chiefly with echoing their constitutional maxims, seldom aspiring to the introduction of any political deductions of his own. There were certain political views which used to be designated as "Whig principles;" and, although these suffered a temporary disturbance by the violent agitation which heralded and accompanied the measure of Reform, still Lord John Russell was to be found, at all possible and convenient times, repeating those principles, and avowing, somewhat ostentatiously, that they formed the foundation of his political creed.

But when the great men of the Reform ministry passed from the scene, or were absorbed in the ranks of their opponents, Lord John Russell shot up into a leader. Whether he took the lead by mere rotation, or whether his party had discovered in him superior talents, the public did not know; but he had not long held the post of manager of the House of Commons—he being then the organ of government there—ere it became evident that under that smooth exterior of quiet imitation, for which he had been ranked as little more than an aristocratic puppet, there lay a steadfastness of character, a power of observation, a skill in debate, and, above all, an habitual tact, which qualified him to play a much more important part than he had hitherto done in the game of politics, and made it worth the while of men of all parties to study his peculiarities, and ascertain his principles. It was observable, too, that with power and its responsibilities came a consciousness of independence from those trammels which a state of comparative political pupilage had imposed. Called upon to act for himself, and held responsible to the country for his opinions, he less frequently spoke the established and hereditary views of his party, and more often those conclusions of his own which he had been for a long time forming, from a careful and extensive observation of the signs of the times and the wants of the people. His speeches still contained much of the old leaven; but there was infused into them a more independent, philosophic, and statesmanlike spirit.

We have already placed Lord John Russell second to Sir Robert Peel in the art of managing the House. He certainly must yield to him in that Protean spirit, that plasticity of temperament, which enables the right honorable baronet to enter at will into, and personate for the time being, the many opposite characters which he has filled during his long career. Although Lord John Russell has at times shown that he is cognizant of all the many shades of difference which mark the opinions of opposite sections of his party—although he, the aristocratic Whig, can sympathize for the hour with the Political Economist, the advocate of Extension of the Suffrage, the Free-trader, or the Dissenter, still the scale of his operations is not to be compared with the magnificent sphere occupied by Sir Robert Peel. Nothing short of what the late Charles Mathews used to call his monopolylogue will satisfy the latter: the former is content with playing all the parts in his own peculiar line; and now and then, perhaps on great occasions, one or two additional, provided always they are in the regular drama. But although Lord John Russell, either from being restrained by principle or from the want of skill, may not attempt those bold and gigantic delusions, those mesmeric practices on the credulity of the House of Commons, which characterize the public career of Sir Robert Peel, yet there are many points in respect of which he may, as a speaker, be regarded as superior to his rival. If he does not accomplish as much by his orations, they often exhibit higher qualities of mind, and produce the immediate result of pleasing the auditory with much less appearance of preparation and effort. Sir Robert gains his end by a tremendous expenditure of words, a sacrifice of straightforward argument, a transparent mystification, and a perpetual repetition of his views, which would be tedious even in a legal advocate. Lord John trusts rather to a simple, clear, and plain exposition of his meaning, unambitious, yet pregnant with thought. He steals in unpretending guise on the attention of his hearers, pursues his undeviating course without apparent effort, unfolds all his views without suspicion of preparation, while leaving no material point undisposed of; and then, suddenly, when such a thing is least expected, he strikes out some original and bold conception, something that rings at once on the intellectual ear as sterling gold ere even it is tested, that bears away the admiration even of those who are most prepared to contest the truth of the proposition it contains, while it charms the whole House into applause. One such accidental and apparently unpremeditated stroke raises him instantly far higher in the esteem of the House than all the labored, though successful, sophistries of an orator like Sir Robert Peel.

In fact, a little more care and attention to obvious rules, to the construction and arrangement of sentences, and the artificial alternation of brilliant with merely level speaking, would render Lord John Russell a finished, if not an elegant speaker. His language is in a high degree correct. His sentences are frequently so constructed as to possess both force and beauty; yet, from the careless adoption of loose, conventional, conversational forms of speech, they at first sight appear clumsy and feeble. A speaker who ushers in some fine philosophical maxim, some concentration of political thought, which is perhaps to become the watchword of party for the season, and to excite the serious criticism of observant men,—he who, having matter to utter of this high order, having already clothed the idea mentally in the most elegant, pointed, or antithetical form of words, introduces it with a "Well, then, I say, sir," hem—ing, and ha—ing, and hesitating, like a school-boy on examination-day, deserves his fate, while willfully provoking it, if careless and unobservant listeners, judging only from superficial inaccuracies of speech, and comparing them with the choice and elegant diction of a Macaulay or a Sheil, or the pure correctness of a Stanley, set him down as a clumsy and imperfect speaker,—one whom fortune, the chance of high birth, not original merit, has placed in his present exalted position. Yet so it is. Lord John Russell will give utterance to sentences worthy, both for the idea and the language, of being embalmed among the remarkable sayings of distinguished men; but he will preface them, and perhaps follow them up, with the common chit-chat verbiage of a gossip's tale.

There is a terseness, simplicity, and brevity, about his annunciations of opinion very similar to the characteristics of the style of the Duke of Wellington; and proceeding, *longo intervallo*, from the same decision of character. He seems to weigh well all he utters. He does not speak from impulse, or only on the suggestion of the moment, but rather seems as if he had a reserve of opinions, giving forth only those portions of his political doctrines which are for the time being suited to the views and interests of his party. He develops just as much as he thinks their wants require, and is seldom or never betrayed into an advance beyond the line of demarkation he has resolved on. It is as if he possessed an armory from which he furnishes just those weapons which from time to time he thinks necessary. He is an admirable debater, from his coolness, readiness, and phlegmatic self-possession. His historical knowledge is as great as that of Sir Robert Peel, and he equals him in his intimate acquaintance with all great constitutional precedents, and the established dicta of former party leaders. He has also a remarkably clear and ready view of the position of parties, both at the present time and formerly, and knows how to avail himself most ably of their many inconsistencies. He has a perfect recollection of the "points" of former debates, and the dilemmas into which the inconsistencies of his adversaries may have thrown them. These he often refers to most happily and unexpectedly, and with a kind of good-natured slyness of allusion wholly free from party animosity. There is not the slightest acrimony in his personal allusions. He is never ungenerous to an opponent. Delicate irony, or the clever juxtaposition of past with present professions, these are the limits of his personality. He is the gentleman even in the greatest heat of debate. His triumphs, won in this easy way by tact and intellectual keenness, unaided by passion, contrast favorably with the costly victories of debaters like Lord Stanley, Mr. Disraeli, or Mr. Roebuck. Yet Lord John Russell is not deficient in dignity or manliness when the occasion calls it forth. He has a great reserve of moral strength and energy. When the acknowledged organ in the House of a tottering ministry, his Radical followers used frequently to take advantage (or, rather, to try to do so) of the weakness of the government. At a time when a vote was a victory, a timid man would have been disposed to submit to this ungenerous treatment. Not so Lord John Russell. Under his quiet exterior of almost proud indifference lies an habitual determination of character. He knew that to seem weak was to become weak; he therefore always spoke out. A remarkable instance of this was the determined way in which he once put down Mr.

Wakley, when he thought to lay his heavy hand upon him. He was flung in an instant. This was when the former Whig government was on its last legs.

Lord John Russell advances his opinions with remarkable modesty of manner. For his standing and parliamentary influence, he is one of the most unassuming speakers in the House of Commons. Yet, withal, you perceive that what he advances he intends to adhere to. Although there is none of that arrogance and presumption of success which so often characterize the exordiums of established speakers, there is evident firmness and self-reliance. The modesty of manner arises from personal peculiarity, or perhaps from deference for the great constitutional character of the assembly; not from mental doubt or hesitation. Lord John Russell's mind is suggestive, not dogmatic. Yet, although he submits his conclusions respectfully to the House, he betrays no want of confidence in their soundness. His deference is personal, not intellectual. On the contrary, he grapples boldly with questions. Unlike Sir Robert Peel, he does not exhaust himself and the patience of the House with elaborate statements of the different courses which he "might" take, as though politics were a mere game of chance or calculation, but he takes his side at once, chooses his course, and stands by his choice. As he never takes extreme views, he is the better able to argue boldly on his avowed principles.

Occasionally, his diction rises into a lofty simplicity of style—a clear-seeing impartiality, showing his mind elevated above the excitements of the hour—which is almost too free from party spirit for the atmosphere of the House of Commons. You might almost suppose you were hearing history read. This does not always suit the vulgar and depraved appetite of some of his supporters, who require that their leader shall be more impregnated with their own political and sectarian animosities. Now and then you hear murmurs of rebellion in their ranks; out-of-doors they are most valiant in their refusal to be any longer led by such a *fainéant*, as they term him; but, when the time for action comes, they are glad enough to range themselves again under his banner. His coolness and tact, they have learned, are better guides than their prejudices or passions. Extreme opinions, they know, however well they may point a speech on the hustings, will not do for the legislature. Accordingly they always repent their insubordination. Their quiet, determined little leader holds himself aloof, till they come on bended knee to claim his forgiveness.

But when it suits Lord John Russell to descend into the arena of party, and adopt a more decided tone, he can do so with remarkable effect. The force of contrast makes his declarations of war more to be feared. As he seldom advances but when there is a chance of making an impression, the raising of his standard is apt to spread alarm among his antagonists. No man in the House is then more ready with a battle-cry. He concentrates and embodies the party hope of the hour with remarkable force of phrase and felicity of diction. Surprise is an element of success in eloquence as it is in humor. Without apparent effort, and while pursuing the unambitious tenor of his ordinary level speaking, on these occasions he suddenly and unexpectedly hits out some short, pithy, pointed sentence, containing, in few words, and readily remembered (sometimes depending for its attraction on the trick of alliteration, sometimes on the inherent force and simplicity of the proposition), the political dogma which finds favor with his party at the moment, or that principle which he intends shall be the object of their united efforts for some time to come. Standing out in bold relief from the monotonous commonplace, or the even simplicity of demonstration, which have formed the rest of the speech, they have all the air of apothegms or maxims, and are caught up and repeated by the noble lord's followers, and made the channels of their own thoughts. Stamped from his mint, they are taken for sterling gold; though, to say the truth, they are not always of the true metal.

He has a remarkably neat mode of turning a phrase. He sometimes, though rarely, sets his ideas in a frame of highly wrought diction. Almost any speech on a great topic will afford instances of this. His choice of language is often felicitous, and more effective from the concealment of effort. His speech on Sir Robert Peel's first free-trade budget, in which he spoke of the premier's plan as "disturbing, but failing to settle," affords some instances of this. Again, he is happy in impromptu,—a very rare quality in our modern parliament, where almost every speaker prepares himself. It may seem superfluous to remind the reader of Lord John's successful hit at Sir Francis Burdett. When that honorable baronet, after having been in the Whig ranks all his life, joined the Conservatives, disgusted at the attempted tampering with Church property, he alluded to some observations of Lord John Russell as being dictated by "the cant of patriotism." The noble lord, with great promptitude, replied, that if there was the "cant of patriotism," there was also such a thing as the "recant" of patriotism. This allusion to the turbulent early life of Sir Francis, although in itself but a trivial play on words, was powerfully effective, because so sudden and apt. A more delicate and pointed, and a less obvious retort would not have told so well in such a congregation of many grades of intelligence as the House of Commons. Again: no man excels Lord John Russell in the difficult art of talking philosophy, or assuming the didactic tone, in a popular assembly, without the appearance of pedantry. His mind is deeply imbued with the hereditary opinions of his party—in fact, he is a sort of model Whig, and although he is compelled by the exigencies of modern politics to take part in a species of agitation, he always seems to view the events of the hour with the eyes of his ancestors. Although the apostle of progress, he is always more disposed to look back than forward. The political child of popular agitation, he seems to be asham-ed of his parent. He would now rather have measures which he approves carried by the authority of the old maxims and principles of his forefathers than by mob will. He is an aristocrat of liberal views playing reluctantly the part of democracy; and his speeches present the medley of principles which such a position would induce.

Notwithstanding the many points of excellence in his speeches, Lord John Russell's personal exterior and style of speaking are most disappointing. Remembering the pleasure he has given you on paper and the prominent position he holds in the House of Commons, your first sensation on seeing and hearing him is one of disappointment. Can that little, quiet, fragile, modest, almost insignificant-looking man, so neat, plain, and formal in his black coat and snow-white neckcloth, who sits with his legs crossed "anyhow" and his hat overshadowing his small sharp features till they are scarcely seen,—can that be Lord John Russell? Is he really the leader of that compact and numerous party? And has he the power or the skill to rule and rein them in; to amalgamate all their discordant varieties; to tame their political violence, of which you have heard and seen so much; to pour the oil of his philosophic spirit on the troubled waters of their excited passions; to beguile them into suspending or giving up their cherished opinions and settled purposes, and cordially uniting in working out his views, and respecting, if not obeying, his will? When you regard the *physique* of Sir Robert Peel; his full, commanding figure, his intellectual face and head, his handsome, expressive countenance, his erect and manly bearing; you are half tempted to believe, on trust, all you have heard of his magical influence over the House of Commons: but no persuasion will induce you to think that the diminutive model of a man who has been pointed out to you as Lord John Russell—whom Lord Palmerston, his next neighbor, might almost dandle in his arms—can possess those qualities which history tells us are necessary in order to sway popular assemblies.

In a few moments he takes off his hat and rises from his seat; advancing to the table to speak. Now, for the first time, you see something that prepossesses. His head, though small, is finely shaped; it is a highly intellectual head, and the brow is wide and deep. The face, broad and firm-set, sphinx-like in shape, is not of faultless outline, but it is strongly marked with character. A thoughtful repose, slightly tinged with melancholy, pervades it. The features are sharply defined; they look more so in the extreme paleness of the complexion—a paleness, not of ill health, but of refined breeding. The mouth is wide, but finely shaped; surrounded with a marked line, as though it were often made the vehicle of expression, while the lips are firmly compressed, as from habitual thought. The eye is quick and intelligent, the nose straight and decided, the eyebrows dark and well arched, and the whole face, which seems smaller still than it is from the absence of whiskers, is surmounted by dark and scanty hair, which leaves disclosed the whole depth of an ample and intellectual forehead. A moment more, and you are struck with the proportions, though small, of his frame—his attitude erect, his chest expanded. You begin to perceive that a little man need not of necessity be insignificant. There is a presence upon him, a firm compactness of outline, a self-possessed manner, a consciousness of latent strength, that lead you to abandon your unfavorable view of his physical attributes, and to hope much from his moral and intellectual qualities.

He speaks, and for a time your disappointment returns. You have seen him make one step forward to the table, look all round the house, then make a step back again into his old place; then with the right arm stretched partly out, and his face half turned to his own supporters, he begins. His voice is feeble in quality, and monotonous. It is thin, and there is a twang upon it which smacks of aristocratic affectation; but it is distinct. He is, perhaps, about to answer some speech, or to attack some measure, of Sir Robert Peel. He goes on in level strain, uttering a few of the most obvious commonplaces of apology or of deprecation, till the idea of mediocrity grows irresistibly upon your mind. Yet the House seem to listen anxiously—they would not do so if they did not know their man. Wait a little. A cheer comes from around him; it bears in it the effeminate laugh of Mr. Ward, the deep bassoon note of Mr. Warburton, the shrill scream of Mr. Sheil, the loud hearty shout of Mr. Wakley, and the delighted chorus of the Radicals and manufacturers. Nay, even on the opposite side, the "point" has not been without its effect, as many a suppressed titter testifies. All the level commonplace, it seems, was but the stringing of the bow; at the moment when least expected, the cool, prepared marksman has shot his arrow of keen and polished sarcasm at Sir Robert Peel, whom it has fleshed, if not transfixed. You follow the speaker a little longer, now fairly interested in him, even though opposed to his opinions, and you find that he has more of those arrows in his quiver. And then he proceeds, during a speech of perhaps an hour and a half, developing those characteristics of his mind which we have described in detail; now earning approval by his enlarged and statesmanlike views, now lowering himself to the level of the various prejudices of his party; alternately compelling respect and admiration or provoking something like contempt; now rousing his own side to cheers against their opponents, and now stimulating those opponents to laugh at or suspect their own leaders; but always exhibiting power, self-possession, tact, skill, parliamentary and political knowledge, command of language, and felicity of diction, surpassed by but a few of the distinguished men of the day.

Meanwhile you have lost sight of the defects of the speaker—defects of voice, manner, and action, which place him as far below Sir Robert Peel, in the merely mechanical part of oratory, as his occasional elevation of thought and happy choice of language place him in these respects above him. If you had not been thus carried away, you would have been speedily wearied by the drawling monotony of voice, the hesitation in delivery, the constant catching up and repetition of words, and even of portions of sentences; and you would have noticed that the only action used was a constant stepping forward from the bench to the table and back again, an occasional thumping of the latter with the right hand, when not rested permanently on it, a folding of the arms akimbo, or an action peculiar to this orator when he rests his left elbow on his right hand, while the left arm, raised perpendicularly, is held up as if in warning at his opponents.

As a party leader, Lord John Russell inspires more confidence, and, if the term may be used, regard, than Sir Robert Peel. This follows naturally from his greater consistency. In submitting to his guidance, men know within some reasonable limit what they will be expected to do. Lord John Russell leads, Sir Robert Peel drives; Lord John Russell is liked, Sir Robert Peel feared. Between the former and the different sections of Liberals there is usually a pretty good understanding. He does not go far enough for the ultras, but as far as he goes they can go with him. He carries his party along with him in his measures—makes them sharers, as it were, in his councils. Sir Robert Peel prefers to rule alone; he matures his plans and calls on his followers to support them if they choose, or to refuse, he cares not which. Therefore they are usually on doubtful terms with each other. On the other hand, with the whole House collectively, the more commanding and decided character of the premier gives him a more extended influence. Sir Robert Peel has more admirers, Lord John Russell more personal followers.

In the struggle for power Lord John Russell has been but the pioneer of Sir Robert Peel. He prepared the public mind for the measures which his rival has passed. The one has borne all the odium of suggesting them, the other has secured the *éclat*, such as it is, of having carried them. Sir Robert Peel's character as a statesman can be judged of because he has held office, with power. What Lord John Russell would do can not be known, because, although he has held office, it has been without power. The former secured the start in the race. He could never before develop his real character, because in the struggle for power he was compelled to hide it. Lord John Russell was in a position to express his wishes and to hint at his policy, but the weakness of his government was such that he could not carry it out.

But, although Lord John Russell has been so far outwitted, he is increasing his influence in the House. It has been shown that he has some qualities which place him as a speaker, in some respects, above Sir Robert Peel. He has maintained his personal influence with his party, and his style of eloquence is eminently suited to them. It is impossible to say of what importance this personal following may be to him hereafter.

THE DUKE OF WELLINGTON.

"THE Duke of Wellington an orator! He who never uttered two consecutive sentences without hesitation; who exhibits a hardy contempt for all the graces of language and style; and in whom the faculty of imagination, if it ever existed in his mind, has been dormant for half-a-century! Do you mean seriously to class him as an orator?"

This would be a very natural question if it were admitted that oratory is a merely extrinsic and superficial art, aiming at skill in the choice of words and the shaping of sentences, and trusting for its hold on the human mind rather to the vehicle in which the thought is conveyed than to the truth or force of the thought itself. But there are degrees and classes of oratory as there are of poetry. The chief object of oratory is to persuade or convince, to bring the mind of the hearer into agreement and coöperation with that of the speaker; and this is often effected with success in proportion to the sincerity and straightforwardness brought to bear on the task. Some of the most effective and influential speakers have been men who never received any regular training to the art of elocution; and among these a place may be claimed for the Duke of Wellington.

Although it is now fifty-six years since the Duke of Wellington was returned as a representative to the Irish parliament, and although, after the Union, he continued, with the exception of some intervals of time, to be a member of the United parliament as representative of an English borough in the House of Commons, until he was raised to the Peerage; we should not forget that it is only within the last twenty or twenty-five years that he has taken so active a part in parliamentary life, or occupied so commanding a position as a politician in the state. In the earlier part of his career, he made no great figure as a speaker. When in the Irish parliament, he gave no promise of that intellectual distinction which he afterward achieved, but some of the most obvious characteristics of his public speaking were as observable then as they are now. There was the same abruptness of delivery, the same plain, straightforward, but unassuming expression of his views, that has since been the distinguishing feature of his speaking in the House of Lords. A contemporary observer speaks of his address as being unpolished, and says, that he showed no promise of his subsequent unparalleled celebrity. During the years that intervened between this period and his second entrance into political life—years which witnessed his successes in India, his steady progress of triumph in Spain, and the final glories of Waterloo, his mind was occupied with thoughts and pursuits far different from those which qualify a man to become an influential public speaker. And when, at length, the course of events forced him into a position of responsibility which compelled him repeatedly to speak in parliament, he had nothing to rely on but the strong natural resources of his mind, the noble candor and sincerity of his disposition, and the consideration which he might hope would be extended to his deficiencies as a speaker, on account of his brilliant services as a soldier. As the character of his mind developed itself, it presented an aspect of strange originality to the civilians around him. They could not at first understand, though they soon learned to appreciate, that admirable organization of mind, matured, if not produced, by the habits of military life; an organization so perfect as to retain all subjects of discussion, all principles of political science, all the facts with which his mind was stored, in that exact subordination which was their relative due; and so well maintained as to enable him to call them up and use them for his purpose, with a readiness to which even the most practiced minds around him were strangers, from their not having been subjected to the same discipline.

The architecture of the duke's system of political opinions was equally simple and equally perfect. As a Tory he built on the foundation of certain fundamental principles, which were to him the articles of a political creed; and the whole of the rest of the structure was in perfect proportion, the ornamental being everywhere secondary to the useful, and a rigid economy being observed of all unnecessary accessories of opinion. But, as if he were again constructing his redoubts or his fortresses, although the masonry of his political system was as solid as if it were intended to last forever, yet, at the word of command from his sovereign, or under the pressure of that iron necessity which a soldier, without fearing it, respects, this elaborate structure would be abandoned, deserted, and a new one commenced with equal earnestness in new fields of action and on a new foundation. The duke, as a statesman, fought bravely and steadfastly in defense of the principles it was his mission to uphold; but when the time came that the invaders could no longer be resisted, he surrendered manfully and without disgrace. He only abandoned one strong defense of the Constitution in order to take his stand behind another. As earnestly as he had fought against Emancipation, so did he renew the battle against Reform. But, true to his military habits, when the king asked him to form a government on the principle of moderate reform, he at once obeyed the word of command, saying, "If he had refused to assist his majesty because he had hitherto been opposed to reform, he could not have shown his face in the streets for shame of having deserted his sovereign in circumstances so painful and alarming." In like manner, in November, 1834, although he declined to become premier, he so far braved popular opprobrium as to undertake, until the arrival of Sir Robert Peel, the four highest civil offices in the state; and in the last great crisis, that of Corn-law Repeal, he equally exhibited this distinguishing trait of his public life, by fighting the battle of the Corn-laws up to the latest moment that his party continued resolute to maintain them, as though utterly ignorant that any great movement for the repeal was being agitated in the Cabinet.

The Duke of Wellington's mind is so constituted as to render it impossible for him to make use of those arts by which public speakers usually seek to influence their audiences. In this sense of the term, he could not be an orator if he would. He has no idea of separating his subject from himself, of looking at it in its external bearings without reference to his own views. He can not, as Lord Brougham or Lord Lyndhurst would, view it as a theme for the exercise of his intellectual ingenuity. He has no idea of design or of coloring; does not look at it with the eye of an artist, studying what will best conduce to a grand effect, or where the light and shade are to be thrown in. He never thinks of preparing exordiums or perorations, or of attenuating parts of his discourse that the strong points may seem stronger. He never plays with a question. Politics are with him a serious reality, not a mere game. Nor are they a passion, as with men of warmer temperament; they are rather part of a grave duty, to be dealt with, not from choice, but because his position in the country requires that he should be mixed up with them. He never speaks for the sake of display, apparently having no vanity of that sort. Whenever he rises to address the House, it is because necessity compels him—because the debate would be incomplete until the most distinguished man of his time had delivered his sentiments.

Being thus obliged to speak, he says no more than the occasion absolutely requires. He gives utterance to the real sentiments of his mind, the unbiased conclusions suggested by a cool head and an almost unparalleled experience. You can see at once that this is done without effort, and, above all, without any desire for effect. It is a labor of duty, not of love. It is not sought by him, yet he is ready when called on. Having said his say, he seems relieved of an unpleasant load, and sits down abruptly as he rose, indifferent whether what he has delivered has pleased or displeased his audience. These, it is quite unnecessary to say, are not the characteristics of professed orators. Yet the duke will produce, on the floor of the House of Lords, as startling and, perchance, a more permanent effect, than the most ingenious and eloquent of them all.

The agencies by which his influence works on the legislature and the public are of a far higher order. Look at the moral weight he brings with him. With a reputation already historical, what man of the day, be he even the greatest, can command the respect which his mere presence inspires? It may seem a trifle, but it is one pregnant with deep meaning, that the only individual in this country, except the members of the royal family, to whom all men, the highest and the lowest, uncover themselves on the public highway, is the Duke of Wellington. If the vulgar, the indifferent, the triflers, the ignorant, pay this homage to him where no homage is due to any man, shall not the same sentiment prevail within the walls of the House of Lords, among those whose privileges and social preëminence rest upon hereditary gratitude?

The Duke of Wellington in his place in the House of Lords, stands apart from and above all the other peers. There may be men of more ancient lineage, there are certainly men of more commanding and brilliant talents of the sort that captivate an assembly, whether composed of the high or the low: but he transcends them all in the possession of that power which is created by a voluntary intellectual submission. Plain, unpretending, venerable, as he is, he seems encircled by an atmosphere of glory. All physical defects, all the infirmities of age, are lost in the light of his great fame. He seems already to belong to the past, and to speak with its authority. Often oracular in his denunciations and in his decisions, strange to say, those who hear him seem to believe that he is so.

And it is not among pigmies that he is thus morally a giant. The deference and respect paid to the Duke of Wellington in the House of Lords come from men of the highest order of minds. Neither political differences nor personal vanities interpose any obstacle to its free expression. Powerful and successful orators and statesmen, aristocratic demagogues, grave lawyers and erratic lawgivers, whatever may be their mutual jealousies or their customary arrogance, all yield at once to his moral supremacy. The man of the present day who stands next to him in the extent, if not the quality of his fame, he who is distinguished among his cotemporaries not more for his parliamentary and political successes than for his mental and moral insubordination—he, too, ostentatiously proclaims himself the devoted admirer and follower of the Duke of Wellington. The homage is too universal not to be sincere.

It is this moral weight or influence that gives to the public speaking of the Duke of Wellington its chief characteristics. He can speak with an authority which no other man would dare to assume, and which, if assumed by any other man, would not be submitted to. For the same reason he can dispense with all the explanation and apology which so often render the speeches of other men ridiculous. He has no need of a hypocritical humility or an affected desire of abstinence from that great necessity of politicians—speech-making. He knows both that he is expected to speak and that what he has to say will be held to be of value. He knows that no decision will be come to till he has been heard, and that the chances are in favor of his opinion prevailing even with those opposed to him, unless the current of political feeling should happen at the time to run very strongly indeed. These incumbrances of ordinary speakers being cast aside, the duke can afford to run at once full tilt at the real question in dispute. To see him stripping the subject of all extraneous and unnecessary adjuncts, until he exposes it to his hearers in its real and natural proportions, is a very rich treat. He scents a fallacy afar off, and hunts it down at once without mercy. He has certain constitutional principles which with him are real standards. He measures propositions or opinions by these standards, and as they come up to the mark or fall short of it, so are they accepted or disposed of. Sometimes, but rarely, he carries this inflexible system too far, and has afterward to retract; but it is remarkable for a man who has wielded such authority, who has been accustomed to implicit deference for so many years, and whose mental organization is so stern and steadfast, how few prejudices he has. Even these will always yield to necessity, often to reason. If he be sometimes dogmatical, the fault is less his than of those who lead him into this natural error, when their respect deters them from even reminding him that he is fallible.

Self-reliance and singleness of purpose induce in him vigor of thought and simplicity of diction. This simplicity, which is not confined to the language only, but extends to the operation of the mind, is unique. You meet nothing like it in any other man now prominently before the public. There is a rigorous economy of both thoughts and words. As a speaker and as a general, the duke equally disincumbers himself of unnecessary agents. He is as little fond of rhetorical flourishes or declamatory arts as he was of useless troops. Every word does its work. Simple, sound, sterling Saxon he seems to choose by instinct, as hitting hardest with least show. Sometimes this self-reliance and simplicity degenerate into an abruptness almost rude. Then the simplicity would almost appear affected, but that the duke is wholly incapable of that culpable weakness. Those curt notes of his to people whom he conceives to be in any way intrusive, or who say or do what does not square with his rigid notions of etiquet, are often more amusing than dignified. Still they are strictly characteristic, and are only eccentric evidences of that spirit which makes the duke in his parliamentary career mark out a course for himself, and, having once persuaded himself that it is right, adhere to it with almost obstinate perseverance.

In attributing to the duke this simplicity of thought and language, it is not intended to imply any narrowness or feebleness of intellect. A plainness and simplicity there is, in dress, in manners, in style of thought, in expression, which might warrant a superficial observer, knowing nothing (if that be possible) of the life and services of the man, in such an assumption. He would be apt to set the duke down as a well meaning, prejudiced, honest, dogmatical, and very impracticable old man, whom you would treat with respect on account of his years, but whom you would on no account allow to meddle in your affairs. But all this is external only. The readers of the duke's dispatches need not be told this. They exhibit proofs of a highly toned and admirably regulated mind. High honor, inflexibility, sagacity, instinctive knowledge of human nature even at an early age, a capacity for the grandest designs and most enlarged views, combined with a readiness for the most minute of military affairs,—these are to be found in every page of those extraordinary productions.

Similar qualities have developed themselves in the duke's political career. He clings to the great principles of the constitution with a tenacity which has the best effect on cotemporary statesmen. His sagacity is the result of a most enlarged experience. With all his apparent simplicity and rigidity, no man more thoroughly keeps pace with his age than the Duke of Wellington. He unites great shrewdness of perception and readiness of observation with a disposition steadfastly to adhere to what is, rather than to yield to what has not been tried. If he rarely rejects a theory, he as rarely adopts one, because it is new. He is not fond of theories, except those which the past and the experience of long practice have sanctioned. He individualizes every thing as much as he can. He prefers a small benefit that is specific and real to the most magnificent promises. The chief characteristic of his mind is common sense; but it is of a very uncommon sort. It becomes a kind of practical philosophy. He requires so much per cent. deposit for every share in the joint stock of modern wisdom. Perhaps he sometimes pushes these peculiarities too far. The prejudices of so powerful a man may sometimes become a great national obstruction. But, on the other hand, it is well that there should be some men with fixed ideas, to prevent the moral world flying off out of its appointed orbit.

It is the moral influence of the Duke of Wellington, and the position in the country which his great services have secured for him, that render him so influential a speaker in the House of Lords. It is felt that his speeches are not merely made for a party purpose, but that they embody the experience of a life. His sincerity and the reliance you have on his sagacity, compensate for the absence of those graces of style and manner, and that choice of language, which are expected from a public speaker. He usually sits in a state of abstraction,—his arms folded, his head sunk on his breast, his legs stretched out: he seems to be asleep. But, in a very few moments, he shows that he has not been an inattentive observer of the debate. He suddenly starts up, advances (sometimes with faltering steps, from his advanced age) to the table, and, without preface or preliminary statement, dashes at once at the real question in dispute. The keenness with which he detects it, and the perseverance of his pursuit, are remarkable proofs of the unimpaired vigor of his understanding. Even with all the physical feebleness which might be expected at his years, he entirely fills the house while he speaks. His utterance is very indistinct; yet by a strong effort of the will he makes himself clearly heard and understood, even though to do so he may have to repeat whole portions of sentences. Not a point of the discourse escapes him; and the most vigorous debater often finds the weakness of his argument, however cleverly masked, suddenly detected and exposed. Some of the short, terse, pointed sentences, fall with a force on the House the more remarkable for the contrast of the matter with the manner. The speeches as a whole, though always extremely brief in comparison with those of more elaborate debaters, strike the hearer with surprise for their sustained tone, the consistency of their argument, and a kind of natural symmetry, the necessary consequence of their being the sincere and spontaneous development of a strong mind and a determined purpose.

Of the political career of the Duke of Wellington it is not desirable to speak where praise or censure would alike savor of presumption. He shares with most of the great men of the day, and with Sir Robert Peel in particular, the blame which it is usual to attach to inconsistency. Posterity will decide on the degree of turpitude attributable to the statesmen of this age, for their manner of guiding the country peaceably through a revolution in opinion and legislation, to attain which would have cost other nations all the frightful penalties of civil strife. Whatever may be the ultimate decision, it will no doubt be borne in mind that the Duke of Wellington, from the very commencement of his active political career, stood above the temptations of ordinary ambition, and is, therefore, exempt from the more ordinary and obvious grounds of reproach.

THE RIGHT HON. T. B. MACAULAY.

The popular voice places Mr. Macaulay in the very first rank of cotemporary speakers. Those who are prepared to admit a distinction between the most distinguished and successful of untrained speakers and the confessed orators, include him, without hesitation, in the latter class. If they form their judgment merely from reading his speeches as reported in the papers, certainly they have ample ground for presuming that he must be a man of no ordinary eloquence; for he scarcely ever rises but to pour a flood of light upon the subject under discussion, which he handles with a masterly skill that brings out all the available points, and sets them off with such a grace of illustration, such a depth and readiness of historical knowledge, as are equaled by no other living orator. His speeches, indeed, looked at apart from all immediate political considerations, are admirable compositions, which may be read and read again with pleasure and profit, long after the party feelings of the moment have subsided; and in this point of view they seem to be regarded by the general public. An equal interest and admiration are felt by that comparatively small and exclusive section who form the audience in the House of Commons. When it gets whispered about that Mr. Macaulay is likely to speak on a particular question, the intelligence acts like a talisman on the members. Those who may not take sufficient interest in the current business to be present in the House, may be seen hovering in its precincts, in the lobbies, in the library, or at Bellamy's, lest they should be out of the way at the right moment, and so lose a great intellectual treat: and it is no sooner known that the cause of all this interest has actually begun to speak, than the House becomes, as if by magic, as much crowded as when the leader for the time being is on his legs. So general an interest in one who has not rendered himself important or conspicuous by any of the more ordinary or vulgar means of obtaining political distinction, or of exciting the popular mind, is of itself proof enough that he must possess very extraordinary claims. In this interest and admiration we most cordially concur. We are not going to question the accuracy of that verdict of the public which places Mr. Macaulay among the very first orators of the day,—though, perhaps, we may be able to suggest grounds for a more discriminating criticism and judgment than he is generally subjected to; but, before proceeding to do so, it may be desirable to notice some peculiarities in Mr. Macaulay's political position, and of the means by which he has arrived at it, which illustrate in a very remarkable manner the working of the constitution, and exemplify the real freedom of our institutions.

The theory of the representative system in this country assumes that members of the House of Commons are elected by the free choice of the people, because of their peculiar fitness for the business of legislation. As a large and important portion of those who form the government are chosen from the representative body, the same theory, if followed out, would further assume that they were so selected because they were more distinguished than their compeers for the possession of those qualities of mind, and that general knowledge of the condition of the country, which would make them good administrative officers. This is the theory; but the practice is far different. It seems almost absurd to recapitulate what every politician assumes as the basis of his calculations, and every newspaper and annual register records. Yet this familiarity with the facts blinds us to their importance; and we are not a little startled when told that under our representative system, which we are so ready to hold up to the world as faultless, intelligence, knowledge of the affairs of the country, and general fitness for the business of the government, are the very last things thought of in a candidate for the suffrages of the people.

Without pushing this view to the extreme conclusions which it will naturally bear, it may be observed, that in practice the rank or property, or local influence, of a candidate, obtains more influence than is exactly consistent with the perfection of the abstract theory of representation. County members are more often returned by this kind of influence than any other. The son of the great local peer, or the head of the preponderating family in the county, is naturally looked to when a vacancy occurs; and he would be regarded as next door to a madman, who proposed a candidate because he believed his intelligence, his experience, his talents in the House of Commons, qualified him for the post of member, unsupported by any particular local influence. In the boroughs, rules not very dissimilar prevail. In many cases, notwithstanding the Reform-bill, the nomination system still exists; and here, as under the old system, the young man of talent who has his political fortune to carve out, may find the door open which is to lead him into parliament. Where the boroughs are in this respect "open," the influence of property, direct or indirect, is very nearly as strong as in the counties. The leading banker, or brewer, or manufacturer here, stands in a position not very dissimilar to that of the man of family in the more extended electoral sphere. He is returned, either on account of his personal and local influence, or because he is the representative of some "interest;" but general legislatorial qualifications are here, as elsewhere, almost the last things required from him. It is true that the borough representation opens the door of parliament to commercial men of high standing, who come forward on their general reputation, and not on any local influence; and that it also ushers into parliament that very important body, the lawyers: but these are only a minority of the whole.

The selections made by the aristocratic or governing body, whether Whig or Tory, of members to recruit from time to time the ranks of the administration, would appear to be influenced by principles or habits not wholly different from those which guide the constituencies. The man of talent, but without an alliance with nobility, or ostensible wealth, has scarcely a fair chance against rivals who may combine those advantages with even far inferior abilities. Whether this be a good or a bad system is not in question, though that it should so universally prevail in the face of a watchful public is *prima facie* evidence in its favor. It does exist, however. A Sir Robert Peel or a Lord John Russell, forming a government, does not first look out for friendless and landless men, even though their lack of wealth might only obscure the genius of a Canning. No, they rather are disposed to patronize the Charles Woods or the Sidney Herberts, whose merits have the additional weight of their near relationship to two several earldoms. The heads of the aristocratic parties are accustomed to look to their own ranks for their pupils in the science of government and their successors as the inheritors of power, unless in those offices, limited in number, which are filled by practicing barristers, whose professional position and success in the House have long since, in the eyes of the initiated, designated their future position as solicitor or attorney-general. For all these reasons, it is seldom indeed that one sees in the higher offices of government men who have not some relationship with the leading nobility, some hereditary political claim, or who are not great city or money lords, or barristers with an acknowledged standing and reputation, and who have already exhibited proofs of parliamentary ability.

Mr. Macaulay is an exception to all these rules. Although he is a barrister, he does not practice as one, —at least, his parliamentary standing in no way depends on his profession. Although indebted to the nomination system for his first admission to parliament, having first sat for the Marquis of Lansdowne's borough of Calne before the Reform-bill, yet he is in no way indebted to any Whig family connection for the start this gave him at the very outset of the race. Still less is he, or has he ever been, in that state of political servitude which might otherwise account for his rapid advance to the highest offices in the gift of an exclusive aristocratic party. He has boldly asserted the most ultra-liberal, almost democratic opinions, always tempered by the refinement of a highly cultivated and well constituted mind, but still independent and uncompromising. It is to his parliamentary talents that he is almost exclusively indebted for his advancement, and in this respect he stands almost alone among his cotemporaries. It is because he is a distinguished orator—an orator developing, perhaps, into a statesman—that he has attained the rank of privy-counselor and cabinet minister. To other great men of the day —to such men as Lord Stanley, Lord Lyndhurst, Lord Brougham, or Sir Robert Peel, the ability to address assemblies of their fellow-men with skill and effect has been a powerful agent of their political success; but in their cases it has been auxiliary only, not, as in the instance of Mr. Macaulay, the sole means of coping with established reputations. They each and all had either birth, social position, or the advantage derived from professional triumphs at the bar, as an introduction to the notice of those who from time to time have been the dispensers of honor and the nominators to office.

The high political rank held by Mr. Macaulay, then, —secured as it has been by no subservience to the aristocracy on the one hand, nor any attempts to build power on democratic influence on the other—is a singular instance of the elasticity of our institutions, and of the opportunity afforded in the practical working of the constitution to men of talent and conduct, of raising themselves to the highest positions in the state. Looked at with reference to the relative constitution of society in England and France, the elevation of Mr. Macaulay, by means so legitimate, is to be regarded as an infinitely greater triumph of mind over aristocratic exclusiveness than the prime-ministership of M. Thiers or of M. Guizot, however dazzling or flattering to literary pride, achieved as each was, in a greater or less degree, amid the disorganization of society following a revolution. Mr. Macaulay's position, too, is of importance, not merely as regards the past, but also with a view to the future. Events seem pointing to a period when the aristocratic influence will be exercised less directly and generally over the representative system and in the legislature. If it is ever destined to be superseded by the commercial, or even the popular influence, how desirable it is that constituencies so tending should choose for their representatives not the mere pledged advocates of rival "interests," or those coarser demagogues who live by pampering the worst appetites of the partially instructed, but men of well trained minds, initiated in the business of government, and far surpassing their accidental competitors in those external arts and graces of the political adventurer, for which, strange to say, the least educated audiences display the keenest relish, while, by so doing, they mark their own just appreciation. The success achieved by Mr. Macaulay—more remarkable and significant that it was in opposition to the prejudices and remonstrances of some of the older members of the Whig party—opens the door to a new and increasing class of public men, who would devote themselves to politics as the business of their lives, as others give themselves up to science or to the regular professions; who from the very nature and origin of their influence would find favor with popular constituencies, as anxious as the aristocrats were under the old system to secure talented and well trained expositors of their wishes and opinions, so that they might become a real and active power in the state, and not merely puppets in the hands of intriguing and ambitious statesmen. It is a significant fact, as connected with this theory, that Mr. Macaulay should be the representative of the second metropolitan constituency in the empire.

The character of Mr. Macaulay's mind, as developed in his various speeches and acknowledged writings, eminently qualified him for the part he has already taken in the political history of his time, and that which he seems destined still to act. It is obvious that a man whom, speaking relatively, one may, without offense, call an adventurer—a title which, it will be seen, is not in his case meant as a reproach, but rather as by comparison an honor—it is obvious that such a man must have some very peculiar qualities of mind, so to have overcome or disarmed the most jealous aristocratic prejudices, at the same time that he has made his country, and at least the literary world in general, ring with his name; while his conduct as a politician has by no means been characterized by that caution and dissimulation which sometimes carry a man safely through the difficulties of political warfare, till the hour has come when he conceives he may safely declare his real sentiments, and stand forth to the world the true man he is. Mr. Macaulay has, almost from the outset of his public life, boldly avowed the most extreme opinions ever countenanced, even in the most desperate manœuvers of faction, by the heads of his party. By the side of landholders and men whose standing depends on elective influence, he has declared himself the open advocate of the ballot. He was always ahead of his party on the Corn-laws; and on all the other great popular questions with which, from time to time, they have tampered. Yet be it ever remembered, as his political position was not created by mob influence, but rather dependent on the favor of those who were socially, though not intellectually, his superiors, he risked every thing by this frankness. He might have played a safer, but not so bold or glorious a game, if he were not far above the political meanness of disguising his opinions.

There is a fine spirit of philosophical statesmanship animating all the political thinking of Mr. Macaulay, which guides him safely in those dangerous tracks to which he is led by his intellectual propensities. His mind has been trained in the old forms, and in its full strength it does not repudiate them. In this respect he is more to be relied on as a politician by the cautious, than even the most obstinate adherent of the *status quo;* who, in most cases, gives a strength to the opinions he affects to shun, and stings to fresh energy opponents he pretends to despise. Mr. Macaulay neither shuns nor despises. He is not to be deterred by warnings derived from the past, or predictions of evil in the future. He grapples with every proposition that comes in his way, meeting it fairly on its own ground. No fear of explosion withholds him from applying his intellectual test to the new element, or from appropriating it to the purposes of political science, if its properties or its facility of combination make it a desirable ally. A new opinion, or a new movement originating in opinion, is either discarded, crushed, disposed of at once, or it is now and forever incorporated in the system he has raised for himself, and which he is always adding to, cementing, strengthening, never weakening or undermining. He looks at the present and the future with the light of the past. However prospective his purposes may be, his mind is retrospective in its organization, and in the intellectual aliment on which it has fed with the most appropriating avidity. However new may be his propositions or his views, they are never crude. If he sometimes appears to question, and, by questioning, to undermine and destroy, the most cherished and universally admitted principles, the chances are that he does it only to divorce them from fallacies which tend to weaken their efficacy. He separates the sound from the unsound, in order to unite it again to fresh and undecayed materials. He is a great reconciler of the new with the old. It is his delight to give new interpretations to old laws and forms of thought, and, by so doing, to restore their original integrity. With all his brilliancy, although it is one of his distinguishing traits to touch the most grave and important topics in that light and graceful spirit which has made him the must popular essayist of his time ; notwithstanding that in his writings, and even in his speeches on congenial themes, he seems led captive by his imagination to an extent that might make the common dull herd fear to yield themselves to his guidance ; there is not among the politicians of the day a more thoroughly practical man than Mr. Macaulay. Although he may adorn a subject with the lights afforded by his rare genius, he never trifles with it. The graceful flowers have strong props and stems beneath, to bear them up against rough weather. His historical research renders him a living link with the old and uncorrupted constitution of the country. He can bring, most unexpectedly, old sanctions to the newest ideas. Thus to ally the present with the past is the valuable instinct of his mind. It operates insensibly as a great guaranty with others not so quick and capable. It is also a living and active principle, the operation of which may be most beneficial in cotemporary politics. By it antiquity conquers and absorbs novelty, which again reanimates the old. If the spirit of inquiry, or of innovation, or of change, or of indomitable English common sense, suddenly breaks away the legislative barriers behind which an established system of political things has intrenched itself, it is a great source of confidence to those alarmed at defeat, as well as those perhaps equally alarmed at success, to know that the invading is in reality older than the invaded; that what is supposed to be a revolution is, in truth, a restoration of something better than that which was swept away. Mr. Macaulay looks at political questions in this reconstructive spirit, and hence the favor with which he is regarded by his aristocratic allies. He has all the holiness, vigor, and originality which democratic opinions inspire, without that leveling spirit which makes them odious and dangerous.

It is this philosophic and statesmanlike tone which gives the speeches of Mr. Macaulay their real interest and value. The more grave and important considerations which it educes from the political events of the hour are admirably intermingled and interwoven with them, so as to do away altogether with the appearance of pedantry and dry historical disquisition on the one hand, or of vague and useless political theory on the other. There is no speaker now before the public who so readily and usefully, and with so little appearance of effort, infuses the results of very extensive reading and very deep research into the common, every-day business of Parliament. But his learning never tyrannizes over his common sense. If he has a parallel ready for almost every great character or great event, or an instance, or a dictum, from some acknowledged authority, his own reason does not, therefore, bow with implicit deference, making the one case a rule for all time. His speeches on the Reform-bill, more especially that on the third reading, were remarkable evidences of the skill and readiness with which he could bring historical instances to bear upon immediate political events, without being at all embarrassed by the precedents. His mind appears so admirably organized, his stores of memory so well filled and so instantaneously at hand, that the right idea or the most happy illustration seems to spring up at exactly the right moment; and the train of thinking thus aroused is dismissed again with equal ease, leaving him at liberty to pursue the general tenor of his argument. There is very great symmetry in his speeches. The subject is admirably handled for the purpose of instructing, delighting, or arousing; and learning, illustration, invective, or declamation, are used with such a happy art, and with so equally happy an abstinence, that, when the speech is concluded, you are left under the impression that every thing material to a just judgment has been said, and the whole theme exhausted. His speeches read like essays, as his essays read like speeches. It is impossible to doubt that they are prepared with the utmost care, and committed to memory before delivery. They bear internal evidences of this, and the mode of delivery confirms the suspicion.

The speeches made by Mr. Macaulay on the spur of the moment, when the subject has suddenly arisen, and preparation is impossible, confirm, by contrast, the belief that his great displays are carefully conned beforehand. There is almost a total absence of that historical allusion, that happy illustration, those antithetical sentences and paradoxical arguments, which characterize his formal orations. They are generally, when thus the spontaneous product of the moment, most able and vigorous arguments on the subject under discussion, which is, in most cases, placed in an entirely new light. After he has spoken on such occasions as these, the debate usually takes a new turn. Members on both sides of the House, and of all ranks, are to be found shaping their remarks, either in confirmation, or refutation of what Mr. Macaulay has said; so influential is his bold, vigorous, uncompromising mode of handling a question; so acute his analysis; so firm his grasp. So that we must not merely look at Mr. Macaulay, in the common point of view, as a "brilliant" speaker and accomplished orator, delivering essays on a given subject, adorned by all the graces of style, and in which the imagination preponderates over all else; we must also regard him as a practical politician, ready at every emergency, and exercising by the superiority of his mind an ascendency over the councils of the nation. He mingles in a remarkable manner the persuasiveness of the advocate with the impartiality of the judge. If a judge were to use eloquence to insinuate on the minds of his hearers the justice of his decision, he might treat his subject in much the same style as that adopted by Mr. Macaulay. His art in concealing the machinery with which he works on his hearers is perfect. There is no appearance of a plan, yet a careful study of his speeches will show that they are constructed, and the subjects and trains of thought disposed, with the utmost skill. There is no apparent straining after graces of style or peculiarities of diction, as in the case of Mr. Sheil. You are thrown off your guard by the simplicity of the language, and the absence of all ambitious effort. He seems rather to trust to the clearness of his case, and the impetuosity and perseverance of his advocacy. Yet no opportunity for working up a "point" is neglected. Exquisite passages are here and there scattered through a speech, yet they seem to fall naturally into the argument, although really the result of the most careful preparation. His perorations, too, are remarkable, in general, for their declamatory energy, their sustained eloquence, and the manner in which they stamp, as it were, the argument or theme of the whole speech on the mind of the audience at parting. Grace of diction is throughout made secondary to vigor of thought. But Mr. Macaulay argues much in metaphor, though never for the metaphor's sake. He will put the whole force of a position into an apt and simple illustration with a suddenness quite startling. These, and an occasional antithesis of the simplest kind, are almost his only departures from the style of ordinary level speaking. His language, at the same time, is always remarkably pure; and for elegance it is unsurpassed. There are, however, faults in his speaking. For instance, he will sometimes spoil the effect of an eloquent passage by a sudden antithetical allusion, involving some vulgar idea, which catches him because of the opportunity it affords for alliteration or contrast, and which he thinks humorous. This is in bad taste, and is so far an evidence of his want of a keen sense of wit and humor. Yet it is seldom that there is even this slight and trivial drawback to the symmetry of his speeches.

Admirable as Mr. Macaulay's speeches are on paper, his delivery of them altogether belies that reputation which they are calculated to obtain for him. It is, perhaps, heightened expectation which causes the deep disappointment one feels on hearing him the first time; or it may be that his defects of manner and style would not be observed were the matter he utters of an inferior order. Whatever the cause, the spell is in a great measure broken. Nature has not gifted him, either in voice or in person, with those attributes of the orator which help to fascinate and kindle a popular assembly. With such a voice and aspect as Lord Denman, how infinitely greater would be the effect on his audience of his undoubted intellectual power! Mr. Macaulay, in his personal appearance, and in the material or physical part of his oratory, contradicts altother the ideal portrait one has formed on reading his speeches. Every man would, of course, have his own especial hallucination; but the chances are ten to one that the majority would have associated with his subject every physical attribute of the intellectual—investing him in imagination with a noble and dignified presence, and especially with a voice fit to give utterance to those fine passages of declamation with which his speeches abound. The contrast of the reality is, in many respects, striking. Nature has grudged Mr. Macaulay height and fine proportion, and his voice is one of the most monotonous and least agreeable of those which usually belong to our countrymen north of the Tweed—a voice well adapted to give utterance with precision to the conclusions of the intellect, but in no way naturally formed to express feeling or passion. Mr. Macaulay is short in stature, round, and with a growing tendency to aldermanic disproportions. His head has the same rotundity as his body, and seems stuck on it as firmly as a pin-head. This is nearly the sum of his personal defects; all else, except the voice, is certainly in his favor. His face seems literally instinct with expression: the eye, above all, full of deep thought and meaning. As he walks, or rather straggles, along the street, he seems as if in a state of total abstraction, unmindful of all that is going on around him, and solely occupied with his own working mind. You can not help thinking that literature with him is not a mere profession or pursuit, but that it has almost grown a part of himself, as though historical problems or analytical criticism were a part of his daily and regular intellectual food.

In the House of Commons, the same abstraction is still his chief characteristic. He enters the House with a certain pole-star to guide him—his seat; how he reaches it seems as if it were a process unknown to him. Seated, he folds his arms and sits in silence, seldom speaking to his colleagues, or appearing to notice what is going forward. If he has prepared himself for a speech, it will be remarked that he comes down much earlier than usual, being very much addicted to speaking before the dinner-hour, when, of course, his memory would be more likely to serve him than at a later hour in the night, after having endured for hours the hot atmosphere of the House, and the disturbing influences of an animated debate. It is observable, too, that, on such occasions, a greater number of members than usual may be seen loitering about the House. An opening is made in the discussion, and he rises, or rather darts up from his seat, plunging at once into the very heart of his subject, without exordium or apologetic preface. In fact, you have for a few seconds heard a voice, pitched in alto, monotonous, and rather shrill, pouring forth words with inconceivable velocity ere you have become aware that a new speaker, and one of no common order, has broken in upon the debate. A few seconds more, and cheers, perhaps from all parts of the House, rouse you completely from your apathy, compelling you to follow that extremely voluble and not enticing voice in its rapid course through the subject on which the speaker is entering with a resolute determination, as it seems, never to pause. You think of an express train which does not stop even at the chief stations. On, on he speeds, in full reliance on his own momentum, never stopping for words, never stopping for thoughts, never halting for an instant, even to take breath, his intellect gathering new vigor as it proceeds, hauling the subject after him, and all its possible attributes and illustrations, with the strength of a giant, leaving a line of light on the pathway his mind has trod, till, unexhausted, and apparently inexhaustible, he brings this remarkable effort to a close by a peroration so highly sustained in its declamatory power, so abounding in illustration, so admirably framed to crown and clench the whole oration, that surprise, if it has even begun to wear off, kindles anew, and the hearer is left utterly prostrate and powerless by the whirlwind of ideas and emotions that has swept over him.

Yet, although you have been astonished, stimulated to intellectual exertion, thoroughly roused, and possibly even convinced, no impression whatever has been made by the orator upon your feelings; nor has he created any confidence in himself apart from the argument he has used. And yet, strange to say, perhaps it is because his oration has been too faultless. He exhibits none of the common weakness of even the greatest speakers. He never entices you, as it were, to help him, by the confession of any difficulty. The intellectual preponderates too much. More heart and less mind would serve his turn better. How different is Lord John Russell! Though with a responsibility so much greater, how often he appears to be in want of a thought, a word, or an illustration! He, as it were, lets you into the secret of his difficulties, and so a sort of friendship grows up. You see him making up for his part; he does not keep you before the curtain, and then try to dazzle you with his spangles and fine feathers;—so you acquire confidence in him. Not so Mr. Macaulay. He astonishes you, quells your faculties; but, at the same time, he keeps you at a distance. Always powerful and influential as he must be in the councils of his party, he would never have a following in the country. He is too didactic. He never thoroughly warms up his audience. It is not his defective voice, for Mr. Sheil is as bad, if not worse off in this respect; yet what a flame he can kindle! The cause lies in his inveterate habit of preparing his speeches, even to the very words and phrases, and committing them to memory long before the hour of delivery. Partial preparation is allowable in the greatest orators. Exordiums, and perorations, and the general sketch of the speech, may well be arranged and shaped beforehand; but et some scope be left for the impulse of the moment. The greatest thoughts are often those struck out by the mind when at heat: in debate they are caught up by minds in a congenial state. Even a lower order of excellence will at such times produce a greater effect. It is wonderful, however, that Mr. Macaulay contrives so well to adapt these cool productions of the closet to temperaments excited by party. If a counterfeit could ever stand competition with the reality, these mock-heroics of Mr. Macaulay would not have the worse chance. When he is called up suddenly, under circumstances forbidding all preparation, his speeches produce a much greater immediate effect. As compositions they may be inferior, but for practical purposes they are much better. On such occasions he has sometimes reached the height of real eloquence—not the eloquence of words and brilliant images, but that fervor and inspiring sincerity which comes direct from the heart, and finds at once a kindred response.

LORD STANLEY.

AMONG cotemporary orators, Lord Stanley is one of the most distinguished. During the many years when he took a leading part in the debates in the House of Commons, he almost always held a very high place among the most eloquent and effective speakers in that assembly; sometimes he raised himself to the very first rank. No one has been so bold as to question his intellectual power; few have dared to match their strength with his. He has, in fact, been almost universally acknowledged to be, as a parliamentary debater, a successful competitor with Sir Robert Peel, Lord John Russell, or Lord Palmerston. Whatever exasperated enemies or cautious friends may have said as to the tendency of his oratorical displays; however they may have been deprecated from time to time as too stimulative of party spirit and too provocative of party animosity, no one has withheld from them the tribute of admiration on intellectual grounds. Lord Stanley was one of the chosen spirits who really led and ruled the House of Commons.

While he continued there, it might have been somewhat difficult to take an impartial view of his claims. He threw himself with such a determined, at times with such a reckless spirit, into all attacks; he so thoroughly and desperately identified himself with his party in all defenses, that it was all but impossible to exclude prejudice from a judgment of his merits as a statesman; so strong was the partiality either for or against him. For during many years, indeed up to within a very short time before his retirement from the lower house, Lord Stanley knew no medium in politics. He threw himself, heart and soul, into whatever he undertook. It was a personal matter with him. He seemed really to believe in that political iniquity of his antagonists which others on his side appeared only to assume for the sake of oratorical invective. He lived in a perfect turmoil of contest. He had certain regular opponents with whom it was always understood the battle was to be fought to the death. Whether the fault was theirs or his is not the question: the fact was so. Beside these, he had always a small array of stragglers, with whom, from time to time, he had to maintain a kind of guerilla warfare—a species of strife which is proportionately as harassing and perilous in debate as it is in the terrible reality of war. It leaves a man no rest. He must be forever prepared. He must, as it were, sleep in his armor and with his sword unsheathed. No allowance is made for the weaknesses and infirmities of humanity. If, by chance, a man so situated should be caught tripping, he is fallen upon at once. If the fatigues of laborious official duties shall have impaired his powers; if some subordinate shall have misinformed him as to facts, or committed him as to opinions or declarations, no allowance whatever is made for such a man. He has made too many enemies. He has conquered, perhaps, in too many contests. The vanquished thirst for revenge. No political courtesies are in reserve for him. He has fought while alive, and fighting he must die.

And in like manner has Lord Stanley been judged by too many of his cotemporaries; by too many of those who envied his splendid talents; as well as by those who, naturally enough, smarted under the inflictions of his sarcastic spirit. He has made more political enemies, and possibly more personal ones, with less real cause, than any other of his cotemporaries.

Everyday events prove this. If we are to judge from the noble lord's extreme and marked quiescence during the latter part of his sojourn in the House of Commons—a political indifference so unwonted as to have given rise to the most singular rumors; for instance, that he was dissatisfied at playing so subordinate a part to Sir Robert Peel, and that his removal to the House of Lords was the price of his continued acknowledgment of that right honorable baronet's superiority—Lord Stanley wished for something like repose after the excitement of the contests of the last few years. It might seem that, having been mainly instrumental in winning the battle which placed the Conservative ministry in office, his proud spirit was so far satisfied, and that he desired now to sign a treaty of peace with his old antagonists. But the deep and bitter enmities which his powerful and unsparing eloquence had aroused were not to be so allayed. Those who had suffered by his former activity would not now let him rest. They sought to avenge themselves for past indignities and defeats, by assailing his character as minister. Never was there yet a member of government, and especially one holding the comparatively remote and retired office of colonial secretary, who was assailed so mercilessly and so indefatigably, or so decidedly and palpably on grounds of a personal nature. He suffered now the reaction of his former triumphs.

All these things make it difficult to deal with Lord Stanley's character as a statesman and an orator. If a man who has played so distinguished a part has made many enemies, he must also have many enthusiastic admirers. Political gratitude may as much exaggerate his merits and services, as political hatred may depreciate them. In either case the parties, whether enemies or friends, deal with the man *as he was.* They look back to the stormy times when the character which they hate or admire was formed and displayed;

and they conceive that character to have remained the same. They refuse to acknowledge, or to see that time and the abatement of many causes of irritation may have materially altered the tendencies of one who early in life exhibited intellectual propensities of a very different kind. That Lord Stanley has been removed from the arena in which his combative habits were so fully developed into a sphere where they are comparatively useless; and that since he has been in his new position he has been more quiescent than even he was during the last year or two of his continuing in the House of Commons, will, however, materially lessen the difficulty, and enable us to look at his character with more impartiality and more fearlessness of arousing hostile opinions on either side, than if we had applied ourselves to the task some six or eight years ago, when his gladiatorial powers were in full play.

It is a bad thing for a young nobleman, and proportionately it is bad for his country, when he leaps suddenly from a minority and private life into the full exercise of legislative functions as a member of the House of Peers. On the other hand, it is advantageous that he should previously undergo a training in the House of Commons. One of the most valuable practical safeguards of the constitution is that provision of the law which makes the sons of peers eligible to election as members of the popular representative body, and that custom of the country which usually gives persons so situated a preference. They are thus brought early into contact with popular opinions; and the natural pride of birth is held in check by the counteracting pride of talent, and of power derived from the people. As a political school, the House of Commons thus forms an admirable preparation for the House of Lords. It familiarizes the young nobleman with the wants, feelings, and opinions of classes with whom he might otherwise never come in contact; and it enables him at a future period, when raised to the peerage and released from the immediate control of popular opinion, to take those wants and feelings into account in the responsible task of legislation.

Whatever may be the political opinions that have been imbibed by young noblemen, bred, perhaps, amid traditions of feudal grandeur, contact with the current sentiments of men springing from the mercantile classes, or representing abstract opinions founded on ideas of popular omnipotence, tends to liberalize them as citizens, and lessens the probability of their being placed in collision with their fellow-subjects, should questions of mutual right ever arise between the privileged class and the people. As an intellectual discipline, too, passing a few sessions in the House of Commons serves the young peer. The discipline preserved in that assembly has a tendency to bring down arrogance; while the constant and temperate discussion of all subjects most interesting to a citizen removes the inexperience by which it is engendered. This training serves him especially when he first enters the House of Lords. From the aristocratic character of that assembly, and the intellect of which it boasts in individual members, a young man making his first appearance there might naturally feel overpowered by the greatness of his audience. A modest nature would be abashed, an arrogant one hopelessly put down—discouraged by an austere silence. Lord Byron felt the extreme difficulty of rising to address such an assembly. A few years' training in the House of Commons prepares a man for this ordeal. It is true, that no audience can, as a whole, be more severe than that of the House of Commons. But then the young orator, especially if he be a peer, is cheered by the reflection, that singly they are not so much to be feared, and, above all, that they are ephemeral. Victory is more, and defeat less, than in the Upper House. He comes up to the House of Lords knowing what his powers are; what he can do, and what he can not. He does not attempt too much; and in what he does attempt, from long practice having given him confidence, he usually succeeds.

Lord Stanley has profited more than most men by this training. Had he mounted at once to the House of Peers, it is more than probable that he would not have acquired the high reputation as an orator which he now enjoys. Of course he would have distinguished himself: such talents as his are not made to be hidden,—they would have forced themselves on public notice in some way or other. But their development would probably have been very different. That energy of character, which, when roused by party conflict with obnoxious individuals, or by antagonism with opinions and principles which he had learned to hold in abhorrence, made him the most powerful debater in the House of Commons, arming his intellect with keen and ready argument, and his tongue with invective or sarcasm, would, in all probability, if he had not been placed in the circumstances which called it forth, have expended itself with equal vigor in other channels. We should have found him as fixed and determined of purpose in his devotion to some scheme of opinions, perhaps to some party, as he was in grappling with the Irish members in the House of Commons. His oratorical efforts would have been of a more purely intellectual character, less mixed up with personal feeling, which, as it is, has given them their distinguishing features. But what they would thus have gained in tone, they would probably have lost in vigor. He might have acquired a reputation for philosophical views as a statesman—these, indeed, might always be detected even in his most fiery speeches; and he might have attained to a considerable purity and elegance of style as an orator. But he would not have stood out among cotemporaries so marked a man as he now is. His name would not have been identified with the sterner features and attributes of party contest. We should not have witnessed that peculiar impatience and restlessness of disposition, in which he is surpassed by but one living orator; nor that indomitable spirit which will not brook defeat, nor be satisfied with less than the utter prostration of the foe, in which he is again to be likened only to the noble and learned ex-chancellor. He would, in all human probability, never have met an antagonist so personally powerful, and at the same time so out of the pale of ordinary parliamentary courtesy, as O'Connell; nor would he, therefore, have been almost the only man to have realized in his person the old practice of party contests, where the strife was between man and man, not between principle and principle, or measure and measure.

But, on the other hand, if Lord Stanley would thus have avoided much of that odium which party hatred, justified, it must be admitted, by circumstances to a certain extent, has attempted, and still attempts, to affix to his name, he would have entered on the duties of legislation with powers far less developed, with experience much more circumscribed, capabilities of usefulness much more confined, than those which, after his stormy career in the Lower House, he now possesses. As it is, he comes to the House of Peers with a reputation which enables him, without offense to the pride of any of his colleagues, to assume the position of a "leader;" with a temperament, all the elasticity of which remains unimpaired, while its irritable tendencies are evidently softened down and ameliorated; with faculties strengthened by use, and a mind stored with every sort of experience in public affairs that can render a man useful in their administration. The longer he continues in the House of Peers, the longer will he be removed from those irritating causes which were the only drawbacks on his complete success in the House of Commons, and the more will he be disposed to view questions—whether of a political or an administrative character—in that statesmanlike spirit which contemplates the necessity of small compromises in order to ward off great contests. It is almost impossible to account for the change that has already taken place in him, except by attributing it to ill health, or to a resolute determination of self-restraint, now that the circumstances surrounding him are so different from what they were when he was in the opposition in the House of Commons. A change there is, unquestionably. When he was in office you could no longer recognize in the quiet, unobtrusive minister who sat under the wing of the Duke of Wellington in the House of Lords, who spoke only when called upon, and then only in the routine discharge of official duty, the fierce, fiery leader who had been named the Hotspur of the Conservative forces; whose parliamentary life had been one long series of party hostilities; who was so prone to attack, that his opponents were obliged in self-defense to be forever on their guard; and who was so ready at retort, that one almost suspected that the sarcasm used in reply must have been prepared for an attack. A singular and striking instance of this change soon occurred. Lord Brougham, by the unrestrained use of his sarcastic powers indiscriminately among friends or foes, had, long before the advent of Lord Stanley to the House of Lords, acquired such a mastery over that assembly, that no man seemed to have the courage to answer him. He lorded it over all, and dealt out his reproofs or his sarcastic irony with a perseverance, a reckless boldness, a fearlessness of retort, that gave him a preeminence apparently most grateful to the combative propensities of his nature. When it became known that Lord Stanley was to be raised to the House of Peers, every one pointed him out as the natural antagonist of Lord Brougham. His well known character, his fearlessness, and extreme aptness and readiness in retort, proclaimed him, now that Lord Lyndhurst had grown too indolent, or too friendly with the common enemy, the most fit person to encounter the giant, and possibly to lay him in the dust.

Nor was Lord Brougham long in provoking a contest. Scarcely had Lord Stanley appeared in the House after having been confined at home by illness, than his noble antagonist rushed to the attack. The exact particulars are unimportant. He offered some sneering and sarcastic remark on Lord Stanley's anxiety to make a second speech on a subject on which he had once delivered his opinion as colonial secretary. The retort was obvious; it was even expected by the House; and had Lord Stanley been the man he was but a few months before, he would have given his assailant a castigation such as perhaps he never received before, for no man but Lord Stanley possessed the same powers. But, instead of so doing, he quietly and calmly submitted to the attack, to what was so personal as almost to amount to an insult, and thus let Lord Brougham retire from the contest, if contest it could be called, with the *éclat* of having conquered so doughty a conqueror, and nerved to future efforts of the same amiable character.

Far different was the Lord Stanley of five or ten years ago. Then, no man in the House of Commons, however distinguished by power of oratory, or however influential with the country, would have thought of making an attack on Lord Stanley without the certain expectation of a retort in kind, possibly carrying sarcasm or ridicule almost beyond the limits of courtesy. Then, he was one of the most, if not the most, actively militant of our public men. He had, as has been said, two classes of opponents: one class the regular constitutional opposition, as represented by the Whig leaders; the other class composed of such men as O'Connell and his immediate satellites, and Mr. Hume, Mr. Wakley, and other representatives of the Radical interest. With one or the other of these he was in a perpetual state of conflict. It was the fashion at the time with his enemies, and indeed they have not forgotten the trick now, to attribute this constant warfare in which the noble lord was engaged to his own infirmity of temper, which made it impossible for him to be on good terms with any one. They invariably made him the assailant, and insinuated that if others did not attack him they would not themselves be left alone. All was laid to the score of his natural irritability and irascibility of disposition, which would not let him rest in quiet himself, as other easy-going statesmen were content to do, or let others be at peace. They overlooked, or would not see, one quality in Lord Stanley's mind which explained the whole. They had been so long accustomed to a kind of moral laxity in the mode adopted by public men of dealing with great questions, that they could not at first understand a man who looked upon politics, not as a mere game of skill in which the reward of success was rank and power, but as a real and serious business, in which the temporal and even the spiritual welfare of the nation was at stake. They did not see that Lord Stanley was in earnest, that there was a sincerity animating all his public acts which made it impossible for him to fence with blunted foils. What was play to others was real, serious, responsible work to him, and hence his disposition to treat men and measures in a spirit which, when misunderstood, appeared to be an angry one. Angry men usually become the slaves of their own passion. The intellectual powers lose their influence, and the victim of this kind of excitement is sure to place himself speedily in a false position. Did Lord Stanley ever exhibit these symptoms of the infirmity attributed to him? No. On the contrary, if not always calm, he was at least collected; and however far a species of moral indignation, which often infused itself into his politics, might carry him, he never lost his self-possession. Though liable to be, to all appearance, carried beyond himself in the excitement of debate, he never forgot his object, or failed to strike the decisive blow at the happy moment. Lord Stanley never really lost his temper. The target as he was, during the stormy period to which we refer, of all the vulgar abuse of the Radicals and particularly of the Irish party, he availed himself of the full limits of parliamentary license in paying off the assailants in their own coin; but that he did this so neatly, keenly, pointedly, and provokingly was proof enough that his intellectual powers had not been blinded or his judgment carried away by strong gusts of passion or ill-temper, as his enemies insinuated. No; it was because Lord Stanley did *not* lose his temper that those who smarted so often under his lash asserted that he did. Had he really been the man they represented, they would have covered him with ridicule, not with reproach.

It was very remarkable, the influence he exercised over the House of Commons while ranked with Sir Robert Peel in opposition to the Whig ministry. Of course his position as a speaker had long since been ascertained. His very first speech of any importance, in the year 1820, on Mr. Hume's motion against the temporalities of the Irish church, stamped him at once as the possessor of no ordinary talents as a debater. Many successive efforts, during the ten or twelve years immediately succeeding, confirmed the opinion then formed; and his speeches and general conduct while secretary for Ireland under the Whig government proved that he would be equal to almost any emergency. He stood the brunt of all the fervid eloquence, the searing invective, the keen sarcasm of Sheil during the great anti-tithe agitation; he withstood the still more terrible because more earnest and impassioned denunciations of O'Connell, who had not then weakened the influence which his emancipation victory had gained for him. No one will deny that Mr. Stanley was then equal to his task, nor that there are few who at that time could have filled his post, or have conducted such difficult affairs with so much firmness or so little of weak compromise. No doubt he made enemies; no doubt he laid the foundation of that hatred of his name which enabled O'Connell to hold him up at a later period to the execration of the whole people of Ireland. But the belief that he was doing his duty to his country in the most enlarged sense sustained him amid all the obloquy he suffered. And so again it was in the great struggle which he maintained side by side with Sir Robert Peel against the Whigs, from the year 1835 to 1840. The power he then exercised was almost magical. There was something so earnest and unpremeditated in his assaults, yet they were sustained with such vigor, such moral momentum and intellectual skill, that he quite took the house by storm. Even foes admired. They could not but confess his power. His oratory, for the great effect he can produce, is unique and unparalleled in its total freedom from affectation or the usual preparation which great speakers resort to. He disdains, too, all the arts which other orators adopt, or, if he uses them, he has also acquired the higher art of concealing their use. If any thing, there is too palpable a rejection of the ordinary graces of manner—that preliminary deference which the artist should always show to his art. He seemed to think his subject too great and important to render any extrinsic appliances necessary. This was in the manner: the matter was far different

After sitting with folded arms, his legs extended to their full length, the heels resting on the Speaker's table, his hat slouched over his face as it were moodily, he would suddenly start up and present himself to the House to speak. A rough, somewhat slovenly and ungraceful exterior and style of dress, features hard, with lines strongly marked, and a frowning, almost scowling expression, these did not at first prepossess you; but another glance reminded you how high, broad, and full of intellect was the forehead, and how keenly piercing was the eye. The mouth, too, told in its clear outline, its firmly compressed lips, and the lines drawn around it, how often, and how successfully it had been made the ally of thought; how often it had helped in the expression of sarcasm, that passion of the intellect. You were instantly struck with the consciousness of mental power displayed in the countenance, and with a marked simplicity of style and manner. There was no attempt at attitude, no preparation as for an oratorical display. But there was a collectedness in the bearing which it was impossible to misunderstand. He seemed to be fully aware what he could do, and to be quietly determined to do it. The next thing which struck an observer (we speak in the past tense, because we are referring more particularly to a former period) was the exquisite clearness of his voice, which was of remarkably fine quality, silvery, yet very manly; almost as musical at times as the notes of an oboe, yet also sonorous when deep themes were touched, or the speaker's moral feeling was aroused. His action, too, was simple in the extreme.

All this, however, was but the external and unimportant part of Lord Stanley's oratory. For, although no man had greater command over his physical powers than he had, though in few were the outlets of expression so completely the willing and immediate slaves of the intellect in conveying the thought or the feeling of the moment, yet Lord Stanley trusted less than most speakers do to the advantages which his voice and countenance gave him. He rather threw himself on his intellectual resources, confident in the justice of his cause, or, at all events, in the soundness and invulnerability of the view he took of it. His oratory was essentially stimulative, agreeably and excitingly so to friends, provokingly so to enemies. No man produced greater results in this way with less apparent effort. His hits at his opponents were the more effective and annoying, because so intangible. Hints, insinuations, sarcasms conveyed by a glance, a sneering tone of voice, or a curl of the lip,—these were thrown off like sparks from the anvil. To notice them was a confession of an opponent of their applicability. Yet they told with the audience; and many a sudden, sharp, and rapturous cheer showed the victims of his tormenting power that the random shots had hit; yet they dared not reply, lest they should increase the ridicule. But these formed only the fringe, as it were, of the speech. The staple was of much sterner and more sterling stuff. No man could argue a question with more exquisite analytical power than Lord Stanley. There was a clearness and precision in his statements which one looks for in vain in cotemporary speakers, except perhaps, in Lord Lyndhurst, who, if possible, excels Lord Stanley in the massive simplicity of his style of argument. Both these speakers produce alike on the mind the idea of great intellectual power, and bespeak a kind of reliance on what they may advance, independently of any exercise of the judgment upon it. This prepossession is the shadow which greatness casts before it.

Lord Stanley has great command of language in the true sense of the phrase. Many men gain credit for having command of language, when in fact they have only a copious flow of words. One of the most distinguished orators in this country—perhaps, taking his early as well as later efforts into account, the most distinguished—has acquired a most undeserved reputation for command of language, when in fact his claim rests on the reckless profusion with which he uses his vocabulary, more especially on his remarkable memory for synonyms. In his writings, it is true, Lord Brougham displays a purer taste. Lord Stanley's command of language is of a very different kind. It deserves the name. He knows the real value of words, not merely as words, but as parts of a sentence. He uses them, to all appearance, naturally and spontaneously, but at the same time with so much taste and art that they appear to possess more value than when used by any other speaker, Mr. Macaulay, perhaps, excepted. He combines unusual force of phrase with elegance of diction, to an extent which would seem to be the result of severe study and premeditation, but that the circumstances of haste and the ephemeral nature of the topics discussed forbid the suspicion of preparation. There is Horatian brevity, delicacy, and force in some of his sentences.

Lord Stanley relies so much on himself, depends so entirely on the workings of his own intellect, stimulated by the hope of triumph, upon the material he has furnished, that he seldom borrows weapons from others. He very rarely quotes, except, indeed, in cases where it is necessary in a statistical point of view, or where he is arguing matters of detail; but when he does quote for oratorical purposes, he does so most effectually. Lord Lyndhurst and Mr. Sheil are his only rivals in this respect; that is to say, in the effect with which they make another man's thoughts their own for the time being.

An instance of Lord Stanley's powers in quotation occurred in one of the Irish debates nearly ten years ago. It had been the policy of the Conservative opposition to show that the Whig government were the mere tools and puppets of O'Connell, who was prepared (as the event proved) to cast them off with contumely as soon as his turn was served. The House was densely crowded, and in a most excited state, at an early hour in the morning, after a most animated debate, in which some of the first speakers had exerted their powers to the utmost. Lord Stanley had been for some time charming and stimulating the House by the eloquent manner in which he attacked his opponents, and the indignant sarcasms he heaped upon them; when suddenly adverting to the position in which they stood toward O'Connell, he broke out in the words of Hotspur to his uncles:—

"But shall it be, that you—that set the crown
Upon the head of this forgetful man;
And, for his sake, wear the detested blot
Of murd'rous subornation—shall it be
That you a world of curses undergo;
Being the agents, or base second means,
The cords, the ladder, or the hangman rather?—
O, pardon me, that I descend so low
To show the line and the predicament,
Wherein you range under *this subtile king*.
Shall it, for shame, be spoken in these days,
Or fill up chronicles in time to come,
That men of your nobility and power,
Did gage them both in an unjust behalf—
As *all* of you, God pardon it! have done?
And shall it, in mere shame, be further spoken,
That you are fool'd, discarded, and shook off
By him, for whom these shames ye underwent?
No; yet time serves, wherein you may redeem
Your banish'd honors, and restore yourselves
Into the good thoughts of the world again:
Revenge the jeering and disdained contempt
Of this proud king; who studies day and night,
To answer all the debt he owes to you,
Even with the speedy payment of your deaths."

It required no ordinary degree of moral courage to

attempt, or of oratorical skill to deliver a quotation so long and so dangerous, to a crowded House at a late hour. Its effect was appalling, from the extraordinary power of emphasis thrown into the delivery. No actor, though his profession be to harmonize the voice and to fascinate the feelings, could have given the passage with more powerful or thrilling effect. The House was completely carried away; and the ministers against whom it was directed seemed really alarmed at the torrent of feeling raised against them. Such debating seemed no longer play.

But Lord Stanley has long ceased these extraordinary efforts. From the nature of his mental organization he requires a great occasion and a worthy antagonist to draw him out, to stimulate him to the full exercise of his power. Lord Brougham is the only man so situated as to be able at present to compete with him, and there the contest seems to have been declined. There is at present no peer opposed to him who is qualified to measure swords with Lord Stanley. Lord Clanricarde, with all the will, has not the requisite power; and Lord Clarendon's mind is of too philosophical a cast. Earl Grey has all the desire to compete with Lord Stanley; but, although powerful in argument, he does not equal his noble rival in the more delicate and refined intellectual attributes of the debater. Causes of irritation thus placed at a distance, it is to be hoped that Lord Stanley will steadily develop those capabilities for statesmanship which we firmly believe him to possess, but which have hitherto been partially obscured in the excitement of party conflict.

LORD PALMERSTON.

In a debate some few years ago in the House of Commons, Sir Robert Peel excited considerable merriment by alluding to Lord Palmerston as having been called "a pure old Whig." The phrase was felt to be an equivocal one. It might be taken as an ironical allusion to the ostentation with which the noble lord then paraded what he termed "Whig principles" before the House—principles which he, at that time, adhered to with the tenacity, and propounded with the zeal, proverbial in recent converts; or, still in the same spirit of quizzing, the right honorable baronet might have meant to refer to the weight of authority which the noble lord added to any intrinsic truth there might be in the political views referred to: because, from the opportunities he has had of testing the opinions of other political parties of which he has, during his long life, been a member, his preference for "Whig principles" might be held to be the result of settled conviction. There was still another sense in which the sly humor which dictated the phrase might have designed it to apply to the noble lord.

The sexagenarian juvenility of Lord Palmerston has been the subject of much good-humored raillery. The public are already sufficiently familiar with the somewhat stale jokes which the newspapers have for some time applied to the noble lord, because they have chosen to assume that he, more than most men, sacrifices to the Graces. Lord Palmerston is too respectable, both in talents and character, to be affected by such harmless nonsense; more especially as it is, in point of fact, founded on error. Nor should we here so particularly refer to the subject, but that if not in his outward man, at least in his mind, the noble lord certainly does reverse some of the usual laws of Nature. Although from early youth he has been, in some capacity or other, before the public, and during the greater part of the time in the service of the state, it is only of late years that he has "come out," either as a statesman or as an orator. Perhaps this may have arisen from constitutional indolence; yet the restless activity of his subsequent ministerial career almost forbids the assumption. It may have been because he did not desire to thrust himself prominently before the public while he still occupied a position in the senate, or filled situations in the government, comparatively subordinate; but a reference to Hansard will show that at no time was the noble lord deficient in a characteristic propensity for self-display, although his efforts in parliament for many years scarcely distinguished him from the ordinary herd of level speakers. Like the blossoming of the aloe, the parliamentary fruition of his genius, though long delayed, is marvelous. Few, indeed, are the men who, after passing through a youth and manhood of indifference, apathy, or, at the utmost, of persevering mediocrity, could, long after the middle age had passed, after the fire of life might be supposed to be almost exhausted, blaze out, like the sacred flame on the altar of the fire-worshiper, at the very moment of decay. In this respect, as in many others, Lord Palmerston is a puzzle. He has begun where most men end. Long passed over and forgotten by Fame, he suddenly recalls her, and arrests her in her flight, compelling her to trumpet forth his name. Not even recognized as a statesman, but classed among the Red Tapists; as a speaker ranked with the steady-paced humdrums; he was almost the very last man in the House of Commons on whom one would have fixed as being likely ever to rival Lord John Russell in the leadership of the Whig party. Suddenly, without apparent cause, without its being discovered that he had become possessed of the elixir of life, he astonished his cotemporaries by the display of a vigor which neither his youth nor middle age had shown: he entered the lists alike with the veterans and the young ardent spirits of the House of Commons, proving himself a very master of the art which he had thus with so tardy a haste essayed, and raising himself to a level with the very best speakers, nay, even ultimately rivaling Lord Lyndhurst himself in the ability and power with which he used the ordinary weapons of party for the annoyance of his foes. Like the sleeping prince in the fairy tale, although by the influence of the spell half an age had passed over his bodily frame, the fire and energy of his early days remained. The heat, the vigor, even the rashness of youth, were in him most strangely combined with the authority and experience of more advanced years. The hero of Godwin's romance did not more secretly or more instantaneously discard the crust of time. It is told of Mathews, that one of his most pleasing pastimes was suddenly, chance-wise, to mingle with any group of boys, asking to join in their play; when he would, by the force of his rare genius for imitation, throw himself completely into the childish character, romp with them, laugh with them, cheat with them, quarrel with them; till, although they could not at first quite fraternize with the very tall stranger, they gradually began to look on him as less unlike themselves, and, at last, admitted him to the full rights of companionship. Similar, one may suppose, were the feelings of the leading men of the House of Commons, when Lord Palmerston, after having willfully hid his powers so long, burst out upon them as a first-rate speaker. It took them some time to believe it possible; but gradually their incredulity gave way under the proofs of his ability and vigor; and they now acknowledge to the utmost of their admiration the mistake which they, in common with the noble lord himself, had made during so many years. Like some diseases, Lord Palmerston's oratorical and political talent was chronic; it required time for its development.

All things taken into account, Lord Palmerston is, perhaps, the best debater among the Whig leaders of the House of Commons. In the different qualities which, when combined, go to render a man an orator, he is excelled by many individuals among his cotemporaries. Lord John Russell shows more tact, more intimate acquaintance with party history (not with parties, for in that knowledge Lord Palmerston beats all men living, having been a member of almost every government within the memory of man), greater skill in pointing allusions to the political errors of opponents, and altogether more refinement in the management of his parliamentary case. In eloquence, both of conception or in delivery, Lord Palmerston is, of course, excelled by Mr. Sheil or Mr. Macaulay, and even by men holding a far inferior rank as speakers. In soundness and vigor of argument he can not stand a moment's comparison with Mr. Cobden or with Earl Grey (when that nobleman does justice to his own powers), or even with Mr. Charles Buller. Each speaker on his own side, in fact, is in advance of him in some particular quality of the orator. Yet no one would for a moment hesitate to place Lord Palmerston among the first speakers in the House of Commons, or would deny that he had derived from hearing one of that nobleman's speeches as much pleasure, of its kind, as if he had listened to the most brilliant efforts of Macaulay, the most spirit-stirring of Sheil, or the most skillful and satisfying of Lord John Russell. The peculiarity of Lord Palmerston which gives him this singular power of charming with an oration as a whole, the several parts of which are not calculated to please, if critically analyzed, is his thorough and hearty spirit of partisanship; not malignant, or angry, or mean, as is that of most zealous advocates of embodied opinion or interests, but frank, manly, open-hearted, and undisguised,—so much so as to assume almost a sportive character; as if parliamentary politics were a mere pastime, a kind of relaxation from the heavier cares or labors of administration or of ordinary political life, in which all men are bound by a sort of mutual compact, answering to the laws of a game, to exert their utmost powers to excel or to overcome each other, for the sake of the distinction and applause which are the reward of success.

This peculiarity must always be borne in mind in forming our opinion of the noble lord. He takes up political questions in parliament in the true forensic spirit, but also with much of that interest which an advocate feels, not so much in the fate of his client as in the success of his own efforts. Lord Palmerston appears to feel in a less degree the importance of "Whig principles" than the advantage of a triumph for the Whig party, and for himself as a member of the party. In this he differs from Lord John Russell, who ministers to party feeling only so far as it is identified with the principles which he considers ought to regulate him. Lord Palmerston, if he is one of the most ready, facile, clever, adroit, among the leaders of the Whigs in either House, appears also to be one of the least earnest. His politics are as a garment, worn because it is thought to be the most becoming. As far as it is possible to divine the motives of public men, hidden as they sometimes are for years under accumulations of almost necessary deceit, this appears to be the ruling tendency of Lord Palmerston's public character. On one subject alone is he always terribly, inconveniently in earnest—the praise of his own foreign policy. However artificial may be his advocacy on other questions, however he may, when he is determined to make a good party speech, spur himself out of the languor which seems to be his habit of body if not of mind, no such aids to his energy are required when the doings of Viscount Palmerston, sometime her majesty's Secretary of State for Foreign Affairs, are concerned. But of this more hereafter.

Lord Palmerston, in a very good speech—a sort of summary of the session, *à la* Lord Lyndhurst, which he made at the close of the parliamentary campaign of 1842—said of Lord Stanley, "No man is a better off-hand debater than the noble lord; but off-hand debaters are apt to say whatever comes in their heads on the spur of the moment, without stopping to consider whether it is strictly the fact." Had the noble lord been engaged in painting his own portrait instead of Lord Stanley's, he could not more successfully have hit on a leading trait. It is chiefly on this very account that Lord Palmerston is so useful to his party as a debater. A more thoroughly sincere politician would be more cautious. He would have more reverence for truth, more respect for political character. Resting his faith on principles, he would be more chary of trifling with the facts on which they are founded. But Lord Palmerston is a debater, not always a statesman; a first-rate gladiator in the great political arena, and usually a successful one: but, gladiator-like, he inquires little whether the cause he fights in be the cause of truth, being only anxious to show his own skill and overcome his rival. The dexterity with which he fences at the case opposed to him, touching its vulnerable points with his sarcastic venom, or triumphing in the power with which he can make a feint of argument answer all the purposes of a real home-thrust, is only equaled by his corresponding watchfulness and agility in parrying the thrusts of an opponent, guarding himself from his attack, or skipping about to avoid being hit. In these qualities, Sir James Graham approaches the nearest to him. But Lord Palmerston, beside all these practiced arts, has also great plausibility, can work himself up admirably to a sham enthusiasm for liberal principles (just as Sir James used, in former days, to give a high coloring to his Conservatism), and can do it so well that it really requires considerable experience and observation to enable one to detect the difference between his clever imitation and the reality. He is almost unsurpassed in the art with which he can manage an argument with a show of fairness and reason, while only carrying it and his admirers far enough to serve the purpose of party in the debate. He seldom commits himself so far as to be laid open to even the most practiced debaters. They may ridicule him upon his excessive official vanity and imperviousness to criticism on that score, but they can hardly discover a flaw in the particular case which it suits him for the time being to make out. On the other hand, he possesses himself considerable power of ridicule; and when he finds the argument of an opponent either unanswerable, or that it could only be answered by alliance with some principle that might be turned against himself, he is a great adept at getting rid of it by a side-wind of absurd allusion. He very well understands the temper of the House of Commons, and especially of his own party. He knows exactly what will win a cheer, and what ought to be avoided as calculated to provoke laughter in an assembly where appreciation of what is elevated in sentiment is by no means common. He is good at parliamentary clap-traps, and an invaluable coadjutor in the leadership of a party, which, for want of some common bond of cohesion, and distracted as the Whig-Radical party was by conflicting opinion and interest, required to be kept in good-humor by the meaningless yet inspiriting generalities of Liberalism. Of the sort of quasi-philosophical language—the slang of undefined but developing democracy—which pleases the crude, unformed minds of those who are self-chosen to decide on public affairs, and on the conduct of trained statesmen and practiced politicians, Lord Palmerston is a master. He is clever at setting traps for such vain and voluntary dupes. Vague and vapid generalities become, under the magical influence of his congenial intellect, high-sounding and inspiring principles. His process of development, unlike that ascribed to the material world by a recent theorist, stops short at the nebulous stage. To resolve these seductive immaterialities into their elements, so that they might form more natural combinations—to allow the misty mass to become concrete—to let relaxed Whigism consolidate itself into Chartism, or even into more congenial and more despised Radicalism, would be most inconvenient and disagreeable to one who, like Lord Palmerston, is a thorough aristocrat in all his real, self-confessed thoughts and prejudices, and who is disposed to treat all *parvenues* in politics with the genuine heartfelt contempt, the hereditary hauteur, of "a pure old Whig."

It partly follows from these things that Lord Palmerston is a good political tactician. He scents keenly and quickly the changing wind. He probably thinks little, but he observes much. A superficial glance is sufficient to decide him on his line of conduct, because the popular feeling of the hour is what he seeks to captivate. He is clever in the arithmetic of party. He counts heads, and with the increase of numbers correspond his swelling periods. This sort of time-serving policy is not usually favorable to political foresight, nor would any one be disposed to accord that quality in any remarkable degree to Lord Palmerston.

Yet we are going to exhibit the noble lord in the character of a prophet. We would much rather attribute to his sagacity what we are, however, compelled to ascribe to some unlucky accident—the fact that he foretold not only the free-trade policy of Sir Robert Peel, but also the period of its adoption. Speaking in September, 1841, Lord Palmerston said,—"The right honorable baronet had said that he was not prepared to declare that he would never propose a change in the Corn-laws; but he certainly should not do so unless at the head of a united cabinet. Why, looking at the persons who form his administration, *he must wait something near five years* before he can do it." It is a remarkable coincidence, that in *four years and eight months* from the date of this prediction, Sir Robert Peel introduced his measure for the repeal of the Corn-laws. So well did the Whigs understand their man.

To securing success as a debater, Lord Palmerston sacrifices the hope of becoming a first-rate orator. It is the province of the orator, while he is appealing to the passions or developing the policy of the hour, also to shape and polish his discourse and to interweave in it what will render it interesting for all time. Such qualities and such objects are not to be distinguished in the excellent party speeches of Lord Palmerston. They are made for the House of Commons, not for posterity. Except in the clap-traps we have mentioned, there is no ambitious language, no pretense of that higher eloquence, which will stir the hearts of men after the particular voice is dumb and the particular man dead. You can not pick extracts out of his speeches which will bear reading, and will excite interest, apart from the context. There are no maxims or aphorisms, nor any political illustrations or passages of declamatory vehemence; but, on the other hand, the language is choice, the style pure and simple, the construction of the sentences correct, even elegant, and the general arrangement of the topics skillful in the extreme. The speeches seem not to be prepared with art, yet they are very artful; and there is a general harmony in the effect, such as might be expected from the spontaneous outpouring in argument of a highly cultivated and well regulated mind. And although, as has been said, he is chargeable with inordinate garrulity on the subject of his foreign administration, yet you will sometimes find him speaking on topics personal to himself in a high and gentlemanly tone, quite unaffected, and which is extremely impressive. It is because his party speeches are a sort of serious pastime that he can at will throw aside all party feeling, and speak in a manly and elevated tone on great public questions. One of his amusing peculiarities is to identify himself with his party in all their great proceedings. "We" acceded to power; "We" brought in such a measure; "We" felt this or that; —a sort of "I-and-my-king" style, which, in the somewhat self-important tones of the noble lord, and associated with his reputation for dictatorship in his own official department, sometimes borders on the ludicrous.

However much Lord Palmerston may fall into the sham-patriotic vein in his usual party speeches, there is one subject on which, as we have said, he is inconveniently in earnest. Touch his foreign policy, and on the instant his soul is in arms. Nay, he does not wait till it is touched, aspen-like though his vanity be on that theme. So intimately possessed is he of the absolute excellence of his foreign administration, and of its importance to mankind, that he is unceasingly, and without being asked, expounding and explaining it. He defends himself spontaneously, without having been attacked; and he never defends himself without gratuitously attacking some one else. Sir Robert Peel once charged him, in well sugared parliamentary phrase, with assurance. The imputation was well aimed; every one instantly responded to it; for, indeed, the noble lord has no unnecessary modesty in speaking of himself or his services. He is assiduous, and altogether unrestrained by delicacy, in trumpeting his own exploits as foreign minister. All the wars he didn't and all the wars he did bring about; all his dextrous manœuvers by which, while proclaiming peace, he was countenancing a kind of war in disguise;—these have been paraded session after session, upon all imaginable pretexts, before the House of Commons, till Lord Palmerston's pertinacity has become proverbial. His *amour propre*, in fact, on the subject of his foreign policy almost takes the shape of a mania. His constant references to it, and the extent to which he has trespassed on the patience of the House, have detracted, to a considerable extent, from the influence which his undeniable talents as a speaker, and even his admitted abilities as a foreign minister, have long since entitled him to and secured for him. He is so easily excited on this topic, that whatever subject he may be talking on, however much his speech may necessarily be confined to subjects of a domestic nature, his mind seems, by a natural affinity, to glide into the one great theme which occupies his thoughts. At a guess, it might be hazarded that, taking the average of his speeches during the last ten or twelve years, four fifths of them, at least, have consisted of self-praise, or self-defense, in connection with his foreign policy.

It must not, however, be supposed that Lord Palmerston is therefore held in any contempt by the House. Quite the reverse. They may think that he shows a want of taste and tact in thus yielding so constantly to the ruling influence of his mind; but they are not the less prepared to award him the full amount of praise, and, what he more values, of attentive listening, to which his position, whether officially or legislatorially, entitles him. They are willing to admit that, as the foreign minister of England, he has shown himself animated by something of the spirit of the great Earl of Chatham, in his magnanimous determination to uphold, at all hazards, the national honor. In his first administration of the Foreign Office, his task was to make a peace-at-any-price party, pursue a war-at-any-price policy. It was his duty, as well as his ardent desire, to make the English name respected throughout the world. He took a high tone with foreign nations; and they felt that, while Lord Palmerston was at the head of foreign affairs, they could not insult us with impunity. The House of Commons were fully aware of these things, and were disposed to respect him accordingly: but while listening to his perpetual explanations and justifications, they could not help feeling that a minister who was thus paltering between peace and war was very likely to illustrate the old adage concerning the ultimate fate of him who tries to sit on two stools. They saw that his manly policy, instead of showing itself in quiet dignity, was detracted from by a restless spirit of intermeddling, a habit of provoking the irritability of foreign nations, as if for the mere purpose of showing our strength to disregard it. An opponent characterized his proceedings by the terms, "restless activity and incessant meddling." Lord Palmerston seems conscious that such is the opinion entertained of his conduct; for he has himself quoted the terms and deprecated such an application of them.

But the verdict seems to have been pronounced by the House of Commons, that the foreign policy of Lord Palmerston has been more spirited, vigorous, expert, than politic, dignified, or wise. It is confessed that he has enlarged views, which, perhaps, he has scarcely had a fair opportunity of developing; but, at the same time, it appears to be felt that the steps he took to carry out those views acted as so many obstructions. He was for universal peace and free commercial intercourse, but he thought to obtain them by bellicose demonstrations. He had Peace in his mouth, but War in his right hand.

Out of doors, Lord Palmerston is very much misunderstood. The popular idea of him represents him as an antiquated dandy. He is really nothing of the sort, but a man of unusual vigor, both of mind and body, upon whom Time has made less impression than usual. He is not more particular in his dress than are most men of his station in society; and if he be charged with sacrificing to the graces, all we can say on the subject is, that we could point out a hundred members of the House of Commons, of all ages, who are more open to ridicule on this score than Lord Palmerston. Any pretension he may have is, in fact, not personal, but mental. His bearing is eminently that of the gentleman, quiet and unassuming, but manly. As a speaker, his physical powers are scarcely equal to what his mind prompts him to achieve. There is a kind of faded air, which you can not help observing; but this impression may, after all, only arise from a constitutional languor of manner, and from the peculiar intonation of his voice, which has a hollow and fluty sound. With all his talents as a debater, he wants that special combination of personal dignity with popular qualities, which alone could qualify him to be the sole leader of his party, should any cause bring about the secession of Lord John Russell.

LORD LYNDHURST.

Our aristocracy act wisely, as well with respect to their own interests as for those of the country, when they allow admission to their ranks and the enjoyment of their exclusive privileges, as the invariable reward, if not the prescriptive right of preëminent ability in the study and practice of the law.

The position of the "law-lords" renders them advisers of the peers in legislation. If they do not originate the laws, though of many they are the real and sole authors, they at least watch over their administration, and prevent the passing of bad ones; while they are practically the guardians of the constitution and the liberty of the subject.

The lord chancellor of England stands in a still more important and responsible position. He is not merely the exponent of the laws when made: he is chief among those who advise the policy which makes them. His *ex-officio* guardianship of the royal conscience may not in these days of utilitarian policy have all the practical efficacy, either for guidance or restraint, which the theoretical importance of the office implies. But lord chancellors during the last century or more have, by the common consent of statesmen, gradually acquired an influence in political affairs, very different, perhaps, from that which the nature of their functions originally warranted; but, in fact, far more real, more extensive, and more important to the interests of the state. Great, too, as their direct and official influence is, their indirect power is still greater. The wisest and most distinguished statesman is but an amateur in the making of law. However great his abilities or correct his principles, his opinion is but that of a gifted or well informed individual, if, indeed its importance be not often derived from his being the head of a party. But the lord chancellor is the living representative in the cabinet of a great system, the growth of centuries of thought and experience, and framed out of events, principles, and the necessities of mankind, by some of the greatest minds the world has produced. His *dictum* is not a mere personal opinion; it carries the weight of that great system with it. As, except in rare instances, he occupies that exalted position in right of his perfect mastership of the law, joined to excellence, if not preëminence, in the general qualifications of statesmanship, it is not possible but that his decision on a question must, to a very great extent, influence the course taken by the executive government in their initiative character as legislators. But his indirect, and, so to speak, extra-official influence does not end here. His position in the cabinet, and as president of the debates of the House of Peers, give him a vast degree of personal importance in an assembly where, of necessity, so many of its members must be guided by personal considerations; from the majority being there by the accident of birth. The species of influence, of course, varies with the personal character of the individual who, for the time being, fills the office of lord chancellor. The more commanding are his personal qualities, the more direct and immediate is the influence of his example. But even the lord chancellor, most indebted for his elevation to his legal knowledge alone, and least to his eloquence or political ability, even he exerts over the acts of the House of Peers, and, through them, over the country, an influence of which the public generally are very little conscious, and which far transcends any power derived from the office of keeper to the conscience of the sovereign.

It is, we repeat, wise in the aristocracy to reserve such an office as a reward for those who have distinguished themselves in the practice of the law—who, after a long course of servitude to that severe study, have at length made themselves thoroughly masters of our whole system of jurisprudence, and of that great fabric of constitutional law upon which so much of the independent character of the people of this country, and their respect for the rights and privileges of each other, is based. A man so elevated to the privileged order becomes Conservative by habit as well as by right. He is likely to be opposed to all innovation for innovation's sake, and is able to bring to bear upon proposed changes the weight of experience and reputation. His interests, ideas, and prejudices, will all be identified with the maintenance of order. He will be disposed rather to stop and realize the past or the present than to tempt the future. It is true that, during the first part of the last fifteen years, a great exception to these rules was exhibited on the woolsack; but even in that instance time and experience have worn away the first rash ardor which novelty and the unexpected possession of vast power engendered; and he who at one time promised to be the greatest and most formidable innovator of his day, has grown to be the greatest upholder of what is, in opposition to what he once thought ought to be. There is no resisting the influence of a thorough legal education on the mind. Political feeling, or other extraneous causes, may disturb it for a time, but, sooner or later, it will exhibit itself in matured thought and steady principle.

For the country it is good that the presiding authority in the Upper House should be the character we have hinted at, even more than for the privileged orders. For he who has mounted up from the assertion and defense of individual rights to the entire comprehension of the collective rights of the people and the relative claims of classes, is not the worst man to be intrusted with the consideration of propositions which, for good or for evil, are to affect those rights and claims. Nor is it less advantageous to the great body of the people that they should have, in the most secret and the highest council in the empire, one who, raised already above the influence of ambition, and conscious that he has a character at stake with posterity, has been throughout life nursed and strengthened in the principles of justice and equity, and who regards them as the law of his mind.

If the foregoing be not considered too exalted an idea of the dignity and power attached to the office of lord chancellor of England, it will not seem that too high a position is claimed for Lord Lyndhurst when we say, that of all men who have held the office within the memory of living men, and of almost all of whom we have record, he has shown himself the best qualified for it. Of course this opinion is advanced with reference only to his learning, judgment, and general ability as a statesman, and profound acquaintance with the law. Party men may take a party line in discussing such subjects, but from the moment that a man of Lord Lyndhurst's order becomes invested with the responsibilities of legislation, he casts aside party feeling, however much it may have animated him in the struggle for power, and devotes himself to the furtherance of those objects which he believes to be most for the good of the country. Public opinion is at once so watchful and so powerful, that even the most ambitious minds are confined within a legitimate sphere of action. We, therefore, confine our consideration to the abilities possessed by public men for carrying out their views, and judge with reference to them alone, regardless of conflicting opinions on the good or evil tendency of those views. This is, in fact, the only ground on which the character of public men can be canvassed with any hope of arriving at truth.

The influence of Lord Lyndhurst in the House of Lords is almost coextensive with that of the Duke of Wellington. Popular institutions favor the only legitimate despotism—that of mind; and these two Conservative statesmen remarkably illustrate this inevitable tendency of the weaker intellect to yield voluntary respect, if not entire submission, to the stronger. Perhaps it would not be going too far to say, that in the condition of the House of Lords for some years past, if the Duke of Wellington and Lord Lyndhurst resolved upon carrying any particular measure, they had the power to do so. That their proceedings are usually characterized by unfailing good sense and judgment, supplies a sufficient reason why they should wield this influence; and renders it unnecessary to inquire whether they would be able to exercise it in the same degree if they proposed measures which the general common sense of the House would repudiate. Of the fact, however, that those two statesmen are now the ruling spirits in the House of Peers, there can be little doubt.

The sources of their influence are different. The duke's power over his obsequious fellow-peers is derived from his great moral weight, his historical reputation, his proved sagacity, and the steadfastness with which he is known to uphold all that can contribute to the consolidation of the national strength. It is a personal influence. Men follow his lead because it is he who leads, not because they have decided in their own minds to go the same road. Lord Lyndhurst's influence, on the other hand, is intellectual—founded upon the evident strength of his mind, his transcendent abilities in debate, and the towering proportions of his general character. His cotemporaries yield him the precedence, because they feel assured that he has brought to bear upon any question before him all the resources of a perfectly organized intellect—that learning, acuteness, experience, and judgment, have done their utmost. The duke, they think, must be right, because a sort of moral instinct directs him to the true policy. Lord Lyndhurst commands their support because they feel that he has investigated all the bearings and exhausted all the modes of which a subject is capable, and that he will take the right course by the pure preference of reason and judgment.

Nor when one looks at the man is it at all wonderful that this homage should be paid to his intellect. If an involuntary respect is prompted by the mere contemplation of his fine countenance; by listening to his deep, manly, sonorous voice; by his evident self-possession and unconscious exhibition of latent strength; if nature has so stamped his outer man with the physical attributes of superiority, it is the less surprising that those who have so often witnessed the effects of his power on others, or felt it on themselves, should be prepared to yield from settled conviction what others less informed tender from immediate impulse. Lord Lyndhurst is a master. There is the sure stamp of superiority on all he says or does. You feel in the presence of a spirit to which art, education, and the powerful workings of an active intellect, have superadded all that the knowledge of man can give. There is mastery in his reasoning, mastery in his declamation, mastery in his judgment, mastery in his humor. To know him is to rely on his power. Like the giants of the heathen mythology, he presents you in his sphere with an ideal of strength. He seems to pursue his aim with such steady momentum of will acting on power, that failure appears impossible. Thus success breeds success, achievement daunts opposition, the imagination magnifies strength and deprecates resistance. This has been the history of his career in the House of Peers. One man only, Lord Brougham, ever competed with him with forces at all equal in power, and even they were inadequate because not so well regulated. But that joust-like combat between the two noble and learned lords, the public opponents and sworn private friends, is over; and now Lord Lyndhurst has no antagonist. It is not, perhaps, that no one could, or no one dare; but continued success and repeated displays of power have gained for him such a reputation and such respect, that no peer chooses to match strength with him. Apparently he knows this, and walks over his cause with careless ease, as the strong man passes along heedless of danger, because not fearing it. But his consciousness of strength is in no respect shown in arrogance. It is not allied to vanity. It is latent, not ostentatiously displayed. It is questionable whether Lord Lyndhurst would care for praise, if it cost him much effort. He is self-relying by a law of his nature. His mind works for itself, and by itself. Nor does temporary suspension of activity lessen its powers. This is one consequence of its native superiority and admirable regulation. His iron takes no rust from not being often worked. He will remain silent for weeks together, or merely play with his parliamentary functions; yet suddenly he arouses himself, and shows that his powers are as full and as vigorous as when he was engaged in nightly contest. He is always armed, though seldom in action.

Enter the House of Lords, and among the first, if not the first who arrests your attention, is Lord Lyndhurst. As your eye wanders round the house, it is suddenly stopped by an aspect that can not belong to an ordinary man. It stands out in bold relief, like the picture of a master on a well hung wall. In the center of a cluster of faces, some of the features familiar, as those of Lord Brougham, Lord Ellenborough, or

Lord Denman, the fine massive head and commanding features of Lord Lyndhurst arrest your attention, and fill your mind at once. When he sat as chancellor and they were set in the heavy framework—the avalanche of powdered curls—which custom requires our judges to wear in court, and the lord chancellor only in the House, their bright intelligence and serene intellectuality fascinated your gaze like a focus of concentrated light. The outline is grand, and the features and proportions of the countenance are at once so massive and so regular, that not even the furrows of many a long year of mental toil, nor the settled lines of habitual thought, ever strong and vivid in expression, have effaced what in youth must have presented a noble specimen of manly beauty. The forehead high and open, the brow wide, the eyebrows broad and strongly marked, the eye keen, quick, pregnant with intellect, the lion-like mouth, and full, firm-set chin: these present a countenance at once so handsome and so masculine, so full of power, yet so exquisitely harmonized, so grandly serene in repose, yet so quick and vivacious in activity, that you are content to dwell upon it as on some fine piece of sculpture or architecture; and to ask at once, unprompted by preconceived reverence, What are the qualities of the mind of which that face is so magnificent an index? If you are an enthusiast, if you are prone to worship the divine image in the features of man, you will say that such a countenance might be chosen by a sculptor for his ideal of Wisdom. Thought sits on it serene, as on a throne; it is, indeed, a temple whence Intellect may utter her oracles—oracles, alas! too often perverted and distorted by the passions of humanity.

If by good fortune your visit to the House should have happened on a night when this remarkable man has resolved to speak, the physical attributes of his oratory still more enchain your attention while confirming your preconceived opinion of his mental supremacy. Nature seems to have organized him for his destiny as a public orator—as one of those singled out to convey the magical influence of intelligence and sympathy from heart to heart and mind to mind. Had he been born in more stirring and dangerous times, when lives and empires, not ministers and measures, were at stake, he must have stood forward as one of the world's intellectual heroes. As it is, contemplating him amid the lurid atmosphere of party, and under the disadvantages of that too close proximity which breeds contempt, he realizes much, if not all we expect from an orator. His voice is full of organ-like music, deep and sonorous, and capable of sufficient modulation for one who rarely appeals either to the passions or the feelings, the stronger or the gentler sympathies of his hearers, but rather to their intellect, their judgment, their sense of the humorous. His bearing is dignified in the extreme: it exhibits the boldness of the Tribune, tempered by the calmness of the Senator. Self-possessed, cool, impressive, he elevates his audience to the level of his own mind, and sustains them there: he never descends from his elevation, as other orators do, to obtain applause by echoing current prejudices or party passions. When he uses those passions and prejudices, he compels them by superior power to his own purpose, and does not become the slave of his own agents. Like the rest of our public men, he is a very different man, as an orator, when in power from what he was when in opposition. Then, he could condescend to be the partisan, and a powerful one he was; but still you could see it was a condescension—a tribute to the necessities of political strife, not an assault made in hot blood and pursued for the pleasure and excitement of the combat. Lord Lyndhurst, rising in his remote corner on the extreme left of the opposition bench and delivering one of those teasing, terrific attacks on the Whig government which formed the staple of his annual review of the session, was a very different man from Lord Lyndhurst the Chancellor, the moderator of the debates, the triumphant warrior indulging in indolent repose, or the statesman delivering the pure dictates of his judgment for the general good of the whole country, instead of the temporary battle-cries of a party. At all times, however, his oratory has displayed a rare union of power and good taste. He is very self-denying for so powerful a speaker. Great as his triumphs have been as an orator, he always left one under the impression that he could effect much more if he chose.

But the essential power of this great man does not always exhibit itself in the same serious way. If he is giant-like in his strength, he is so also in a tendency to the most playful humor. Strong minds are prone thus to relax the severe tension of their faculties; and Lord Lyndhurst does so to an extent which those who only regard him as the senator or the judge would hardly conceive possible. And here, by the way, it may be observed that an error has gone abroad, favored by party animosities, to the effect that Lord Lyndhurst is an ill-natured or bad-tempered man. There could not be a greater mistake; yet it is a very natural one, for the vanquished are always prone to attribute some malign power to the conqueror. That Lord Lyndhurst has, from time to time, made his opponents feel the lash of his ridicule can not be denied; nay, it is something for his admirers to be proud of. But all sarcasm is not necessarily malignant, nor calculated to inflict personal wounds. The most careful search through Lord Lyndhurst's speeches would fail to discover a single instance in which the noble lord has indulged in ill-natured or unfair allusions to his opponents. But, on the other hand, there are multitudes of instances—and our sides ache again at the remembrance of them—where, with good-natured irony and allowable keenness, he has exposed their inconsistencies or their weaknesses. In fact, Lord Lyndhurst's character is too dignified for ill-nature. His sarcasms may be biting, but they are never withering. This constitutes the great difference between his irony and that of Lord Brougham.

To return, however, to Lord Lyndhurst's habit of relaxing in playful humor from the over-tension of application. We only allude to what has occurred in public when he sat as Chancellor. We merely look at him as he appeared in the House of Lords, where, in the intervals of important business, his stirring jest and hearty laugh were infectious among the peers who crowded round the woolsack to join in the little private gossiping that often goes on there. These things occurred in the noble lord's sportive moods, when he seems like a lion at play. Perhaps the rigid may observe, that these jokes and gambols (for, really, they sometimes almost partook of that character) were unworthy the great dignity of the judgment seat, or the constitutional importance of the senate. To say the truth they were sometimes carried quite far enough; but it should be remembered, that these things never occurred when there was any really important business coming on; and that during a great portion of the time of the ordinary sittings, when mere formal business is disposed of, the House is more like a very large drawing-room, where a dozen or so of gentlemen are taking their ease, than the hereditary chamber of legislature of a great empire.

If power be a striking characteristic of Lord Lyndhurst, judgment is not less so. He knows exactly what he ought to do, and what to leave undone,—how far to advance, and when to recede. In this quality he even excels the Duke of Wellington; for he never makes declarations under the influence of temporary excitement which he afterward sees reason to regret, or to recall. His so-called "alien" speech is no proof to the contrary; for it has been satisfactorily shown that he was on that occasion misunderstood. It is this quality of judgment—at once the most rare and the most valuable in human affairs—that, together with his intellectual preëminence, give him his weight and influence in the House of Peers. It regulates his words and his deeds.

Good taste, or the same judgment applied in another sphere, characterizes his speeches. There is a massive simplicity about them highly characteristic of the man. The ideas are plain, forcible, clear to the simplest comprehension; the language terse, simple, vigorous, and epigrammatic. When epigrammatic, it is not the less natural, as the particular form of expression is evidently not studied, but is shaped spontaneously in the mold of his mind. It is almost superfluous to add, that his reasoning is vigorous and unassailable; his perception acute; his comprehension large and capacious. He never travels far wide from his subject, either in thought or language. He has a task to perform, and no temptation to display will turn him aside from his path. His eloquence does not run wild in tangled luxuriance, like Lord Brougham's. Nor does he "get up" speeches, like Mr. Macaulay or Mr. Sheil. There are very few prepared rhetorical passages, but all is simple, nervous exposition. Every word does its work, and no more work is undertaken than the subject requires, or that can be well performed with justice to it. For this reason, his isolated speeches will not excite so much admiration as those of some of his cotemporaries. There are few of those striking passages which bear quotation for their independent beauty. His eloquence must be considered in connection with his whole political career; it is an integral part of his character, not an attribute adopted for display or distinction.

As a statesman, Lord Lyndhurst must share with most of his cotemporaries the blame of inconsistency. Where there is such equality of offense, censure ceases to be invidious, perhaps to be effectual. Lord Lyndhurst, like his brethren in the ministry, was a conscientious anti-emancipationist in August, 1828; he was a stanch supporter of the Emancipation Act in April, 1829. He took up both sides with equal facility. Again, he was one of the most powerful and effective agents of the Conservative party in undermining and overthrowing the Whig government; he then became one of the foremost of those who were acting as a government on Whig policy. But these grounds of criticism are beside our present purpose. We desire rather to estimate his capabilities as a minister, and these are transcendent. Admitting the principle of expediency, a more efficient exponent of it, or one more able to carry it out, is not to be found in the country. In a practical age, he is eminently a practical man. He does not allow even the most cherished opinions to interfere with what he conceives to be inevitable necessity. He meets political difficulties face to face, and grapples with them, or accommodates himself to them, as the case may be. His facility as a legislator and a statesman is only equaled by his extensive knowledge of the laws, the constitution, and the necessities of the country, and his matured experience. His influence on the minds of his countrymen, through the sway he exercises over the judgment of the peers, is enormous. He has realized more than any lord chancellor, within the memory of the present generation, those large and undefined privileges and powers which at the opening of these remarks we have assigned as part of the unrecognized functions of the office he holds. He also excels his immediate predecessors in the degree of confidence he inspires in the House of Lords. Such influence, such power, without direct responsibility, would be dangerous, if intrusted to a man of ordinary mind, with ambition, and passion, and deep-rooted prejudices. But it becomes innocuous in proportion to the intellectual and (politically speaking) moral worth of the holder of it. It is the offspring of personal respect, and, therefore, can scarcely be accorded to an unworthy or undeserving object. Its origin is a guaranty for its harmlessness. If it were not deserved, it would not be conceded. This deference and confidence follow as an almost necessary consequence in the case of such a man as Lord Lyndhurst.

EARL GREY.

The Whigs recognize the principle of an hereditary succession even in party leadership: an office under government, and ultimately a seat in the cabinet, with occasionally an advance in the peerage, are as certainly secured by a kind of law of entail to the Whig lordling who turns his attention to politics, as is his paternal estate. Public honors and power, under the favoring forms of the constitution, have become, to a few families, almost a private property. We do not say that they inherit these things without deserving them; far from it: the sons of the great Whig families have often developed into statesmen, becoming by the force of their talents entitled to fresh honors; and in their turn founding new families, all with the like claims on their party. But they certainly have had a preference in the first start into life which has not been enjoyed by commoners generally, nor even by the scions of other noble families professing, perhaps, liberal politics, but not being within the charmed circle. An exclusiveness in the distribution of offices, and the initiation into the service of the state, has characterized the Whig party since it first became possessed of power under the constitutional form of government; nor, until the bold offer of Lord John Russell to Mr. Cobden, of an office under government, when that noble lord was forming an administration on the resignation of Sir Robert Peel, before introducing his free-trade plan, has there been any material symptom of a relaxation of that rigid rule of almost family preference. Mr. Macaulay's elevation to the cabinet is a brilliant exception; but the ground of his promotion has been, as we have shown, exceptional also.

The practice of sending the eldest sons of peers, who hold by courtesy titles of nobility, into the House of Commons as representatives of the people, is one of the most singular of those compromises which are the very essence of political and social life in England. Of the advantage derived by the public from this arrangement there can not be the slightest doubt. A senate composed of men inexperienced in public affairs, from their very station comparatively ignorant of public wants, and who would legislate more by their will than their reason, without being subjected to restraint or responsibility,—such a body of privileged dictators would be almost as dangerous as a purely democratic assembly. Their laws would have no moral sanction. However the constitution might assert or strive to enforce their claim to hereditary wisdom, the merest crudities of a purely popular representative would find more willing support from the people than the most elaborate productions of such king-made oracles. But when they have previously served and undergone training in the House of Commons, they have secured a personal as well as a legal claim on the respect of the nation. They are then recognized by their deeds, not by their titles only. The history of the chief party contests of their time is a record of their speeches and votes: they are identified in the minds of the people, of whatever classes—Tory, Whig, or Radical, it is all the same—with the triumph of some favorite principle; or it may be only with its defeats, yet defeats which are not the less cherished, for they are looked upon as the precursors of future victories. Long before the time comes at which, in the order of nature, they are elevated to the peerage, their intellectual and political standing becomes ascertained, and they take a position at once. Their claim comes backed by the suffrage of the public; and it is yielded to at once. The most active among the peers, those most entitled by rank and experience in the Upper House to hold permanently the lead on either side, at once give way when one of these chosen men of the House of Commons comes up with his certificate of superiority.

Beside the education in practical statesmanship which young noblemen so situated receive during a few years' campaigning in the House of Commons, a moral influence is exercised over them which is also of the highest advantage to the nation. They learn, both by precept and example, the value of public opinion, that indefinite but omnipotent and omnipresent agent in the political affairs of free countries. Few greater calamities can befall a nation than a necessary separation and antagonism, both of feeling and of interest, between the privileged and the unprivileged classes. If a nobility so situated be high-spirited, powerful, and deeply imbued with a sense of hereditary right, they will restlessly strive at an oligarchical tyranny. Revolution, in states so situated, is always more than a possibility, and democracy lours in the distance. On the other hand, if this privileged and isolated nobility be not animated by the higher range of ambitious motives, they will, from combining too much leisure with too much wealth, become depraved in their moral habits; spreading the poison of a vicious example through the whole social system. Of each evil, history, past and present, affords too many fatal instances. There must be a safety-valve for the passions, whether political or personal. In our system it is provided. The young noble, by the law and the constitution a commoner, can only obtain his right to sit and speak in the representative assembly by an appeal, more or less real and sincere, to the free suffrages of the people. Coriolanus must sue for votes in the market-place, or his ambition will chafe and his talents rust, while meaner men sway. Therefore (the simile is rude) his nose must come to the grindstone. Once in Parliament, emulation quells the baser passions in the soul, and the whole of the intellectual and moral powers of the young aristocrat, according to his degree of talent and intelligence, are devoted to the one great object—distinction. That distinction can only be obtained by commanding public opinion; first, that of the House; then, that of the country at large. Fortunately, the steady character and practical genius of the British people render appeals to political passions comparatively useless. In the House they are a sham—oratorical flourishes, pretenses to turn a period, laughed at for what they mean, admired for how they are expressed. In the country, they evaporate with the excitement of the election; disappear, like the fleeting glories of the traveling theater, with the removal of the last plank of the hustings. It is turn and turn with such people: I am beaten to-day; it will be yours to-morrow: so they laugh at each other, for the defeat that has been or is to be. Something real is wanted, then, to give the young peer in masquerade influence in this, the largest, greatest, highest permanent assembly of his fellow-men, there is in the country. He must be well read in the laws of the past and the facts of the present. He must not only be more philosophical than the lawyers, but also more practical than the practical men, or neither will submit to be led by him. He finds, too, that here, where all men are equal, certain principles of freedom are held in common. His mind becomes imbued with them. If he began in play, he ends in earnest. Men fresh from the factory or the desk are, he finds, as well versed in affairs as he: nay, some of them almost equal him in his school-learning and his oratory. There is no patent, no privilege, in talent. If he would be a great man, he must work, too,—work with the head and heart. He, too, competes in the noble strife, tasks his intellect, trains his powers, to rise to the height of statesmanship and eloquence—to make his personal, warrant his social, superiority. His heart, too, warms in the contest; insensibly he becomes more national, less exclusive. Nay, by the time he enters the exclusive walls, the privileged assembly, he almost wishes he could dispense with his rights. Acted upon thus by public feeling in the Lower House, he reacts upon it. By his example of liberalism (not political but social) he makes them love the aristocratic. And how can democracy show itself, where the future nobles of the land are to be found stretching the most free of all free constitutions almost to its extreme point of tension?

But if the country gains by this system of political training, it is attended with some disadvantages to the individual statesman or orator who is thus removed to the Upper House. Men who have made a great figure in the House of Commons often fail in the House of Lords. The habits, the tone of thinking, the style of eloquence, that are adapted to the one do not suit the other. What wonder if a man, who has laboriously trained himself up to one standard, should be at fault when suddenly required to adapt himself to another which is quite different? Lord Brougham has in this respect succeeded admirably in effecting his transformation from the commoner into the peer. At first, he was not sufficiently aware of this necessity of his new position, and some very strange scenes occurred; but now he is quite another man. It is not every one, however, that has the same plasticity of mind: and hence that very usual question, when a popular leader becomes elevated to the peerage, "How will he do in the Lords?"

Earl Grey has of late been very often made the subject of this question: partly because, by the death of his celebrated parent, he has been so recently raised to the Upper House, and partly because it is generally understood that an attempt will be made to elevate him to the position of leader of the Whigs in the House of Peers, on the Marquis of Lansdowne hereafter resigning in his favor that sometimes most arduous post. There is reason to believe, also, that Earl Grey conceives himself to be, as a debater, a match for Lord Stanley, — in short, a sort of natural antagonist (of course, in a parliamentary sense) of that distinguished speaker; so that when causes now existing shall have ceased to operate, and when Lord Stanley shall have assumed that position in the House of Lords which, in a reorganization of parties, will become at once a right and a sphere of duty, Earl Grey will be enabled to stand up as the assertor of principles materially differing from those which Lord Stanley is known to entertain, and thus once more realize those old ideas of party opposition which recent events have so much tended to postpone, if not to neutralize. If these assumptions be true, if Lord Lansdowne be really disposed to yield to Earl Grey the management of what is certainly at the present time the most compactly organized party in the country, it is a step peculiarly interesting to the people of England, from the great influence which the acknowledged head of a party, whatever may or may not be his talents, has upon the course of legislation It becomes important to inquire, Whether the probable elevation of Earl Grey to this high-priesthood of Whig principles be justifiable or desirable on the score of his possession of commanding talents, or superior political wisdom, or whether it is only a new instance of the hereditary succession of the Whig families to power and honors?

There is one other ground on which the promotion of Lord Grey might be justified: that there is no Whig in the Upper House with so many claims. Mere rank alone, without oratorical powers, or some commanding qualities to which deference would instinctively be yielded, will not in these days justify a man being placed at the head of a party. The Marquis of Lansdowne's claims are not founded on his rank alone. Although his stilted and somewhat pompous style of oratory is now rather out of date, yet there was a period when he was looked upon as one of the foremost men of his time. If he has scarcely fulfilled that promise of future excellence which led his cotemporaries to compare Lord Henry Petty with William Pitt, still his past successes are not forgotten; and he has also that kind of personal weight, derived from his age and political experience, which inspires respect among those who have grown up around him, and who have for so many years stood toward him almost in the relation of pupils. Setting him for the moment on one side, who is there to take his place? Lord Melbourne, of course, must be looked upon as having virtually given up the contest; his name is only associated with an administration whose political history was, in spite of some good intentions, little more than a series of defeats. The Marquis of Clanricarde, though at times he displays great vigor and considerable tact, fails to inspire that personal respect which is necessary in a leader. Lord Normanby, although he has filled high official posts, has no weight in the House of Peers. The Earl of Clarendon is in every way superior, as a thinker and as a debater; there is the stamp of sterling talent on all he says and does. But he is to all appearance either an indolent or an unambitious man, or his ambition is confined in its objects; he has done too much to be altogether passed over, yet not enough to secure our admiration, and induce us to fix on him as even a probable person to be the future head of his party. With these names, we have exhausted the list of Whig leaders in the House of Peers, who in any degree are prominent for their talents. The oratorical strength of the Whigs lies in the House of Commons; nor is it likely that those who there exercise so much influence over the public mind would be in any hurry to leave it. Lord Morpeth will, in the course of things, be obliged to do so; but wherever there is a choice, it is not probable that it will lie in the direction of being, as a popular phrase terms it, "pitchforked." If, then (Earl Grey's personal ambition being seconded by the suffrages of his own party), he shall aim to take and (what would be more difficult) to keep the lead of the Whigs in the House of Lords, it is obvious that the difficulties of his task will be very much diminished by the comparative mediocrity of those with whom he will be placed in immediate competition.

With the political mantle of his father, the present Earl Grey would by no means inherit his responsibilities. The conditions of eminence are not what they were twenty or thirty years ago. Then, to be a party leader—of the chosen few, at least, whom history deigns to notice—impled the possession of an absolute mastery over the elements of political warfare. He to whom his compeers yielded precedence was distinguishable from them, not merely by his talent but also by the degree of his talent. There was in him a marked individuality of character; his intellect was of such towering proportions, that like the stature of a giant it was confessed at once; and all men gave way, by an instinct of deference, to one in whom they recognized a superior. He had not to work his way to the command by slow and laborious efforts and shifting tactics, carrying with him the traces and disgraces of many defeats, of many yieldings, of many compromises, such as men must suffer who seek to attain the height by the tortuous path. He took the initiative in government, stamped the impress of his mind upon that of his countrymen. He laid down principles — principles which, if they were not the creation of his own mind, were at least taken at first-hand from the well stored armory of the constitution ; and never ceased his efforts, or swerved from the course he had marked out, till he had brought his fellow-subjects either to acknowledge them as true, or at all events, to array themselves against him, and trust the issue to a combat in which he was himself at the head of his own following, and where he also secured the glory of the victory. Then, the political history of an age was written in the movements of parliamentary leaders : office gave power, and the real head of a party was at once the medium of its principles, the source of its arguments, and the regulator of all its minutest movements. There was dignity in his high station.

Statesmen then were the pupils of statesmen till they attained their full vigor, till they were politically of age, and fit to begin the world for themselves. They had not yet become the full grown puppets of agitators out of doors—the glittering tools of more hard-handed and determined men than themselves. Things, and, to say truth, men also, have changed since them. A party leader is now an anomaly; the very name itself a perversion of language. The initiative in legislation is assumed, not in the cabinet, but in the market-place, or at the hustings. The loudest voice, the longest purse, the most self-denying demagogueism, the most cautious audacity, the most calculating treason—these are now the qualifications for that mastership of the nation, which used till recent times to be the certain property of those men alone who possessed the loftiest intellect, the most far seeing views, the most prominent integrity of character, the most determined spirit in asserting and maintaining the principles in the truth of which they believed, the most commanding or the most persuasive oratory; who rallied round them the sympathies of their politically hereditary followers, and were elevated to power alike by the affection of the people and the confidence of the crown. Whatever their politics, they were to be depended upon as men; if they could not be relied on and followed for their wisdom, their consistency could be calculated on, and their principles counteracted.

But it is the perverse practice of party leaders in the present day—forced on them, perhaps, by an unhappy necessity of carrying measures by new uses of constitutional powers—to abandon the highest privileges of the statesman, to destroy the noble and exalted ideal which history leaves us, and of which even memory recalls living examples. And this is as true (though, perhaps, in a modified degree) of the Whig as of the Conservative leaders, of the Lord Melbournes and Lord John Russells, as of the Sir Robert Peels and the Lord Lyndhursts. They lead but to mislead. Their principle of political action—the recognition of the pressure from without—perils the credit of either their understanding or their character. Each great era of their political life is divided by an abrupt line of demarkation. Up to a certain day, they oppose with a hypocritical earnestness, or, according to their intellectual and moral idiosyncrasy, they attack with a bold (almost a virulent) fierceness, certain principles and opinions which are before the public, whether in or out of parliament. In the mildest instances, they offer to them an obstinate obstruction. But from that particular day they become altered men. With an earnestness which we are justified in supposing to be equally hypocritical, as being so sudden, they advocate the principles they before opposed, while all their virulence and fierceness are reserved for those they have abandoned. In the milder instances, they yield with an alarming but a contemptible alacrity. To illustrate the relative position of statesmen of the old order and of the new, one has but to compare the course of the late Earl

Grey as to the question of parliamentary reform, with that of Sir Robert Peel as to Roman Catholic emancipation and repeal of the Corn-laws. Putting all party-feeling on one side, this question is far too important to the well-being of the country to be much longer disregarded. The PRIDE of public men alone, if political morality has ceased to influence them, must bring about a change.

Earl Grey's prospects as a politician, and still more if he should be the leader of the Whigs in the House of Lords, will, however, be materially advanced by this lowering of the standard of parliamentary and political greatness. Compared with the giants who have passed away, he is a dwarf in parliamentary ability; but among the shifting shadows who play before us in the little sphere marked out of a blank future by the magic-lantern of a Cobden or an O'Connell, he assumes something like body and consistency. Nay, he has some qualities of mind which, if not exactly amiable and admirable in themselves, at least spring from a moral integrity which will not yield to external influences, and, therefore, indicate his possession of that firmness and frankness of character which one would desire in either an enemy or a friend. On one ground the public may always feel perfectly safe with Earl Grey. However unpopular his opinions may be, either with his own party or with the great bulk of the nation, he always fearlessly avows them; so that, as far as public discussion goes (we speak not of cabinet squabbles), you always know the man with whom you have to deal. He will not shirk an avowal to-day, when it might damage him, to make it openly to-morrow, when it will be profitable. So much for the morality of his political character; his discretion is another affair. Perhaps his frankness may sometimes be too self-seeking, bordering on the reckless.

Earl Grey has been denounced as "crotchety," because, on one or two occasions, he has taken a course or held an opinion adverse to that of his colleagues. That on such occasions he has sealed his verbal dissent by a resignation of his office, has afforded one guaranty of his sincerity. It may fairly be assumed, that a resistance or an independence which terminates in a self-chosen political martyrdom (for such is the loss of office to young ambition), is not mere intractability or restiveness, but that it springs from some more deeply rooted sentiment. At all events, it augurs political disinterestedness, and contrasts favorably with the conduct of those who wheel round suddenly at the word of command, voting to-day against the creed of yesterday, with a callous indifference or an audacious infidelity. We rather dwell upon this virtue of Earl Grey, because he is in want of a good word; in the paucity of his political attractions he needs every favorable construction that can with any degree of decency be extended to him. In the cases just referred to, he was charged with vanity and arrogance. As being comparatively an official subordinate, it was said that he thought too much of himself, as though statesmen or public servants of the second or third degree were not entitled even to lay claim to a conscience, much less to indulge in the moral luxury of a life of hypocrisy. But circumstances alter cases. Earl Gray, as Lord Howick, in the House of Commons, never seemed to look on himself as a subordinate, except as some young prince of the blood might play the ensign or the midshipman. From the first, he has appeared to have his eye steadily fixed on some position to which he aspired, and to have trusted to his rank, the gratitude of party, and the force of his own intellectual energies, as the means of securing it. He scorned to be an apprentice, but rather regarded himself as one of the master's family, ready to be taken into the firm when his time came. Whether this spirit of independence was really arrogance, or whether it was a self-reliance, premature only in the occasion of its exhibition, must be decided by the future conduct of Earl Grey, when his responsibilities shall have been increased; and criticism will be guided, not by the little jealousies of party, but by the observation and the good sense of the public.

Earl Grey can never take the highest rank as an orator. An effective speaker, and a ready, practiced debater, he already is; but he wants those personal attributes which are so essential in completing the full charm of eloquence, that there is scarcely an instance on record of a man becoming a first-rate orator without them. Yet it would not seem that there is any necessary connection between the personal peculiarities, whether favorable or unfavorable, of a speaker, and the intellect, the imagination, or the passions of his audience. One would suppose that mind would address itself at once to mind, that the kindred spirit would communicate with no direct dependence on the physical medium. Indeed there is not any positive proof on record that physical defects, whether of voice, of person, or of aspect, have neutralized the effect of eloquence when the spirit that kindles it was really within a man—deep-seated in the soul. The intellectual pride of man would rather favor the opposite view, seeking to establish the dominant power of the intellect, and making the body a merely secondary and subservient vehicle. But the fact is, that you seldom see a man even aspiring to eminence as a speaker, much less succeeding, unless he has been in some degree befriended by Nature, either in the gift of an harmonious or sonorous voice, or an imposing, or at least not unattractive countenance, and a tolerably well formed person. It may be that an instinct guides such men to their more natural vocation, or that the predilection created by their personal advantages in a first attempt nerves them to others, and so on till they attain to that degree of excellence which would enable them to charm, even were they suddenly deprived of those advantages. In the case of Earl Grey, the want of a prepossessing exterior and of a flexible, harmonious voice very materially detracts from his effectiveness as a speaker, and precludes the hope of his attaining the first rank among cotemporary orators, however great may be his intellectual superiority over many of them. All references to personal defects are invidious, and should certainly be as slight as possible. They might, in this case, be passed over almost entirely, but that it is desirable to correct one impression which party feeling has circulated in the public mind, that Lord Grey is an ill-tempered man. That he *looks* morose, even at times ill-tempered, can not be denied; but the tone and temper of his speeches, and his general conduct as a member of parliament, belie the assumption that this expression is any thing else than a settled form taken by his features, not from mental but from purely physical causes. We think we could point to one or two noble lords, and more than one or two honorable gentlemen, who are infinitely more irritable, morose, jaundiced with apparent disappointment, than Earl Grey, only that Nature has given them a mask to conceal their thoughts, more perfect in its proportions and more deceitful in its expression.

But in spite of the load of adverse circumstances against which Earl Grey has to bear up,—notwithstanding his harsh, shrill, discordant voice, his unexpressive countenance, and features so far removed from the standard of manly beauty, he has proved himself no ineffective antagonist of the chief speakers of the day. His intellectual powers, aided by very extensive knowledge of the most varied kind, which he can bring to bear alike upon abstract questions of policy or the most minute affairs of daily legislation, have carried him through the natural difficulties of his position. When he left the House of Commons he had worked himself up, by his talents alone, to a position among the Whig speakers scarcely inferior to that of Lord Palmerston, and decidedly above that held by many others who started with him in the race. If he had not yet arrived at that point in parliamentary importance when a member is, as a matter of course, "expected" to speak —when the debate is not considered complete till he has contributed his share to the general stock of argument or illustration—at least he seldom or never rose but to cast a new light on the subject, to throw down the gauntlet of opinion, to give a new and unexpected turn to the debate, or, at all events, to compel speakers who succeeded him to notice his views. With a very analytical mind (in this respect he stands out in favorable contrast with his cotemporaries), he was remarkably skillful in hunting out and exposing a fallacy, quite remorseless in controverting any proposition or opinion contrary to those principles of constitutional government or political economy which he holds, partly by hereditary descent, and partly by his own free adoption. In this pursuit he seemed to feel a keen intellectual pleasure, as though he spoke not merely as a duty to party, but also as a personal satisfaction to himself. His views were always clear and defined, from his having laid down in his own mind certain principles as what ought to be the basis of public polity, up to which he reasoned. His public course appears to have been uniformly guided by his sincere convictions, whether right or wrong; not, as in the case of some of his colleagues, by the desire to obtain popularity. If any thing, he is disposed to push the doctrines of the political economists too far—to take human nature too little into account.

Forced to depend for influence as a speaker, not on his personal but his mental powers, one consequence is, that the reasoning faculty too much predominates. A demonstration is all-sufficient with him. No allowance is made for the wants or the weaknesses of human nature; for temporary detracting causes; for those infirmities of our race which make the perfect practical application of abstract propositions, however true they may be, a great difficulty, if not an impossibility. He takes existing facts too little into account. That which is to politicians generally a most important element, scarcely enters into Earl Grey's calculations. With him, whatever ought to be, must be. He is altogether too confident, not so much in himself, as in the all-sufficiency of reason to decide on any case that may be subjected to it. He does not seem to be conscious of that higher wisdom which is, in most respects, above the ken of the mere reasoning faculty, being founded upon experience and strengthened by humility, till it becomes a kind of intellectual faith. He has none of the philosophy of Edmund Burke. He lays down excellent principles, but, unlike Lord John Russell, at inconvenient times. It is his fault to be too fond of argument; nay, of what a popular expression terms, not unhappily, "argufying." At times this habit degenerates into mere captiousness. Like Lord Denman, he will fix with earnestness and intensity on some minor point, which he will elevate into undue importance, but which a more enlarged mind would pass over as being among the necessary conditions of a proposition, to be admitted without question. On the other hand, this disposition to cavil and dispute, to rest great questions upon trifling points, this microscopic view of constitutional principles, often becomes of great public value when the rights of the subject are concerned, at a period when a general confidence in the integrity and public spirit of public men leads us to acquiesce in a relaxation of those safeguards of liberty which our more suspicious ancestors watched in a spirit of obstinate obstruction.

With such peculiarities of person, of temperament,

and of intellectual bias, it is not probable that Earl Grey will be able to take the lead of the Whig party in the House of Peers. He wants dignity, both personally and mentally. The very qualities which made him useful as a subordinate, or as a colleague in the House of Commons, would unfit him for a position of command or responsibility in the Upper House. The political philosophy which prevails among the peers is very different from that chance-medley which is the natural result of popular election in the other place. A species of free-masonary is established there. They can afford better to dispense with popular fallacies. Much more is taken for granted than in the House of Commons; and a man like Earl Grey would be apt to find his weapons get rusty for want of use, unless, indeed, he were to keep them in play by demolishing the select few whose garrulity is recognized and kept up for the general amusement. His powers of argumentation would be almost thrown away upon such men as Lord Lyndhurst, or even Lord Brougham; and the principles which he used to lay down with so much authority, and so little fear of contradiction, in the House of Commons, would stand but a poor chance with the Duke of Wellington on one hand, or the Bishops of London or of Exeter on the other. He will find the straw-splitting system of little use in the House of Lords. If he is permanently to take his place among the chief men in that assembly, he must altogether elevate his tone, enlarge his views, purge his intellectual prejudices, consolidate his principles. He must exhibit less of speculative democracy, less of the tyranny of the political economist, less devotion to theory, more amenity to the practical necessities of a compromising age. Above all, he must not expect from the House of Lords that consideration he received from the House of Commons, as the son of the man who carried the Reform-bill.

SIR JAMES GRAHAM.

WHATEVER may be suggested to the contiary by personal or political antipathy, it will be very generally admitted by men of all parties, who are conversant with the subject, that Sir James Graham stands next to Sir Robert Peel and Lord John Russell in the degree of influence he exercises over the debates in the House of Commons. It is not as an orator, more than respectable though his pretensions be, that he ranks thus high: for there are many, even among his inferiors as statesmen, who in eloquence far transcend him. Nor is it because he has, in the course of his long and checkered career, developed those higher qualities, either of character or of intellect, which lead men in the aggregate to wait upon the judgment of the individual, yielding themselves to his guidance; for the public life of Sir James Graham has been singularly unpropitious to the accomplishment of that glorious distinction. Nor is it that his reputation has grown with the growth or identified itself with the successes of any great national party, whose gratitude would have given him a following, and that following an audience prepossessed in his favor; for there is scarcely a public man of the day who has been so deeply and irrecoverably inconstant to political alliances, or the virulence of whose temporary opposition may with more precision be gauged by the fervency of his former support. On none of the received grounds, in fact, can his influence—popularity it can not be called

—with the House of Commons be accounted for. Such as it is, it depends on himself alone. It is anomalous, like his position.

The solitary, self-created, almost undisputed sway wielded by Sir Robert Peel, one can understand. He has been the foremost man of his time. Always the leader of, even in adversity, the most powerful party of his countrymen, he has never, except, perhaps, in the single instance of the Reform question, run counter to the feelings of the nation. There are principles and sentiments which, even in the hour of the uttermost estrangement, he held in common with his opponents; there was always some neutral ground for reconciliation. If events proved that his advocacy could not always have been sincere, no one could point to habitual virulence and acrimony assumed to give the color of earnestness. He soothed, flattered, cajoled, played off parties and opinions against each other with delicate finesse, but never directly outraged deep-rooted prejudices or long established opinions. And so, indeed, it is with him in the present hour. While ruling his political cotemporaries with a power so absolute as to be almost without parallel in representative assemblies, and, at the same time, so well masked as to require all the envenomed ingenuity of a disappointed partisan ere it could be discovered, much less believed in, Sir Robert Peel has contrived to avoid exhibiting most of the harsher symbols of his sway. His despotism has not been obtrusive, or his tyranny odious. He has made men enslave each other, without himself standing forth as the confessed cause of the general degradation. If he has no natural or personal followers, so also he has no organized opponents, —at least, their organization melts away at his approach: they are valiant only behind his back.

The more genial, mild, and natural influence of Lord John Russell with his followers is also to be accounted for; nor is it at all surprising that he should be a favorite as a speaker with the House generally. Of the Whig party, first the *protégé*, then the pupil, and now the leader, he has always been the firm and consistent supporter. Of one side of the House he possesses the favor by every right of political service; and party is not slow to be grateful, however wanting it may be in other political virtues. To his opponents and the House generally he has always exhibited a deference and respectful consideration, which, if it sprung from policy, was wise in the extreme, for it has secured a degree of prepossession on personal grounds which is not enjoyed even by Sir Robert Peel himself, and often acts as a counterbalancing make-weight for mental and physical short-comings in his oratory.

Sir James Graham's influence in the representative branch of the legislature is not to be attributed to any of the causes which have secured its favors for these two distinguished men. Like Sir Robert Peel, he has constantly been in antagonism with parties and opinions to which he has at some other time, before or since, given his most hearty support. But his changes of opinion and of policy have been made under very different circumstances, and the tone and character of his advocacy and opposition have been of a very different nature. Sir Robert Peel's first great act of inconsistency, however it may have exasperated his followers at the time, still bore the stamp of statesmanship; inasmuch as it was the application of a great, and, in some respects, a desperate remedy to a state of things, to which the history of the constitution afforded no parallel. It carried with it, also, to most minds the justification of an overpowering necessity. His subsequent deviations from the line of policy professed by him in early life, and while still the leader of the old Tory party, have, in like manner, been to a great extent the result of circumstances which he could not control. Many compromises of principle are forgiven in the regenerator of a great party. And Sir Robert Peel, too, has always kept his motives so free from suspicion. His ambition is, at least, of an ennobling and exalting character. He has never been the mere partisan, or allowed politics to become a passion with him, but has preserved his dignity amid all the heats of party strife. Personal motives are seldom assigned to him when he sees fit to change his policy. He has preserved in an eminent degree the respect both of parliament and the public.

Not so Sir James Graham. He has not, amid his many changes of opinion and party, preserved the same high character, the same freedom from the imputation of partisanship, the same presumption of stainless motive, that have upheld Sir Robert Peel, and retained for him the personal favor of the House of Commons, even in the most critical and dangerous periods of his fortunes. Still less has he observed that steady devotion to early received and professed opinions, that tolerant and liberal appreciation of the principles and views of opponents, that gently repulsive retirement from stage to stage of party defense in the face of the advancing enemy, which, together with many personal qualities of an amiable character, have secured for Lord John Russell so much of the regard of foes as well as of friends. Sir James Graham has acted on wholly opposite tactics. There has been more (so to speak) of brigandage, more of the loose policy of the Free Lance, in his political life. His attacks have always been fierce and virulent in inverse proportion to what has proved to be the depth of his convictions, and to the apparent necessity of the case; his defenses have always been distinguished by a blind and passionate obstinacy; his compromises and abandonments of professed opinions have always been sudden. These are great defects of character in the eyes of Englishmen, and they react upon Sir James Graham, and lessen his consequence as a statesman, to this hour, in spite of his commanding talents and great position.

Sir James Graham has made enemies of almost every party in the legislature. It has not been because he has opposed them from time to time, for other men who are much more popular have for many years done so more effectually; but it has been on account of the extreme virulence of his opposition. His fighting has always been *à l'outrance.* He has been too prone to disdain the courtesies of political warfare; fictions though they be, yet agreeable ones and humanizing. He has always appeared to import his passions into party conflicts, as though he were not merely fighting the battle of opinions, but also maintaining his own personal quarrel. And yet he has never succeeded in impressing one with the idea of his being in earnest. That would have rendered pardonable, language otherwise too severe. His harangues while in opposition, and indeed all his party speeches, rather seem the elaborate efforts of one having little real sympathy with the themes he is discussing or the views he is urging, but who has worked himself up to a state of fictitious enthusiasm or moral indignation, in order the more effectually to gratify political vindictiveness, or advance personal ambition, by obtaining the applause of audiences willing to be misled under cover of those high-sounding pretenses. But, whether simulated or real, some of the speeches here more particularly referred to — and to which, it must be added, no one could listen without being struck with admiration at their boldness, skill, and sustained energy—were scarcely reconcilable with that liberal and charitable interpretation of the motives of opponents, which is one of the first duties of public men to each other. Nor has Sir James Graham, while conducting his combats in this spirit, been at all choice in the weapons he used. Any missive that came to hand was hurled indiscriminately at the foe. No epithet, however heavy its imputation (always, of course, saving that it is parliamentary); no taunt, however bitter or exasperating, whether to individuals, to parties, to opinions, or even to whole nations; no general charge, however grave as against the policy of a party, or however damnatory of the motives of his opponents in their councils or their conduct; and, finally, no manœuver that could by any stretch of license be accounted not inconsistent with parliamentary honor, even to the extent of partial statements of opponents' opinions, or partial quotations or withholdings of justificatory matter; not one such expedient, however little to be approved in fair and free public discussion, by which a temporary triumph could be won, or a rival for the hour put down, was ever rejected by Sir James Graham from any delicacy of temperament, or from any high and fastidious sense of honor, such as restrains some men from grasping the victory which is theirs on such conditions; or even from that constitutional love of fair play and open, stand-up fighting which is the Englishman's boast, and which is covertly the guiding principle in all the debates in parliament.

It will be observed that blame is imputed to Sir James Graham, not merely because in the course of a long and very stormy political life he has changed his opinions. Men have always been held at liberty to do that; and of late it is becoming quite a fashion. It is on account of the extreme virulence and unscrupulousness with which he has from time to time advocated the opinion or the party object of the hour, and the suddenness with which he has changed those opinions and objects, that he has failed to secure his fair share of the respect of his cotemporaries, at least for more than his great talent. A very cursory glance at his speeches will fully confirm the view here put forward. Look at his earlier political career, when, as "the Cumberland Baronet," he frighted the isle from its propriety by the violent and unconstitutional tendency of his writings and speeches. Who could have suspected that a man whose sentiments breathed so much of the very spirit of license would, in comparatively few years, stand before the world one of the favored leaders of the party he was then denouncing so violently, and as the most arbitrary Home-secretary the country had known for many years? Again, his attacks upon the landed interest in the earlier part of his career were so harsh and virulent, that one can scarcely believe, though the fact stares one in the face, that the same man has been, for twelve or fourteen years, one of the chief counselors and leaders of those whom he then treated as the pests and enemies of their country. Furthermore, let us look at the zealous partisanship with which, when he was a member of the Whig government, he attacked on the one hand the Radicals, of whom, at least in opinion, he might once have been accounted a leader; and on the other the Conservatives, in whose ranks he was so soon to hold one of the most distinguished posts. Nor can it be forgotten how, when in power as a Conservative minister, he stood out in marked relief from his colleagues, in the virulence of his attacks on those with whom he had so lately held office, and toward whom he at least, and Lord Stanley, should have been restrained in resorting to the more envenomed hostilities of party. It can not be attributing too much importance to the effects of this constant antagonism on his part to the convictions or the self-love of his cotemporaries, when we say that they detract very materially from the estimation in which he is held, and preclude the possibility of his being popular in the House of Commons, however much his eloquence, his debating powers, or his extraordinary aptitude for business, may cause him to be admired, and render him valuable as a minister and a statesman.

It has been in the face of all these self-created obstacles, in spite of drawbacks and disadvantages which would have long since consigned an ordinary man to oblivion, that Sir James Graham, after having deserted his post in the van of one party—the party with whom his early political life was spent, and to whom he was indebted for his position—has forced his way to the very leadership of another; of a party distinguished for the possession of talent legitimately occupying its ranks, and not at all dependent upon chance recruits for the figure it makes before the country. Without a following, after having violently discarded the political friendships of his youth and manhood, and in spite of an habitual, almost a studied avoidance of all the ordinary arts of popularity, which at times has almost gone the length of courting public odium, we find Sir James Graham the right-hand and confidential counselor of the most powerful minister this country had known since Pitt; the absolute dictator of all the internal administration, and of much of the internal policy; and the originator, or at all events the arbiter, of the internal legislation, of this great kingdom. More than of any other living statesman, it may be said of him, that he has made his own position. It was probably the object of his early ambition; yet, if we look at his career, how unpropitious was its commencement for such a close! So much the more merit, then, in an intellectual point of view, is due to him who could thus compel circumstances to his purposes. It is to his talents alone that he is indebted for the high posts he has held, and the distinguished position he enjoys among his cotemporaries. He has literally fought his way up; and a hard fight he has had. If he has multiplied the natural obstacles of such a career, so much the greater is the talent and the determination of purpose by which they have been overcome. What Mr. Macaulay has won by his eloquence and capacity for statesmanship, Sir James Graham has attained by the same spirit of self-dependence, working out its mission in the more active and stormy scenes of political excitement, by more bold and dangerous ventures, and more skillful and daring pilotage.

Sir James Graham has always been equal to his position. Various as have been the parts he has played in the political drama of his time, he has always glided naturally into them, and distinguished himself as one of the first actors, rising naturally to the top. His speeches from time to time afforded an accurate barometer of his political position. On whichever side of politics they were made, they have always been marked by great aptitude, readiness, tact, vigor, and power. Except Lord Brougham and O'Connell, he has been, perhaps, the most actively militant orator of his day. When he is down, he attacks those who are uppermost; when he is in power, he wages perpetual war with those who are out. Whether attacking institutions or defending them, however, he has shown equal ability and determination to conquer at all hazards. When he was a Radical, or at least so very ultra a Whig that the steady ones of the party were almost ashamed, or at least afraid of him, he was so thoroughly uncompromising in his denunciations, that Mr. Duncombe, whom he nightly strove to extinguish with all the awful terrors of law and order, would have been by his side but a mere wretched shadow of a demagogue. In fact, we have no such Radicals now as Sir James was then. They are all fat, jocular men, growing wealthy upon coronerships, and such-like abominations; or *blasé* dandies in search of an excitement. Some of the speeches of Sir James Graham, whether in parliament, at the hustings, or at public meetings, at the time referred to, would in the present day be accounted almost too bold for the most determined aspirant for the honors of political martyrdom. For they were unredeemed by the philosophy of liberalism; they had not even the dignity and tone of Chartism. They were simple, unadulterated, partisan speeches, made to serve a purpose, and forgotten by the speaker as soon as uttered. But about their talent there was no mistake. It was not that they were distinguished for high eloquence, but for power and downright hard hitting. They gave the speaker a claim on the rising party of the time; and in a few years the *quasi*-demagogue shot up into a minister.

And a capital minister he made. His most determined enemies do not deny this. Whatever may be thought of Sir James Graham as a politician, no one hesitates to admit that he is one of the best administrative officers this country has for many years produced. The same talent, the tact and aptitude, which had made him so clever an assailant of the former government, rendered him immediately fit for office. He was here, as before, equal to his position. As a speaker on behalf of the government, too, he proved himself a most valuable ally,—turning the flank of his quondam Radical associates with provoking skill and unerring precision. But the prior claims of those who were already designated as the successors to the chief posts in the Whig party still kept Sir James in the background, and forbade the hope of his taking that distinguished position for which his talents and ambition alike indicated him. The reorganization of the party at that time, and their adoption of a policy of dangerous progress, afforded an opportunity for a change; and accordingly, very soon after, we find Sir James Graham (after a short time spent in a chrysalis state) a full-blown Conservative. Here, again, he was fully equal to his position; and as it was during the long and glorious struggle of the Conservative opposition, headed by Sir Robert Peel, Lord Stanley, and Sir James Graham, that the latter made his best speeches, a better opportunity can not be taken to treat of his peculiarities as an orator—which was the part he then laid himself out to fill—before attempting to describe him as home secretary, in his character of repressor-general of the insubordinates in the House of Commons, or "crusher"-in-chief to the ministry.

The Conservative speeches of Sir James Graham, made when fighting side by side with Sir Robert Peel and Lord Stanley against the Whigs, were admirable specimens of what may be done by highly cultivated powers, extensive acquaintance with the best models of eloquence, persevering care, and elaborate preparation, without oratorical genius, or that earnestness and sincerity of purpose which will often advantageously supply its place. Assuming them to have been deliberately got up to serve a certain purpose, it would be impossible to withhold admiration from the power, tact, and aptitude, with which the means were made subservient to the end. Upon the supposition that the speaker was really sincere, it was difficult to account for the absence, even in the most solemn appeals to the religious feelings of the auditory, or to their cherished constitutional prepossessions, of those touches of deep feeling which are the utterances of the soul, not the promptings of art, and which act like a talisman upon the sympathies. The speeches referred to were, many of them, superior as compositions to those of Sir Robert Peel or Lord Stanley, containing more of the great argument on which the whole movement of the Conservative party was based: for, although Sir James Graham evinces so little readiness to bend his will to those around him, he shows an almost chameleon-like power of reflecting their sympathies, opinions, or prejudices. They were in this respect admirable manuals for the party, and no doubt did good service in the country. But the impetuous eloquence of Lord Stanley, and the admirable persuasive art of Sir Robert Peel, enabled them to achieve more, with materials which, in justice to Sir James Graham, we must admit were not superior to those which are to be found in his speeches of that period. What detracted from the effect of the declamatory passages was a somewhat pompous and stilted tone, a too evident affectation of solemnity and earnestness; which might have been partly natural, arising from physical causes, and therefore not fairly the object of criticism, though materially marring the effect of the speeches. But allowing for all these defects, they were yet remarkable efforts of oratorical skill, which raised Sir James to a level with the best speakers in the House of Commons. The exordiums and perorations always bore marks of the most careful preparation, and were usually models of fine composition; the quotations were most apt, and often from recondite sources; the poetical passages delivered with a fine emphasis and full appreciation of the rhythm. As a debater, rising at a late hour, perhaps, to reply suddenly to the arguments of a previous speaker or speakers, where the novelty of the topics precludes all preparation, and the real powers of the orator are therefore tried to the utmost, Sir James showed himself the possessor of the very highest order of talent,—in readiness of argument, retentiveness of memory, suddenness of quotation, quickness of retort, in invective, sarcasm, repartee, declamation, he was seldom or never at fault, and was always the antagonist most dreaded by the Whigs. Perhaps one reason for this might be the virulence of tone, and unscrupulousness in the use of weapons, of which mention has already been made, as one of the chief faults of Sir James Graham.

But all these successes as a politician, and all these triumphs as a speaker, will not account for or justify the assertion with which these observations commenced —that Sir James Graham's influence over the House of Commons is only second to that of Sir R. Peel or Lord John Russell. For influence he does possess, although, in the face of all that has been here said to his disadvantage, it is most difficult to trace it to its source, seeing that there is no man in the House who appears less to court popular favor than Sir James Graham. Looking back at his career while joint leader of the Conservative opposition, it was certainly then impossible to predict that he would develop into the sort of character he has exhibited as minister and home secretary. Prominent as his position then was, he was rather the servitor of party than otherwise: he never assumed to take the lead. Still less would you have supposed that he would have had the boldness to flout the House as he has since done; or so ostentatiously to defy the sovereign people through their representatives. All honor to him for his courage, though it might have been exercised in a better cause. It is because Sir James Graham affects, or really feels, an indifference to the good opinion of the House, that they submit so spaniel-like to his caprices or his studied coldness and indifference, and pay so much attention, often so much deference, to his opinion.

A hardness and impassibility of temperament, which is to censure or obloquy as adamant or rhinoceros-hide, joined to a wonderful knowledge of human nature, great talents, clear perception, readiness, determination of purpose, and a steady resolution to seize all opportunities and yield none, give him great advantage in an assembly where the average of ability is not above mediocrity, and where there are so few who have the courage or feel the inclination to stand forth as champions. With the exception of Mr. Duncombe, Mr.

Ferrand, and Mr. Wakley, the members generally bent before his consistent will and determination of purpose as home secretary; qualities which, in such a place, are almost tantamount to a strong or superior mind. If they would say the truth, they are not a little afraid of him. At the same time, it must not be forgotten that such a man as Sir James is in these times particularly useful. Utilitarianism, on which are grafted some of the colder and harsher doctrines of political economy, has become the political religion of our public men. Centralization, with its train of paralyzing evils, has become the fashionable machinery of government. The farther the ear and eye are removed from the actual scene, the less chance there is of the evil being seen or the complaint heard. The selfishness of classes needs excuses. It thinks to hide its naked hideousness in systems. Weaker natures fear to lay down, still more to carry out, principles, which this selfishness would fain see adopted. A firmer spirit, which, perhaps because it has faith in such principles, asserts them broadly, and maintains them intact, through good and evil report, becomes a powerful and valuable ally. A Sir James Graham will be clung to, in an instinctive deference for his vigor of mind and boldness of purpose. Such a man serves, to rule. Less remote causes of his influence may, however, be found; causes on the surface, quite sufficient in the present state of things to account for his contradicting all the usual calculations on which ministerial popularity is based.

We are still considering him in his capacity as a minister. His demeanor in the House is a study. As he enters below the bar, his red dispatch-box in hand, his figure towers above most of the members, notwithstanding that of late years he has contracted a slight stoop. Extreme hauteur, tempered by a half-sarcastic superciliousness, is his prevailing characteristic; and, as he slowly drags along his tail and massive frame, which still retains much of the fine proportion of youth, in his heavy, measured, almost slipshod tread, toward his seat at the right of the Speaker's table, there is a self-satisfied, almost inane expression of the countenance, produced by a peculiar fall of the nether lip and a distorted elevation of the eyebrows, that does not by any means prepossess you in his favor, or suggest any high idea of his intellect. He rather looks like some red-tape minister of the Tadpole school, or some pompous placeman, conceited of his acres. But by and by you learn to separate the more fixed habit of the features from this odd expression of the countenance, till you see that the superciliousness is real, though exaggerated by the physical peculiarity. There are no traces of ill-nature in the face; but, on the other hand, there is nothing to encourage. Meanwhile, he has seated himself, placed his red box on the table before him, stretched himself out to his full length, and awaits, with arms folded and hat slouched over his face, the questioning to which he knows he will be subjected at this particular hour, from half-past four to half-past five. He is not left long in his moody silence. Some one has put a question to him. It is Mr. Duncombe, who, if one is to judge by the malicious twinkle in his eye and his affected tone of moral indignation, has got hold of some grievance—some letter-opening delinquency, or some case of magisterial cruelty and Home-Office indifference, with which he has worked upon the members who do the "British-public" part in these little political dramas, for they are crying "hear, hear!" with a forty-John-Bull power. Does the home secretary start up to answer? Is he indignant at the insinuations thrown out by his smart and ready antagonist? Does he burn to relieve himself of the odium of having sanctioned a system of espionage, or of having neglected to redress some wrong—as he, the poor man's *ex-officio* trustee, is bound to do? Oh, no! he is in no hurry. The breath of the questioner has full time to cool, and the voice of moral indignation to abate its energy, ere he stirs. Then he uncoils himself, rising slowly to his full height, and confronting his antagonist with a well assumed consciousness of the extreme absurdity of his question, and the absolute impregnability of the defense, if, indeed, he shall condescend to make any answer at all; for you are left in doubt a moment, whether he will not allow his assumed surprise to dwindle into a contemptuous laugh, and so sit down again. However, such things not being allowed by the sovereign people, and as ministers, however despotically disposed, must answer questions, the next thing to be accomplished is to give as homeopathic a dose of information as possible, conveyed in the largest possible amount of indifference, cool, quizzing, and wholesome parliamentary contempt. There are stereotyped forms. The initiated know almost the words. The cool, phlegmatic, impassible style is, of course, peculiar to the particular minister of whom we speak. His idea of the functions of his office seems to be, that he is to exercise the utmost possible power with the least possible accountability. He is to know nothing, see nothing, do nothing, but what he is absolutely compelled to know, see, or do. If the enemy can ferret out a fact and prove it, so much the better for his case. Then, perhaps, it *may* be admitted. But the usual course is for Sir James, in his low, monotonous voice, and steady, determined manner, to give an elaborate, formal statement of words, with as few facts as possible, and leaving the matter as nearly as possible where he found it. This course has its advantage; for the questions put are often unmeaning, and even detrimental to the public service. Sometimes, however, matters grow more serious. The cool, hard, impassible functionary is compelled by a sense of duty to make a more elaborate statement, and then it is you perceive his superiority as a minister. The clearness, firmness, extent of information and sound knowledge of his duty, he displays, show him to be not deficient, either in act or in explanation, when he thinks it necessary. His questioner is then put *hors de combat*, and he himself gets a sort of license for that superciliousness and apathetic indifference to popular censure, which are so fatally urged to his prejudice. In still more dubious cases, as, for instance, in that of Mazzini, Sir James Graham has carried this impassibility and indifference to an insulting extent. If he believed himself right, of course he showed great moral courage; but moral courage in a bad cause is scarcely distinguishable from obstinacy; and Sir James Graham's conduct in that case laid him open to great obloquy, much of which was deserved. Yet the determination he showed under such circumstances rather increased than diminished his influence with the House. If it made him, politically speaking, hated by many, it also made him feared. Such steady self-possession, joined to such talents and information, and to such debating powers as he has in his former career displayed, though now he rarely exercises them, are quite sufficient to account for that influence which we have ascribed to him, in the absence of personal respect, which, generally speaking, he does not command; or of party gratitude, which he has done little to deserve on the one hand, and so much to forfeit on the other.

LORD MORPETH.

Lord Morpeth's position as a public man must be peculiarly gratifying to his personal feelings. His ambition ought to be more than satisfied with the rank he holds as an orator in the House of Commons, while the personal esteem and respect entertained for him by his own party afford to a man of his peculiar temperament a far more agreeable reward than even the admiration which his displays of intellectual ability have elicited. In the hardness engendered by party strife, it is rare to find personal qualities so much regarded in a public man as they are in the case of Lord Morpeth; and still more so where the individual has entered, as the noble lord has done, with keenness, and as much heat as his nature will allow, into almost all the conflicts of the time. The circumstances attending his retirement some few years ago from public life, and those which have characterized his return, have contributed still further to invest him with a personal, more than even a political interest. When he was ejected from Yorkshire on the final downfall of the Whig party, and when he made that somewhat rash resolution never to reënter the House of Commons unless as representative of the same county, few men could have supposed, in the then triumphant state of the Conservative party, that circumstances would have arisen so soon to restore him to the post he had before held, or to take away from the rashness of that vow by accomplishing its fulfillment. That a man evidently so ambitious of distinction as a statesman and an orator, should have voluntarily debarred himself from his greatest enjoyment on what might seem so sentimental a ground, is at the same time in itself a strong proof of some very decided personal character, some qualities of the heart as well as of the mind, distinguishing him from those who prove the difference by their astonishment, or by their depreciation of what might seem such Quixotic conduct. But Lord Morpeth almost stands alone in this privilege of exciting personal regard, while he at the same time secures political esteem. It is a regard felt by those even who in politics differ most widely from him; who, in fact, were disposed to look at his former coquetings with democracy as involving a most dangerous example. This involuntary blending of the personal with the political character, when accompanied by intellectual claims, and not carried to excess, is very agreeable to the English people, who love to see men sincere and in earnest, even if against them, and who can not be brought to understand that cold abstraction of character by which the man removes himself from the direct agency of human sympathies, living in the intellect and the reason alone, a mere intelligent machine for working out propositions. State-craft, to their apprehension, is nothing but downright hypocrisy; and no state necessity excuses, in their eyes, double-faced policy or tergiversation of principle. A great proportion of Lord Morpeth's popularity with all sections of the Liberal party is to be traced to his instinctive, unfailing honesty of purpose. He might be sometimes personally ridiculed, or oratorically he might absurdly illustrate that vaulting ambition which o'erleaps itself, but he was always morally respectable.

Lord Morpeth contrasts favorably with other Whig noblemen in either House of Parliament, in being, to all appearance, wholly free from the pride of rank or class. In the assertion of those views and principles which are popular with the middle and lower classes, he has gone farther than any of his colleagues; and his evident sincerity of disposition compels us to believe that he feels all he utters. He not only entertains popular opinions, but, what is infinitely more captivating with the multitude, he expresses them popularly. There is a frankness, a warmth, a courtesy, unaccompanied by insulting condescension, that attaches to him men of all shades of opinion. In this respect the young nobleman who most resembles him is Lord John Manners. Starting from wholly opposite points in the political arena, their course seems to run together thus far: that they think the time is come for social, more than for political, concession on the part of men of rank and station, to those who, in the singular changes this age has seen, have secured to themselves so much of the real power of the country.

As a politician, Lord Morpeth has already run nearly to the full length of the tether allowed by the principles of his party; as an orator, he is still in process of development. The Lord Morpeth returned to Parliament in 1846 was such an improvement on the Lord Morpeth who was ejected in 1841, that still greater advances toward perfection may be hoped for. Whether the grafts which the vigorous native stock has received from republicanism in the United States, and from class self-seeking in the Anti-Corn-law League, will bring with them strength or weakness, can not at present be ascertained; but there is a good, sound root and stem of John Bullism in the noble lord's mind, on which one may place great faith. At present, he seems to be rather feeling his own strength; playing with his new-found muscle and sinew; trying experiments with edged tools, of the real danger of which he is not yet fully cognizant. His speeches are as yet powerful efforts, rather than finished works of oratorical art. It is the peculiarity of some men always to be thought young, or at least immature. A privilege in private life, this is in the political world rather a disadvantage. Who ever thinks of Lord Morpeth or Mr Disraeli as steady, staid, middle-aged men—the one of forty, the other of forty-four? Of the readers of Lord Morpeth's speeches, who regard him as a sort of parliamentary pupil of Lord John Russell, but few reflect that he has been in the House of Commons (an interval excepted) now twenty years. Those who are accustomed constantly to see and hear him, if the fact did not stare them in the face, would scarcely give the noble lord credit for the experience which so long a public life ought to have brought with it. They would expect from him ultra-liberal opinions; or warm, hearty, English sympathy, always bordering on rashness; or ambitious efforts at political philosophy; or high-flown attempts at the sublime in oratory: any thing, in short, but wisdom or common sense. When Lord Morpeth was in parliament before, the idea of youthfulness and crudity (as in the case of Mr. Disraeli) had obtained such full possession of the minds of those accustomed to watch those matters, that even superior power scarcely received its due meed of respect when at intervals it was displayed, but was postponed in the general estimation to the claims of unambitious but consistent dullness. Time alone will remove this ridiculous but provoking prejudice. It is fast giving way already.

Carry back the imagination six or seven years. You are walking down to the House of Commons, looking inquiringly, in the stream of horsemen and pedestrians that flows continuously toward St. Stephen's between the hours of four and five, for the notables of the day. Some one strides rapidly toward you in the distance. Heavens, at what a rate he walks! Nearer he comes. He must be *somebody*; but you will scarce have time to take a steady view, ere he will shoot past you. Has he something on his mind, that those two large, wide-open eyes stare so fixedly on vacancy, half-starting from their sockets? Or is it only that he *will* tie his white cravat so tight that his full long face and toppling hat look like a large thistle on its fragile stem? And why stalketh he on (unmindful of the July sun!) with that blank, fixed look, as of unutterable pain? Is he possessed? Hath he a demon? or a steam leg? or thinketh he that he bestrides a velocipĕde? No sign! On, on! the figure comes, Old-Hamlet-like, but t'other way, and with a sharp, quick noise of iron heels. Another instant and it has whisked by you—disappeared, past the tall Hibernian porter, through the little door of the House of Commons—a brief but startling apparition of two eyes, a flushed face (which you think you must have seen before, or something very like it), a fawn-like figure with tapering legs, in a swallow-tailed coat, and fautless inexpressibles!

Having made your way into the strangers' gallery by means of an order, you are observing the different great men of the day. There he is! standing by the side of a little green table near the bar, with papers in his hand, waiting to catch the Speaker's eye. How restless the light, graceful figure is! Is he going to dance? The feet seem as if moving to some "ditty of no tone." Positively, if the Speaker does not call upon him soon, he will pirouette with airy bound along the floor, and come down with an *à plomb* upon the table. Ah! he is at last released from pain—the pain of standing still. He trips gracefully up to the gentlemen in wigs, the Speaker's deputies in martyrdom, delivers his papers, and drops into his seat; for he is in office. A little later and our tantalizing friend rises to speak, standing at the table with his ministerial dispatch-box before him, a mountain of papers, and two oranges snug in a corner—awful symptoms of a long speech. Now you have a moment to study his countenance: surely it is familiar to you! Did you, in the old days, visit the Haymarket Theater? Did you ever see Liston as Apollo Belvi? Do you ever ponder on the graphic works of our great limner-satirist, the mysterious "HB."—he who foreshadows political events, grasping their hidden causes, or seizing on their ridiculous aspects, with such wondrous sagacity and wit? No; nor have you, to your knowledge, ever seen Lord Morpeth before. Yet you know those lineaments! Sir, it is *the other* face you are thinking of.

He has begun to speak. He has delivered an ambitious exordium, stilted and high-flown in language, but elevated and generous in sentiment. His voice is rather harshly high in its tone, and too uniform in its sound. But there is vigor and earnestness, and here and there a touch of manly feeling, that almost startles by its contrast with the odd, overgrown-boyish, yet not unprepossessing, figure and manner. The action, also, is too formal; it has too much of the schools; and there is altogether an artificial and ambitious effort at eloquence that makes one wish Lord Morpeth would trust more to his own unfettered impulses, and not so much to the lessons he has learned of some elocution-master, who has tried to teach him what never yet was taught, and never will be. The style is too much that of the "young gentlemen's academies" on examination-day. But the more you hear, the more you like both the speaker and the seentiments: in spite of all his peculiarities he has warmed you up. If you don't think with him, at least you feel with him. You have forgotten, too, the little traits of the ludicrous, in the palpable moral integrity of the man before you, instinct with a consciousness of the deep responsibilities of his exalted rank and station.

Such was the Lord Morpeth of 1840. To come at the Lord Morpeth of the present day, you have but to soften down the ludicrous ideas, and extend the influence of those which are associated with respect for high moral and intellectual qualities. Five years, while they have added some silver to the gray hairs which it seems is the hereditary peculiarity of his family, have smoothed off many of the angularities, and strengthened the tone, of his mind. His language, still ambitious, is less inflated; his manner less bombastic; his style generally more finished. He is certainly developing, not, perhaps, into a great orator, but, at all events, into a powerful and accomplished speaker, with great sway over the feelings of his auditory. There are in him the materials of a statesman, but of a statesman in whom the good rather than the great will predominate.

Contrasted with Earl Grey, he gains by the comparison. Although the former had the start of him in official life, he is equally, if not more efficient, from his greater patience and amenity. Lord Morpeth never excites bitterness of feeling; Lord Grey does. With equal honesty of purpose, he takes circumstances more into view, and does not run counter to public feeling where no good, but rather harm, would ensue. He takes broader views, more germane to the great object of all statesmanship and legislation than the strict logical conclusions of Earl Grey. He reasons, to a great extent, through his feelings; Lord Grey subdues all feeling to the harsh necessities of experimental policy. The one gives the rein in a great measure to his sympathies, feeling that they will not lead him far wrong: with the other, to think, to reason, to prove, is to be wise; he sets up the wisdom of man's limited capacity above that higher wisdom which is based on our moral instincts. The one warms, inspires you; the other convinces, perhaps, but chills. The one makes the (untried) principles of modern political economists subservient to general policy and the wants of human nature; the other has a cast-iron mold for all things. The one would expand legislation as far as possible, trusting much to the good old forms in which the English nation has grown up; the other would centralize, and, by centralizing, paralyze. The one trusts, perhaps, a little too much to the heart; but certainly the other depends too entirely on the head. It almost follows that the one should be more popular than the other,—at least, so is the fact. Both, no doubt, deserve credit for good intentions. Their future career will be, at no very great distance of time, perhaps, again side by side. It is to be hoped that neither the popular sympathies of Lord Morpeth, nor the personal ambition of Earl Grey, will lead them to disregard or undervalue the dangers to which their own characters as statesmen and the welfare of their country will be exposed, if they too readily yield, on insufficient grounds, to the "pressure from without."

THE DUKE OF BUCKINGHAM.

It has become a deliberate practice with some political writers, who, under the mask of an ardent zeal for the commercial greatness of this empire, seem to conceal sinister designs against the constitutional influence of the landed aristocracy, to sneer at the public displays of noblemen who take an earnest interest in the affairs of the country. Their ridicule is directed not so much against individuals, as against the class to which they belong,—the design evidently being to lead John Bull to believe that those to whom the guardianship of the legislative interests of the country is particularly confided by hereditary right, are not so fit for the work they have to perform as are the more practical men, who have sprung from the middle classes, and have had a personal experience on all the subjects upon which they are required to legislate. During the great Anti-Corn-law agitation, especially, a marked crusade of ridicule was directed against "the dukes." It happened at that time, that one or two members of the highest rank in the peerage threw themselves with unusual ardor into the contest going on out of doors; and portions of their speeches, perverted for interested purposes, were seized upon as foundations for the most monstrous and absurd imputations. Among the rest, the Duke of Buckingham, as being one of the most distinguished of the friends of protection to agriculture, could not hope to escape. The more zealous and disinterested his support of protection, the more certain was he to be held up to public odium, and, what was worse, contempt. Self-interest, pride, a dictatorial spirit, blind ignorance, and arrogant pretension,—these were a few of the motives ascribed to the noble duke and some of his coadjutors; and, as if it were not enough thus to malign and disguise their intentions, an unfair criticism extended itself to their power of enforcing their opinions, until they were described as almost unable to acquit themselves of an ordinary after-dinner speech, except in a style that would disgrace a debating-club.

Now nobody expects a duke to be a great orator. If nature or education make him one, so much the better; but otherwise his position scarcely requires it. The constitution places the peers in a different position from their fellow-countrymen. It is voluntary with a man his being a member of the House of Commons; a member of the Upper House has no choice. Nature wills that he shall be a legislator, whether he likes it or not. It is his duty to form an opinion on every subject that is, in the natural course of things, brought before the House of Lords; he must give his vote if called on, and on great questions he can scarcely vote without explaining the grounds on which he does so. To find fault with a man so situated, because he can not compete with those whom emulation or ambition has made orators, would be in the extreme unfair. The opinions of an hereditary peer are of value, not merely for their intrinsic worth, but also because they come from a man in his position. Every word he utters comes backed by the weight of a delegated authority. Even when he only expresses the interested views of a class, he has constituents as much as any member of the House of Commons; and what he says has importance even on that ground alone. And if he espouse an obstructive policy, it should be remembered that to do that when occasion requires, is one of the duties imposed on him by the constitution. To object, therefore, to men like the Duke of Buckingham or the Duke of Richmond, that their speeches are mere stale reproductions of old ideas, is really not to throw an effectual ridicule upon them. To do so occasionally, and with a due regard to the new ideas engendered by new circumstances, is more a necessity of their legislative rank than any evidence of infirmity in their mind.

But the Duke of Buckingham, although from his high rank and his influence with the landed interest he has been peculiarly laid open to these charges, has really been most unfairly made the victim of political animosity. Sufficient credit has not been given him for his talents even as an orator, much less as a politician. Because it was easy to deceive the vulgar into believing that he was "a duke, and nothing more," those whose object it is to bring the aristocracy into public contempt did not hesitate at the ungracious task. It was of no use that those who were in the habit of hearing the Marquis of Chandos speak, whether at agricultural meetings or in parliament, bore testimony to that frank and open-hearted eloquence which made him beloved as much as he was respected, and constituted him "the farmer's friend" in a personal as well as a political sense. They were comparatively few, and their voices were not heard in the vulgar roar of those interested in running down the agricultural leaders. Yet, as a speaker on ordinary occasions, whether in parliament or at agricultural meetings, the noble duke stands on a par with all but the prepared and professed orators. He can lower the tone of his ideas, and adapt the degrees of his courtesy, to the level agreeable to the feelings or the understandings of an agricultural tenantry; or he can elevate and refine his language and thoughts to the pitch required in the more congenial atmosphere of the House of Lords.

He does both without the slightest appearance of effort; and is, therefore, in all probability, equally sincere, whether his demeanor be that of a ducal legislator or that of a simple country gentleman.

He is charged with having all the pride of a feudal nobleman. At least, he does not display it, either in the House of Lords or when among his agricultural friends. A more pleasing example of the modern feudal relations between the aristocracy and the cultivators of the soil there can not be, than when the Duke of Buckingham meets his agricultural neighbors,—say, at a public dinner at Buckingham, to which he has walked in leisurely in the afternoon from his princely mansion of Stowe. Less display, less pride, less even of the pride which apes cordiality and humility, it would be difficult to conceive. The plain, unpretending dress, the frank, open countenance, the free, manly, courteous bearing, the friendly salutation, the well timed jest, and the hearty laugh at the shrewd response of some old and long tried tenant,—all bespeak a healthy state of the relations between the duke and his neigh bors, utterly repugnant to all suggestions of undue pride or presumption. And when the after-dinner proceed ings—the speeches—begin, you find him entering on his task in the true English spirit, without assumption or affectation, but with a kind of tacit recognition of an equality under the law and the constitution between himself and his hearers, notwithstanding their difference of rank and the power which his position in the county might give him over them. He talks to them, not as a duke to commoners, or as a landlord to his tenants, but as an agriculturist speaking to agriculturists; and his speeches are plain, manly, shrewd, and practical; just the sort of speeches they would make to each other over their pipes and ale. And when he touches on politics, there is none of the *magnifico* in his promises of aid. He knows well that they look up to him as their parliamentary leader; but there is no appearance on his part that he presumes on their regard and respect. He talks to them as a member of parliament might talk to his constituents—*for they are his constituents*—and he willingly renders them an account of his stewardship. The courtier becomes the farmer at these meetings, till the farmers almost become courtiers.

In the House of Lords the duke is more than respectable as a speaker. He addresses the House seldom, but always with effect. When he was in the House of Commons as the Marquis of Chandos, he spoke much more frequently; and held a very distinguished position as a party leader. He was to the agriculturists what Sir Robert Inglis is to the Church—a steady, consistent, and recognized champion. If Sir Robert Inglis has hitherto been more successful in his championship of the Church than the duke has been as the advocate of agriculture, it must be remembered that he has not yet been placed in circumstances of so much trial. The duke's speeches are not of a character to provoke much criticism. He makes no pretensions to oratory, but always produces an impressive effect. Simple and forcible language, a clear and manly voice, a good delivery, and an air of unquestionable sincerity, render him an agreeable speaker to listen to. More dignified and temperate than the Duke of Richmond, he does not so often provoke comment or retort; but what he says has weight with the House from his known integrity, his long and devoted service to the cause of agriculture, and the high position which, whether as an individual member of parliament or a minister of the crown, he has always held in the public estimation.

THE EARL OF RADNOR.

There is not much to be said touching the Earl of Radnor. With the settlement of the Corn-law question a great portion of his parliamentary importance will have subsided. As an opponent of protection to agriculture, he occupied relatively the same position toward the question that was held by the Duke of Buckingham or the Duke of Richmond as its supporters. For a great number of years he has been the steady advocate of the repeal of the Corn-laws; and although his advocacy has never attained that dignity and weight which attended the opinion of Earl Spencer on the same subject, he has at least earned and obtained that kind of moral weight and respect which is always reserved for consistency, even when it has only been the blind impulse or the unreasoning persistence of a confined mind. The Earl of Radnor has always held an anomalous position in the House of Peers; he was, to all intents and purposes, a "Radical," advocating democratic objects, if not democratic opinions, in the very heart of an aristocratic body.

Every observer of mankind will have met in the course of his career some persons of the class to which Lord Radnor belongs as a thinker,—men old in years and experience, but inveterately young and unripe in mind. They are generally extremely honest in their intentions, whether as regards their personal conduct or their belief that the opinions they hold will work for the public good; but those opinions scarcely keep pace with the wants or the intelligence of the time. It is a well founded objection to some politicians, that they are too much addicted to looking backward, that they are blind worshipers of the past, and have no place in their mind either for the facts of the present or for sound and healthy anticipations of the future. Such men are the bigots of a reasoning age; they live amid the tombs of their ancestors; they flourish with a sinister vitality, like weeds of rank luxuriance, amid the ruins of old opinions and institutions. Now the class to which Lord Radnor belongs is the counterpart of this, only that their prejudices run rather in favor of the future—a future created by their own imaginations—than of the past. They are equally bigots—bigots to speculative philosophy and hazardous politics. They are as deeply enamored of the new and the untried, as the others are devoted to the old and the exhausted. The one class are the poets of a fabulous and over estimated past; the others, the prophets of an unattainable future. It may be said on their behalf, that they anticipate their cotemporaries,—that principles which, fifty years ago, were denounced as the vain dreams of enthusiasts, have now grown to be the faith of practical men. And you will often hear them boasting—these few remnants, when they hold their periodical *rěunions*—that what they ran the risk of being outlawed for when they were youths, is now the foundation of the fame of statesmen; that they, despised and ridiculed as they used to be, were, after all, right from the first; while those who ridiculed them confessed in the long run that they were so. But such men can never be persuaded that, except in the abstract sciences, it is possible to discover truth too soon; that in politics, sound principles do not so much prevail as the aggregate necessities of a people; that the application of their principles at the time they urged them with the greatest zeal, would, in all probability, have endangered the safety of the nation; and that, therefore, although as thinkers they might have been right, as statesmen they were wrong. Another point which makes against them is, that however much they may at a former period have been, as theorists, before their age, their minds do not advance with those of their cotemporaries. Their early aims accomplished, they do not, as more healthy and practical minds would, press forward to new discoveries in political science. They rather halt ere even the whole work is done, clinging obstinately to old dogmas and projects, and looking back with senile fondness to those darling offsprings of their youth and prime, once so magnified in importance to their intellectual eye, but now dwarfed in the receding tide of Time.

In truth they are men of fixed ideas, often of one idea, and that not their own. The particular class of politicians to which we now refer—a sparse and scattered few, of whom Lord Radnor is a sort of Coryphæus—may be said to date their existence from about the period of the first French Revolution. The seductive theories by which that great event was heralded and succeeded, seized early on their immature minds, but were not, as with more practical men, discarded as soon as their crude uselessness was made apparent. The opinions, more or less modified, which they imbibed then, they retain undigested at the present hour. They stand—a kind of moral landmarks, showing the height to which exaggerated hopes and unfounded fears carried our fathers. They still look upon Church and State as one enormous hypocrisy; on Ministers, as covert enemies of liberty; on the People as the abstraction of infallible, unerring wisdom and goodness; on the Law, as a complicated machine of tyranny; on Statesmen, as public plunderers; on an Aristocracy as public usurpers; and on all distinctions of rank, as so many badges of slavery. Other men grow out of these youthful prepossessions, these bug-bears of their early fears: not so the young-old-men we speak of; their minds never ripen in the sun of nationality, or gain strength by the fertilizing influence of philosophy. Such as they were when they first imbibed their notions, so are they now. For them Time has no magic of silent change. As their first impressions were prejudices or the impulses of hasty passion only, conviction has worked no result on their minds, and never will.

Of the Earl of Radnor as an orator, but little need be said. He makes no pretensions to the character, and, therefore, could not be offended at its not being awarded to him. But there are few members of the House of Peers, except those in ministerial offices, who so often favor their fellow-legislators with their opinions. As has been already said, the noble earl was always a stout and consistent advocate of the repeal of the Corn-laws; and it was in the constant recurrence, in some shape or other, to those views, that he was most frequently before the House of Peers. At one time he was a sort of squire, or rather, perhaps, the *socius*, of Lord Brougham; afterward he contracted a strict alliance, offensive and defensive, with Lord Kinnaird. The two noble lords were the organs and advocates of the League in the House of Lords. The Earl of Radnor, too, is always great at a grievance. Any case of oppression, particularly should a government officer be the agent of the supposed injury, is a delightful stimulant to the inherent Quixotism of his nature. Nothing will persuade him that either the times or public men are altered; he persists in looking at the case with the light of forty years ago. Visions float before his mind's eye of savage attorney-generals, corrupt judges, and immaculate and oppressed defendants. Hardy's case, or Horne Tooke's, is the pivot on which he turns his whole constitutional knowledge when any question of political liberty is involved. All his efforts are dictated by the most noble and honest feelings; but his zeal sometimes gets the better of his discretion. At these times, or when he is pursuing his favorite theme of repeal of the Corn-laws, he pours forth an interminable flood of talk, a strange mixture of assertion, one-sided reasoning, and shrewd illustration, in which every now and then you hear an argument of singular sense and applicability, or an idea of striking originality, but overwhelmed in a mass of what, without wishing to use an offensive term, we fear can only be described as twaddle. Advanced in years, and with the loquacious habits which age often entails, an enfeebled voice, and a rambling, almost incoherent style of speaking, Lord Radnor does not at first inspire much confidence or respect as a public man. But, amid all his prejudices, and notwithstanding his propensity to talk you to death with them, there is some sterling stuff in him after all. He means well, he is thoroughly sincere; and it should always be borne in mind, whatever may be thought of the wisdom of his uncompromising advocacy of extreme Liberal opinions, that he has, at least, the merit of having urged them on both branches of the legislature through a long period of time, and in a condition of political parties when to do so required a persevering and oblivious honesty of character, if it did not almost involve a loss of caste.

THE DUKE OF RICHMOND.

THERE is more "character" about the Duke of Richmond than even in his ducal coadjutor in the agricultural leadership. He throws himself with more warmth and hearty earnestness into the arena of political strife; and, although quite as kind-hearted, affable, and courteous, as the Duke of Buckingham, he does not so much study and regard the amenities of life, whether in the political world or in his private personal bearing. His courtesy is more frank and blunt. For every two men who would be charmed with the manners of the Duke of Buckingham, one, at least, might, at first sight, consider the Duke of Richmond rude and dictatorial. The kindness of the Duke of Buckingham might be construed into condescension—never that of the Duke of Richmond. He has but one language, one manner, one mode of address for all men. He speaks in the same blunt, downright tone to his equals as to his inferiors; he addresses the House of Lords in precisely the same terms and tone of voice that he would use to a servant. He meets you face to face, foot to foot, as man to man, casting all factitious distinctions of rank aside, and trusting to his cause alone. If you get into a quarrel with him, you must look to receive good hard hits from good hard hands. Like Lord Brougham, he thinks that an argument levels all distinctions; and if he can give you a knock-down blow, he will not pause to inquire whether you are a prince or a pedler, a duke or a manufacturer. He is no orator, any more than his brother duke; but his earnestness, practical knowledge, and sound common sense, make him a formidable antagonist to even the most practiced and powerful speakers.

The Duke of Richmond takes a more general interest in public affairs than the Duke of Buckingham, mixes himself up more with agriculture as a science, and identifies himself with the objects and proceedings of different classes of the community. Although of so high a rank, he is essentially one of the people; he would be a general favorite for his sterling English qualities, even had he no dukedom to recommend him. He has an active, stirring mind, and is quite as much up to the mark in every kind of business as the most practical man of the day. His whole life and conduct are a palpable contradiction to the vulgar ideas about "the dukes." Few among those who are engaged in running down the order would have much chance against the Duke of Richmond, if they were to try a fall with him in argument. Among his other qualifications he is a good magistrate at quarter-sessions, identifying himself more with the people than with the law, and construing the latter as favorably as he can to the offender; and he makes a first-rate chairman at a public meeting or a public dinner. At the latter, he throws himself heart and soul into the proceedings, whether from liking or a desire to put people at their ease; and a succession of short, rattling, appropriate speeches, introduce the several toasts in a manner that dissuades others from prolixity, and keeps up the flow of good feeling uninterruptedly. He is also in great strength at the meetings of the Agricultural Society, of which he has been president. There he thoroughly identifies himself with the feelings and interests of the farmers, and when it is his duty to preside, contrives to keep things together, whether at the business meetings or the purely convivial assemblages, in a style that renders him a general favorite. These matters are trivial in themselves, and would be scarcely worth notice in any man who had been less maligned and misrepresented, less charged with a monopolizing and dictatorial spirit, than the Duke of Richmond.

His chief field of action is, of course, the House of Lords; but he has also distinguished himself at periodical agricultural meetings, and at the meetings of the Central Protection Society. As to his oratory in the House of Lords, the same remarks apply that were made on the Duke of Buckingham—his position should be taken into account in estimating the value of his speeches. It is chiefly as the stanch and consistent advocate of the interests of agriculture that he is distinguished. To the one principle of protection to agriculture he has sacrificed all party and political ties, establishing himself on the cross-benches, and watching the movements of either of the great parties with an eager and suspicious eye. When he was a Whig, he left office and his party because he thought they were about to sacrifice the interests of agriculture; he has again left the Conservatives on their conversion to free-trade. This accounts for the extreme energy, almost amounting to virulence, of his opposition to the Peel government at the free-trade crisis. He was but acting on his memorable, but somewhat intemperate threat, that "those who had brought Sir Robert Peel in would turn him out again." But he has not a particle of rancor in his nature: he is too upright and high-minded to entertain such feelings. He is, however, quite capable of the extremes of an honest indignation; and this feeling it is which seems to have dictated his proceedings in the House of Lords in the decided course he took against those whom he believed to have betrayed their trust.

He is a better speaker than the Duke of Buckingham. There is more force and originality in his ideas, and his language sometimes rises far above the ordinary level. There is less conventionality in his style than in that of any member of the House of Peers. Like Lord Melbourne or Lord Brougham, he uses his illustrations recklessly, regardless whence they come, so that they be pointed and effective. There is vigor in his speeches, derived from the frankness of his character. He talks out boldly whatever he thinks or feels, and as he has a well regulated mind the result is not disagreeable. The same style he uses at a meeting of farmers or at a public dinner serves him also for the House of Lords. He uses no preparation, nor does he attempt to produce effect by means of rhetorical art, and his speeches are more forcible and persuasive from the absence of all appearance of effort. On the other hand, if his language and illustrations are often homely, he can, when occasion demands it, use a more lofty tone, one more in harmony with the position and responsibilities of a peer of parliament. A speech he made against the Corn-bill of Sir Robert Peel, prophesying its consequences and denouncing its authors, was of a very high order of natural eloquence, in the ideas, the diction, and the delivery.

His mode of delivering his sentiments is as peculiar to himself as the sentiments themselves are unaffected and forcible. He plunges into his subject as if in desperation. When he has resolved to address the House, he starts up suddenly, and makes a rush at once at the very pith and marrow of the question, without exordium or apology, or any of those explanations by which ordinary speakers seek to propitiate their auditory. He stands bolt upright, disdains all action, and fires off his sentences in short, quick volleys, like those of a steam-gun. From his loud voice and excited manner you are tempted to think he is in a great passion, and to fear that there may be ere long some unpleasant and unparliamentary explosion. No such thing. The peers are used to this. It is only a constitutional irritability which means nothing, or, what is more likely, a habit of which he can not divest himself. His loud tone of voice helps the belief that he is in a high state of excitement, while its monotony is at times disagreeable. He has a practice, too, of clipping his words, and of pronouncing them with a nasal twang —a sort of compound of the Cockney and Yankee. A more careful man, one more anxious to curry favor by attention to appearances, would correct these blemishes; but there is an unique simplicity in the character of the Duke of Richmond which makes him indifferent to such considerations, or disdainful of them. Upon the whole, we do not know that a more admirable model of what should be the character of the British nobleman could be found among our aristocracy. As a politician he is not a mere theorist, nor does he merely come forward in the arena, as so many do, to defend his order when attacked. He is essentially a working man, laboring as hard and as effectually in his station (and with all the moral weight attaching to voluntary service) as the most humble man in the realm; and we look to see him hereafter devoting his valuable time and aid in the business of government or of legislation, without reference to either personal or party considerations.

MR. BRIGHT.

THE position of Mr. Bright, as a public man, is at present undefined. Returned to parliament under peculiar and almost unprecedented circumstances, a factitious importance was attached to his movements, —an importance which we are far from saying was unwarranted, but which implies a standing among cotemporary politicians that is not yet awarded by the common consent of those who are qualified to judge, or earned by any success as a speaker, whether sudden and brilliant, or steady and progressive. His defects were likely to have been overlooked in the strong light which the triumphant success of the Anti-Corn-law agitation threw around the chief leaders in that movement; and he has not yet had sufficient opportunity of displaying his general qualifications as a legislator or as a debater to enable and to determine, with any positive accuracy, the rank he ought to hold.

Mr. Bright may be said to have been dragged upward by Mr. Cobden, in his rapid and remarkable ascent to fame and notoriety. Had he been left to pursue his path alone, it is more than probable that he would never have emerged from the dead level of society—or that, if he had attained any eminence at all, it would have been to achieve a distinction not more illustrious than that of the most noisy and arrogant orator of a parish vestry, in whom strength of lungs, and an indomitable determination not to be out-bullied, are the most prominent qualifications. If common report be true, it was in some field of action not very dissimilar to this that Mr. Bright first developed his talking powers, and first acquired his relish for the coarser ovations of vulgar fame. But fortune willed that he should live to figure in a much more important sphere; and that he should be the co-tribune of Mr. Cobden in the most decidedly anti-aristocratic movement of modern days—at least of the period which dates from the commencement of the present century.

Although, however, Mr. Bright has been usually associated with Mr. Cobden, as being, next to him, the most prominent leader in this great peaceful revolution, it should be understood that there is a great difference in the mental caliber of the two men. Perhaps Mr. Bright, who has at times exhibited much frankness of nature, would be one of the first to admit this, and to yield the palm of leadership to his nominal as well as real superior in the agitation. While their joint efforts were mainly confined to the platform, when they were still only enforcing bold dogmas and impudent fallacies upon uneducated but prepossessed audiences, the difference was not so perceptible. One demagogue is in the main as good as another, except that he who has the loudest voice and the greatest amount of assurance will often shine in this sphere, to the eclipsing of men of greater modesty and less physical power, but far more extended views and intrinsic value. Therefore, it is more than probable, that if the audiences at free-trade tea-parties, or even at the weekly meetings at Covent Garden theater, could have been polled, at least a very large minority would have declared their preference for the stentorian Bright. But in parliament the case was far different. There the peculiar characteristics of Mr. Bright which were calculated to captivate a mob—the readiness to attack constituted authority, the habitual vilification of the superior classes of society—all made against him rather than in his favor; more especially as there was no charm in his mode of addressing himself to his hearers, but only a mere rude outpouring, sometimes vigorous and powerful, but more often only offensively candid, of the accumulated hatreds engendered by years of unwilling subordination to those who were uppermost, by reason not only of their social position but also of their superior moral and intellectual claims. Yet, even in the House of Commons, Mr. Bright more than once created a sensation and drew down deserved applause. However offensive his leveling spirit may be when he is in a position of attack, every license, of course, is afforded him when he is compelled to speak in self-defense; and on the occasions referred to, he, and the class to which he belongs, had been made the subjects of assaults by members of the agricultural party, which were scarcely excusable. In these instances, Mr. Bright showed such determined spirit, and spoke with such vigor and readiness, occasionally with such cleverness of retort, that he did much to remove the prejudices which some earlier efforts of his, following closely on the unfavorable impression created by his out-of-door proceedings, had produced. Again, his speech on moving for a committee to inquire into the operation of the Game-laws attracted favorable notice, partly because he handled his subject so well, and partly because he achieved a success. It constitutes a sort of breastwork, from which he may pursue that system of attack on the landed aristocracy which, suggested of course by his class-prejudices as a manufacturer, and possibly by his sectarian feelings as a Quaker, seems to be the great object of his public life. Still, with all these symptoms of a growing reputation in the House, he will not bear to be compared with Mr. Cobden, who, as a statesman even, as well as a speaker, stands on higher ground—on an altitude which Mr. Bright could never hope to reach. Mr. Bright would better hear comparison or contrast with Mr. Villiers, who, like himself, has a more confined range than Mr. Cobden.

Mr. Villiers, too, was a determined and persevering advocate of repeal of the Corn-laws; but Mr. Bright has more of character and originality than Mr. Villiers. Sprung from the people, and representing in feeling, as well as by the law of parliament, the commercial classes, Mr. Bright imported more of passion and political feeling into his agitation against the Corn-laws than did his more aristocratic coadjutor. There is a rough, coarse vigor in his style of speaking, which, while it is attractive at a public meeting, rather puzzles the House of Commons. It does not exactly square with their ideas of what the demeanor of a member of parliament ought to be, and yet they can not quarrel with the bold and uncompromising expression of opinion, when restrained and regulated by that respect which even *parvenues* have for custom, from one who, by the suffrage of a legally constituted body of his fellow-countrymen, has acquired the right to speak. The truth is, that Mr. Bright does not pay any very great respect to those enervating conventionalities of debate which are held in so much reverence by the House of Commons. He comes there to perform a duty, which he has been taught to consider a sacred duty—a reality, not a mere form; and that moral impetus bears him onward till he sometimes forgets what is due to the House of Commons on the score of its authority and essential importance, and is not content with merely telling them truths, but must also tell those truths in a manner not always to be defended.

Mr. Bright is dogmatic; Mr. Villiers, argumentative. Upon the former the question of free-trade was forced by the necessities of his position as a manufacturer; the latter "took it up," either from a conviction of what just was, or a foresight of what would be advantageous.

The one spent less ingenuity on his case than the other, because, perhaps, he trusted more to what he believed to be its justice; but, on the other hand, his appeals, whether at the meetings of the League or in parliament, received more attention or commanded more sympathy, because he was felt to be more in earnest and to have better grounds for his advocacy. Mr. Bright's eloquence (if such it can be called) derives its interest from the connection of the speaker with the subject. He is not giving utterance to theories, but to necessities. It is a pounds-shillings-and-pence question that he is arguing, in which every fact is worth all the tropes and figures of the rhetorician. In such a case great allowances will, of course, be made. They are often required by Mr. Bright, who sometimes—not so much in language as in spirit—brings the democratic tone a little too much into parliamentary discussion.

MR. SHEIL.

EVERY public speaker who can arrest the attention and act upon the feelings of an audience is, in the most loose or enlarged acceptation of the term, an orator; even in its strict and literal sense, the same definition would almost apply. But it is needless to remind our readers that there are almost as many gradations of excellence included in that general term as there are in similar ones used in reference to painting or sculpture, or poetry or acting. As the circle of public intelligence becomes expanded, by the greater spread of general knowledge among the people, and the more universal interest of all classes in questions of a political or social nature in reference to legislation, the number of public speakers who excite attention and maintain a hold upon the feelings of the people becomes almost indefinitely multiplied; the intellectual quality of their speeches is deteriorated in proportion as their practical utility is increased; and it becomes more and more difficult to settle the old and often disputed question, "What is an orator?" Several speakers have already been included in this series, whom it would have been absurd to place upon the list of those, so few in names but so brilliant in performances, who, by the common consent of mankind, by the testimony of history and the evidence of their works, happily undestroyed, are recognized as being the great masters in the art of oratory. Yet, on the other hand, the individuals so excluded exercise a direct and powerful influence over their fellow-countrymen scarcely paralleled, and certainly not exceeded, by the higher order of public speakers. Their utilitarian value fully compensates to the general mind for their want of artificial enhancement. The public, perhaps, would care little to know what were the brilliant excellences of Mr. Sheil or Mr. Macaulay, or what a critical analysis would discover of their defects; if the plan of the writer gave them that information on the condition that, in the exercise of a somewhat hypercritical judgment, he left them in ignorance of the oratorical qualifications of Lord John Russell, or Sir Robert Peel, or Mr. Cobden, or even Lord George Bentinck, men with whose names the whole country is ringing. Yet a speech from Lord Lyndhurst, Lord Brougham, Mr. Sheil, Mr. Macaulay, or Mr. Disraeli, or from Mr. Fox and some of the most distinguished platform speakers, wholly differs, not merely in the degree but also in the nature of its excellence, from those of the more practical orators, they who really lead the public mind. The one is a study for the intellect and a pleasure to the imagination, for its intrinsic excellence or beauty, while the other derives its interest from extraneous causes, ceasing with the excitement of the hour; such as the position of the speaker, the nature and aspect of the subject he is handling, and, generally, from the exciting political causes which every year of struggling perpetuates. But the men of the higher order have their ultimate reward. The others have the applause of the present hour alone. Their lumbering speeches are duly reported in the newspapers, in their inglorious rivalry which shall produce the greater number of columns of print; but after the lapse of a week they are forgotten, or only remembered that they may be quoted at a future time against themselves, when, in the mutations of modern politics, they shall find it necessary to contradict all their former assertions and argue against all their former opinions. But the real orator of the highest class—he who had a nobler end in view than forensic sophistry or mere clap-trap and cajolery—not only is admired at the time he utters his speech, but is remembered long after his temporary rivals are forgotten. His effusions are read and studied as models by successive aspirants to fame; they are admired by the poet, as he admires his Milton, his Wordsworth, or his Tennyson; by the artist, as he admires his Titian or his Turner; and it is to them, also, that the most valuable praise of all is accorded—that of posterity. The practical men secure the present only, the men of genius enjoy both the present and the future.

Mr. Sheil is a man of genius, and making allowance for some defects which shall be hereafter adverted to, an orator of the highest order. Whether his speeches be read in the closet years after they were delivered, or whether they be heard with all the advantages of that burning eloquence, that brilliancy of diction, that fiery impetuosity of action, which have now become almost associated with the name of Sheil, they are still the same powerful, beautiful, soul-stirring works, still models of the finest rhetorical art. Scarcely any terms of admiration would be too strong as applied to some of his speeches, while even those which do not rise to the highest pitch of excellence have, nevertheless, so decided and so distinctive a character, that they may be at once known to be the production not only of a superior mind, but of the particular man from whom they have proceeded. The very faults of his style cease to be defects when regarded in connection with the pervading tone of his mind, and the leading features of his character.

Mr. Sheil's parliamentary reputation is now of about fifteen years' standing. For that period he has reigned without a rival as the most brilliant and imaginative speaker, and the most accomplished rhetorician, in the

House of Commons. That assembly—heterogeneous as are the materials of which it is composed—possesses a marvelous instinct in the discovery and the appreciation of oratorical talent. It is their interest that they should have among them those who can occasionally charm them from the plodding realities of legislation, and the dull lucubrations of the practical men. Therefore they are always alive to excellence, and stamp it at once. Not very long since a new member, a Mr. Cardwell, made a remarkably valuable speech on a question of a practical nature, full of powerful reasoning, concentration, and mastery of the facts. Till the evening when he made that speech, he was comparatively unknown; but he had not been on his legs a quarter of an hour, before the unerring instinct of the House (which operates as closely upon good business speeches as on the most eloquent) discovered that, in his degree, he was a superior man, and the cheering with which he was greeted at the close of his address was the stamp they set on his ability. Sir Robert Peel was among the listeners, and in a few weeks afterward Mr. Cardwell became a minister. If, in these days of statistics and sophistry, a modest and undistinguished individual was thus singled out, *à fortiori* it could not have been long before such an orator as Mr. Sheil was elevated to the highest point in the admiration of the House, at a time when high oratory was more valued. He came but to be heard and to be triumphant. Heralded by the hyperbolical praise of his Irish admirers, his first speech was looked for with a curiosity not unmingled with doubt. But he passed the ordeal successfully, and from that hour has been regarded as one of the most distinguished and remarkable of the many great orators which his country, fertile in genius as in natural riches, has ever produced.

Our mention of the Hibernian admirers of Mr. Sheil reminds us that we have somothing to say of that gentleman beyond what is prompted by a recollection of his speeches in the House of Commons. For, unlike most of our distinguished men, Mr. Sheil was famous as an orator long before he entered Parliament. His eloquence had not been the least important element in causing that unanimity of feeling among the people of Ireland which ultimately led to the great political and religious revolution of 1829. There are very few instances on record of men who have become famous as speakers at the bar, or at the hustings, or at public meetings, having equally stood the test of the House of Commons. It is one of Mr. Sheil's many claims on our admiration, that having been an energetic, enthusiastic, and successful leader in a great popular, or rather a great national movement, he should have had the taste and tact so to subdue his nature in the very hour of triumph, as afterward to adapt his speaking to the tone most agreeable to the House, and to charm them as much by the fire of his eloquence as by the delicacy of his rhetorical artifices, without the aid of those stronger and more stirring stimulants to the passions which form the very essence of successful mob-oratory. In very few instances, indeed, has he ever discarded these voluntary fetters on the exuberant vigor of his patriotism and nationality.

Not as an orator merely will Mr. Sheil assist to rescue this age from the charge of mediocrity. Thirty years ago he began to be known and appreciated as a poet—when he was only looking forward to the bar as a profession, and long ere visions of applauding millions, or of high ministerial office, or a place in the councils of his sovereign, ever crossed his ardent and aspiring soul. As the author of the tragedies "Evadne" and "The Apostate," Mr. Sheil already occupied a high place among the writers who were then his cotemporaries—a place not very much unlike that now held by Talfourd. In the intervals of those productions, and for some time afterward, he contributed to the periodicals of the day, and had altogether, even at the early age of twenty-two, made himself that kind of reputation for originality and a high order of talent which floats about society, and interests, by some means or other, more certain in their action than perceptible, the general mind in the career of particular individuals. Still, although there were at all times vague predictions that he would "do something" some day or other, no one seems at that time to have suspected that he contained within him the powers which soon afterward made him second but to one man as a leader of the Irish people, and ultimately have enabled him to compete with the most illustrious men of the day in those qualifications which insure parliamentary success.

But with the time came the man. The Roman Catholic question had of late years assumed a great parliamentary importance. The stalking-horse of an ambitious party, the cause had come at last to be regarded as "respectable." English statesmen and orators —men who in a few years became the rulers of the country—succeeded those great and eloquent Irishmen in whom the advocacy of Roman Catholic freedom from civil disabilities had always been regarded as justifiable —nay, a matter of duty. In the mean while, all the legal dexterity of Mr. O'Connell had been devoted to the construction of an artful but comprehensive scheme of agitation, by which the people of Ireland might be organized, and an unanimous call be made on the English parliament for emancipation. This organization went on, with more or less success, for years. Under the name of the Roman Catholic Association it rose from the most insignificant revival (after a temporary dispersion) in the year 1823, until it assumed that gigantic shape which ultimately terrified the government of England into an undignified submission. It was in that year, 1823, that Mr. Sheil and Mr. O'Connell, who were destined at no very distant time to be the great leaders of the Association, first met, under circumstances somewhat romantic, at the house of a mutual friend in the mountains of Wicklow. There a congeniality of object overcame the natural repulsion of antagonist minds, and they laid down the plan of a new agitation. That their meeting was purely an accidental one, made the results which followed still more remarkable.

Their first efforts were received with indifference by the people; but in a very few weeks the Association was formed, and the rolling stone was set in motion. To those who are curious in such matters, it will be instructive and amusing to observe the parallel circumstances of the origination of the Roman Catholic Association by some six or seven enthusiasts at a bookseller's shop in Dublin, and that of the Anti-Cornlaw League by a few merchants at Manchester or at Preston—for the cotton-heroes have not yet determined at which place the nucleus was formed.

We have alluded to the natural repulsion of antagonist minds. Contrast more marked could scarcely exist than that which was exhibited by the two great leaders of the Association. That their mental qualities were so different, and the sources of the admiration which each in his sphere excited so opposite, may be held to be one of the causes of the great success the Association achieved. If Mr. Sheil was great in rhetoric,—if his impassioned appeals to his countrymen and to the world stood the test, not merely of Hibernian enthusiasm but also of English criticism, Mr. O'Connell was greater in planning, in organization, in action, and he had in his rough and vigorous eloquence a lever which moved the passions of the Irish people. He, perhaps, had the good sense to see that as an orator, in the higher sense of the term, he could never equal his more brilliant and intellectual colleague. His triumphs lay in the council-chamber on the one hand, and in the market-place or the hillside on the other. It was in the forum or on the platform that the more elevated and refined eloquence of Sheil, adorned with all the graces of art, charmed while it astonished a higher and more cultivated audience. Thus they never clashed. While all Europe rung with the fame of the "peaceful agitator," who had taught his countrymen to use the forms of the constitution to the subversion of its spirit and objects, every scholar, every statesman, every lover of the beautiful in oratory as an art, had already learned to admire that new, thrilling, imaginative, yet forcible style of eloquence, which, ever and anon, amid the din and clamor of noisier warfare, sounded the spirit-stirring tocsin of nationality and religious liberty, breaking forth like intermittent lightning-flashes amid the thunders of the agitation. Mr. Sheil, on the other hand, looked up to Mr. O'Connell for his indomitable energy and perseverance, his craft, cunning, caution, his thorough nationality and identification with the feelings of the people, and would as little have thought of substantially opposing his decision, or resisting his general control over the proceedings of the Association, as the other would have attempted to vie with him in eloquence. So they went on together, side by side, though really exercising so distinct an influence, with scarcely any of that jealousy or rivalry which has so often stifled similar undertakings in their very infancy. If Mr. Sheil's ideas of agitation were more grand and comprehensive; if he would fain have gone by a more direct and manly, but more dangerous, road to the intelligence of the English parliament and people; if, in his anxiety to impress on the world a deep and startling conviction of the union and nationality of the Irish people, and their absolute, even their slavish devotion to their leaders,—if in this his superabundant energy and velocity of purpose, he would have drawn the Association into the meshes of the law, there was Mr. O'Connell at his right hand to repress and guide, to steer clear of the rocks and shoals, to accomplish by that crafty prudence and keen dexterity in escape which savors so much of political cowardice, those objects which, in the other case, would have been realized by a more manly display of political audacity. Mr. Sheil might be the braver man at the boarding-pike or the gun, but Mr. O'Connell was the safer at the helm.

To Mr. Sheil was owing the idea of at once teaching the people of Ireland union and a sense of their strength, while obtaining a universal expression of their wish for emancipation, by means of simultaneous meetings throughout Ireland, in every parish in the kingdom, for the purpose of petitioning parliament to concede the Catholic claims. He would have gone farther. He would have had a form of prayer prepared, by means of which, in every chapel in Ireland the people might simultaneously join in an appeal to Heaven for the advancement of what *they* had been taught to believe was a sacred cause; that millions of men and women might breathe the same aspiration to their Creator, at the same moment, throughout the length and breadth of the land. The conception, apart from its impropriety in a religious point of view, was a grand one, and strongly illustrative of its author's character. It was an idea more likely to occur to an enthusiastic and ardent imagination like that of Mr. Sheil, than to the more practical mind of Mr. O'Connell; who again was much more at home in framing a resolution, or organizing an association, or holding a meeting, in such a manner as to evade the law. It was his successful boast that there was no act of parliament through which he would not drive a coach-and-six. Mr. Sheil had a poet's conception of agitation and organization; Mr. O'Connell's was that of a lawyer. Characters more opposed could scarcely have been brought together; that they harmonized so well, notwithstanding the many daily causes of instinctive antagonism that must have arisen, is a miracle only to be accounted for by the influence which a popular movement always exercises on its leaders, so long as they are all pressing forward toward the same goal.

The Mr. Sheil who now sits and speaks in the House of Commons, who is a right honorable member of her majesty's privy council, and has been from time to time one of the most ornamental, if not quite the most useful, of the members of the Whig cabinet, is, however, a very different personage, indeed, from the young, enthusiastic Irishman, barrister, poet, orator, agitator, whose fiery spirit fused into one silver flow of brilliant eloquence so many pure elements of democratic power. Except at intervals, when the old habit recurs, or when some tempting opportuuity presents itself to urge the wrongs of Ireland without compromising his new associates, Mr. Sheil is one of the most quiet, silent, unobtrusive members of the House of Commons. Indeed, he has become so identified with the Whigs, that you scarcely remember him even as an Irishman, still less as one of those who, for so many years, defied the whole parliamentary power of the empire. He has of late years thrown himself almost entirely into the conventionalities of the House of Commons, and has undergone mutation from a popular leader into a partisan. This is said in no spirit of disparagement; on the contrary, however "Young Ireland" may affect to scorn such apparent lukewarmness and subservience to circumstances, it is really one of Mr. Sheil's most solid claims to our respect. Nor is his oratorical power diminished when, on occasion, he deigns to resort to it. On several occasions he has delivered speeches on great questions, not affecting

Ireland alone, but the whole empire, which for vigor, beauty of imagery, boldness of conception, and sarcastic power, will vie with the best of those made in the very heat and fervor of his patriotism. It is not that his strength is diminished, but that it is more under the regulation of his taste and judgment.

Some of the speeches—harangues they would bear to be called—made by Mr. Sheil at the meetings of the Roman Catholic Association, will bear comparison with the most memorable ever called forth by the spirit of democracy. Almost from the first day he appeared on the platform of the Association, the attention of the political world, indeed of all thinking men, was fixed upon him. Those who could not be present to witness the powerful aid lent to his burning words by his striking and original action, still saw unquestionable genius in the exquisite language, the novel metaphors, so bold yet so well controlled, the forcible antithesis, the luxuriant imagery, the unapproachable sarcastic power, and, above all, in an irrepressible spirit of patriotism, and indignant sense of insulted national honor, that bore onward the stream of his thoughts with a wild and reckless abandonment, perilous at every fall, yet, torrent-like, free again at a fresh bound, and rushing far away in flashing beauty. By the side of the deep, steady current of Mr. O'Connell's eloquence, slow moving like a mighty river, the rapid flow of Mr. Sheil's pure, clear, political diction, gave a delightful and refreshing relief to the mind. Take up the proceedings of those meetings, and the very sentences, so short and exquisitely framed, seem as it were to gleam and glitter. Never was sedition clothed in more seductive language, or democratic principles made more fascinating to the most fastidious intellect. In his strong conviction of the justice of his cause, he would certainly at times broach doctrines as to the means to be employed, which it required all the moral weight of Mr. O'Connell and his timorous prudence to counteract. But if the fiery and impetuous young advocate of a people was sometimes thus hurried on by the ardor of his imagination to lengths which his calmer judgment would have hesitated to confront, it was so clearly only the irrepressible enthusiasm of the poet-agitator, not the significant appeal of the designing demagogue, that the poison of the thought had its antidote along with it in the chosen and beautiful words through which it was conveyed. But, with all their faults, and in spite of the meager and imperfect reports of them which appeared in the newspapers and the published proceedings of the Roman Catholic Association, those speeches spread the reputation of Mr. Sheil far and wide, wherever public opinion was aroused on the Roman Catholic question —a question which to the opponents as well as to the supporters of the Roman Catholic claims, was growing to be one of the most vital importance. Their faults were, indeed, many. The politician might be able to find excuses in the singular position of the then leaders of the Irish people, and the momentous nathre and exciting interest of the contest, for the occasional bursts of anti-English feeling, the exultation over English faults and follies, the unconstitutional tone of many of those orations, by which the suppressed hatreds of centuries were arrayed against the comparatively innocent statesmen and people of a single age; the poisoned arrows of the rash rhetorician might rebound from the mail of principle in which the Protestant legislator encased himself, confident in its strength against all but the artillery of popular enthusiasm poured in by the more crafty and designing genius of O'Connell: but the citric, fastidious in eloquence, could not forgive in one whose genius he was compelled to admire, the frequent violations of good taste which the rising orator had not then learned to avoid—the use, without selection or abstinence, of metaphors, whose extravagance could not be excused, however their boldness might be felt or their force acknowledged, and sacrifice to political passions of the symmetry and poetical harmony of what, but for those errors of a luxuriant fancy, might have been grand models of oratorical perfection for all time, each, for its eloquent history of national wrongs, an epic, not spoken only to listening thousands, but recorded as at once a delight and a warning to millions yet to come. And, indeed, we do not overrate the political value of those speeches while thus looking back at their faults. Time has obliterated their immediate effects: there are not many who remember to have heard them; and of the multitudes who read them and felt their power at the time they were delivered, the majority have forgotten, in the excitement of subsequent contests, the great moral influence which they once exercised. But history is already recording their results, and, happily for his own fame and for the gratification of his countrymen, he who delivered them is yet strong, ay, still stronger in those powers which he possesses in such rare perfection, toned down and chastened as they now are in their exercise by increased intercourse with mankind, and the natural effect which time and the absence of all causes of excitement have produced on an ardent and irritable temperament. The speeches to which we more particularly refer were delivered at intervals between 1823 and 1829. Bad as the reports of these speeches are, still their intrinsic worth, their powerful eloquence, and exquisite beauty, make themselves felt through ever so debased a medium. Perhaps the most remarkable of his speeches—the most original and characteristic of his peculiar mind—were those he made at the different aggregate meetings of the Roman Catholics, which took place at intervals during the agitation for emancipation. Then he had a wider field and a more inspiring audience than even at the meetings of the Association; for, at the latter, the cautious spirit of O'Connell prevailed almost without restraint; the jealous eye of the government watched, with lynx-like precision, every movement of so dangerous an organization; and even the enthusiasm and valorous fancy of a Sheil were restrained within the limits of a technical construction of the liberty of public speech. But the aggregate meetings were more a matter of open, public, constitutional right, and there the enthusiastic and indignant orator revelled in the wild freedom of conscious power and irresistible impulse. The full force and beauty of those speeches can now scarcely be appreciated but by those who were so fortunate as to hear them. They left an impression which has never been effaced by even the more perfect and chastened productions of the maturer mind of the orator. One of his greatest triumphs was on the occasion of that miracle—morally, still more than politically, a miracle—the Clare election. Nor should we forget to mention, among his great orations, his speech at a great meeting (at Carlow, if we remember rightly), where, taking the first chapter of Exodus for his theme, and with the Bible in his hand, he quoted, with a solemnity and effect electrical on the sympathies of a religious and enthusiastic people, the words of the inspired writer, and founded on them an impassioned appeal to his countrymen to persevere in their career—to press onward to the goal appointed for them, heedless of the fears of the timid or the suggestions of the compromising. Words are inadequate to convey the effect of this speech; nor was the speech one of words only; it was the action, the fine harmony between the thoughts and the expression, when the feelings were wrought up to the highest pitch of tension in the enthusiasm inspired by the cause, and the sympathy of the multitude around; all these drew forth the hidden strength of his nature, till he poured forth the full force of his fervid soul into his solemn theme.

A very short period found him in the House of Commons. As soon as the Emancipation-bill qualified him, as a Roman Catholic, to sit, his ambition, or the tactics of the Association, led to his being put forward for the county of Louth. He was unsuccessful; and was ultimately content to slip into parliament for a nomination borough—that of Milburne Port. In 1831, on the 21st of March, he made his first speech in the House of Commons, on the second reading of the Reform-bill. He had not long proceeded with his address ere the House perceived, and acknowledged by their cheers, that they had in him, as in Mr. Macaulay, a mine of oratorical wealth, and a perpetual source of the highest gratification. His reputation for power and originality as a speaker had preceded him: and the utmost anxiety was manifested to hear his maiden essay. In this respect he was differently situated from his eloquent rival. From Mr. Sheil, all men expected much; Mr. Macaulay's powers, except, of course, as an essayist, were known only to a comparatively few of his personal friends, and those who had been his cotemporaries at Cambridge. If he therefore made, by comparison, a more brilliant speech, and achieved a more complete triumph, great allowance must be made for surprise. Mr. Sheil, notwithstanding the extravagant expectations formed of him, also achieved a triumph; but it took him a longer time to acquire his absolute ascendency as an orator. People, too, were always afraid that his nationality, which had been so useful in the agitation, would every now and then break out in some anti-English demonstration.

But Mr. Sheil showed himself almost as great a

tactician as he was a rhetorician. The war over and the victory won, he buried the sword and forbore to exult over the vanquished. Throughout his subsequent parliamentary career, he has identified himself with an English party; and while still advocating, with eloquence as energetic but more chastened, the "wrongs" of Ireland, he has never run counter to the feelings of the English as a nation. In this respect he differs from Mr. O'Connell and the *parti prêtre* as much as from "Young Ireland" or the party republican. Gratitude for emancipation made him, together with the new Irish Catholic members, vote with the mass of the English people on the Reform question. That gratitude has never died within him. The penal laws on the Roman Catholics he conceived to be the real badge of national subjugation; those once abrogated, he considered himself one of the people of the British empire, and while still urging on parliament the gradual fulfillment of the contract of 1829, in what he would call its spirit as well as its letter, he never forgot that justice to England was quite as sacred a duty as justice to Ireland: not so all his friends.

This tact and abstinence in Mr. Sheil very materially lessen the difficulty of criticising the speeches he made in parliament. If they are ever disfigured, it is not by wrong sentiment or the undue infusion of political feeling: their blemishes are obvious only in a critical point of view, and are at the same time so entirely counterbalanced by their beauties, that they might be passed over, were it not that their exposure might possibly prevent a very seductive example being followed by others. It should be added, too, that our remarks apply to Mr. Sheil's speeches *as delivered*, not as printed in the newspapers. From the extraordinary rapidity of his utterance, and the abrupt transitions of voice in which his enthusiasm and ardor lead him to indulge, even the most experienced reporters find a difficulty in rendering his speeches with perfect fidelity and freedom. It is obvious that an orator whose beauties of style depend so much upon the most slight and evanescent touches, the nicest discrimination of language, the artful collocation of words and sentences, so as to make emphasis supply in many cases the thought which parliamentary custom will not permit to be expressed in words, must suffer irrevocable damage, if in the process of transmutation the fine aroma is lost, or the exquisite tints and shades confounded in a general flatness and tameness of coloring. Nor is the case mended when he afterward writes his own speeches. He then falls into nearly the same error. The heat of his mind has cooled, and he can not so speedily reproduce it. Sometimes an intelligent and able reporter will produce a better version than his own.

An analysis of Mr. Sheil's speeches would show them to be in the highest degree artificial. It is his object to produce, by the most elaborate selection of themes, the most chosen forms of phrase, and the most refined art in their arrangement, the same effect which the spontaneous efforts of an earnest orator would have had in the highest powers always at command. Mr. Sheil speaks but seldom, and takes much time to prepare his speeches, which, though delivered with all the air of passion and abandonment which the enthusiasm of the moment might be supposed to inspire, are studied even in the most minute particulars, —in the words chosen, the contrasts of ideas and imagery, the tone of voice, the very gesture. This preparation may not extend, perhaps, to every part of the speech: in the level portions, or in those allusions which are called forth by what has happened during the debate, he trusts in a great measure to the impulse or the judgment of the moment, though even nere you may every now and then detect a phrase or a thought which smells of the lamp; but the great passages of the speech—those which the world afterward admires, and which, in fact, form the foundation of the fame of the orator—these are hewn, chiseled, and polished with all the tender care of a sculptor, rehearsed with all their possible effects, and kept in reserve until the moment when they may be incorporated, in all their brilliancy and perfection, with the less conspicuous parts, where they shine forth resplendently, like bright gems in a dull setting. It is in rhetoric and sarcasm that he is most distinguished. As a rhetorician he is almost perfect. No man whom this generation has ever heard speak equals him in the power with which he works out an idea, an argument, or an illustration, so as to make it carry all the force and weight of which it can possibly be made capable; and this, although it is really the result of such art, is done by means apparently so simple that the hearer's mind is unconsciously captivated. A happy adaptation of some common thought, an infusion of nervous metaphor, which gives a coloring to a whole passage without leaving open any point tangible to opposition; delicate antithesis, the more effective from its not appearing forced;—these are among the many arts which Mr. Sheil uses to insinuate his views and feelings into the mind, while avoiding the appearance of making a deliberate assault, or laying himself out to entrap or to persuade. Occasionally there are bursts of passionate eloquence, which it requires all your skepticism to make you believe are not the warm outpourings of an excited mind: but so you may say of a Kemble or a Macready. In his speeches on Irish subjects especially this apparent sincerity is most conspicuous. His heart always appears to be in his appeals to the English nation on behalf of his country; and no doubt at many times he must fling off his habits of preparation, and give rein to his feelings or his imagination. In speaking of Ireland, he personifies her—talks of her and her wrongs as he would of some lovely and injured woman, whose cause he was espousing. Sometimes his propensity to personify runs him into extremes. Speaking of the address for a Coercion-bill in 1833, he characterized it as one "which struck Ireland dumb, and clapped a padlock on her lips; though it never could stop the throbbing of her big and indignant heart!" One of his most remarkable and beautiful outbursts of nationality was in 1837, in his celebrated attack on Lord Lyndhurst for his "alien" speech. Alluding to the alledged charge that the Irish were aliens in blood and religion, he delivered this magnificent burst:—

"Where was Arthur, Duke of Wellington, when those words were uttered? Methinks he should have started up to disclaim them.

'The battles, seiges, fortunes that he'd pass'd,'

ought to have come back upon him. He ought to have remembered that, from the earliest achievement in which he displayed that military genius which has placed him foremost in the annals of modern warfare, down to that last and surpassing combat which has made his name imperishable—from Assaye to Waterloo—the Irish soldiers with whom your armies were filled, were the inseparable auxiliaries to the glory with which his unparalleled successes have been crowned. Whose were the athletic arms that drove your bayonets at Vimiera through the phalanxes that never reeled in the shock of war before? What desperate valor climbed the steeps and filled the moats of Badajos? All, all his victories should have rushed and crowded back upon his memory—Vimiera, Badajos, Salamanca, Albuera, Toulouse—and, last of all, the greatest. Tell me, for you were there—I appeal to the gallant soldier before me (pointing to Sir Henry

Hardinge), who bears, I know, a generous heart in an intrepid breast—tell me, for you must needs remember, on that day when the destinies of mankind were trembling in the balance, while death fell in showers upon them; when the artillery of France, leveled with the precision of the most deadly science, played upon them; when her legions, incited by the voice, inspired by the example of their mighty leader, rushed again and again to the contest;—tell me if, for an instant (when to hesitate for an instant was to be lost), the 'aliens' blanched? And when, at length, the moment for the last decisive movement had arrived; when the valor so long wisely checked, was at last let loose; when, with words familiar but immortal, the great captain exclaimed, 'Up, lads, and at them!'—tell me if Catholic Ireland with less heroic valor than the natives of your own glorious isle precipitated herself upon the foe! The blood of England, Scotland, Ireland, flowed in the same stream, on the same field; when the chill morning dawned, their dead lay cold and stark together; in the same deep pit their bodies were deposited; the green arm of spring is now breaking on their commingled dust; the dew falls from heaven upon their union in the grave. Partakers in every peril, in the glory shall we not participate? And shall we be told, as a requital, that we are estranged from the noble country for whose salvation our life-blood was poured out?"

The effect produced by this passage will not be easily forgotten. The passionate vehemence of the speaker and the mournful music of his voice were a living echo to the deep emotions with which his soul seemed charged. Lord Lyndhurst was in the House at the time, and although conscious that the whole passage was only a beautiful phantasmagoria raised by the art of the rhetorician, still he could not but admire. It would seem invidious to attempt to neutralize so fine a burst of feeling, but a few words of truth will go far to do it: it unfortunately happens that Mr. Sheil himself, in a speech at the Roman Catholic Association in January, 1823, laid down in distinct and unequivocal terms the very same doctrine—that the Irish were aliens—for giving currency to which he so successfully assailed Lord Lyndhurst with the keen arrows of his oblivious passion.

Metaphor and antithesis are the chief agents he uses in his speeches. Sometimes the latter is exquisitely perfect; sometimes, on the other hand, labored and clumsy, and so forced as to defeat itself. Too often he is run away with by the seduction of this pleasing but mechanical mode of pointing thoughts, to the manifest injury and weakening of his argument, or of the general tone he wishes to convey. Then you see that he is only the orator, the sentence-maker, the painter of brilliant pictures; that he wishes his triumphs to be more over the passions or the imagination than over the reason or the judgment. His style has other defects akin to these. For instance, he will often sacrifice the real strength of a phrase, and endanger the success of the thought or argument it conveys, led away by the seductive sound of some word or words rhythmically pleasing in combination, but the application of which in such a manner the judgment rejects; and he will also lose the force and beauty of real antithesis in the glitter or the novelty of its false counterpart. For an odd paradoxical phrase he will risk the simplicity and truth of a sentence. Speaking of the Whig Tithe-bill, he exclaimed, "Tithes are to be abolished. How? By providing for them a sepulcher, from which they are to rise in an *immortal resuscitation!*" This is an abuse of language. His metaphors are bold and striking. Among many brilliant things in his speeches against Lord Stanley, he said, "The people of Ireland behold the pinnacles of the

Establishment shattered by the lightning of Grattan's eloquence."

He excels in sarcastic humor, which is generally conveyed in the most delicate touches. He is like Lord Lyndhurst in the apparent ease and artlessness with which he infuses the most keen and cutting allusions, by the addition of a word or the turn of a sentence in the midst of the most level argument. He seldom makes a "dead set" at his victim, like Lord Brougham, and he therefore produces the more effect. Some of his smartest hits of this kind were at Lord Stanley. It was he who spoke of that minister as "the then Secretary-at-war with Ireland;" and, when alluding to Sir James Graham in council with the noble lord, he spoke of them as "Lord Stanley and *his confederate.*" On another occasion, speaking of "divine service," as referred to in act of parliament, he jetted in a parenthesis ("Divine is an *alias* for Protestant") well understood by Roman Catholics, and having as much force as twenty elaborate speeches. He is not very reverent in his jokes. Alluding to the Temporalities-act, he observed that "Lord Stanley had struck off ten bishops at one blow: he blew off ten mitres from the head of the hierarchy at a single puff." If he can make a witty point or shape a felicitous phrase, no fastidiousness of taste or delicacy of feeling restrains him from wreaking his wit on an antagonist. There are several instances on record where it has done this toward individuals, though never in an ill-natured or spiteful spirit. He is equally liberal in his sarcastic allusions to classes or bodies of men, and not more delicate. We remember an instance, in one of his speeches, which illustrates this peculiarity in his style: he had been drawing a somewhat glowing and overcharged picture of the good results to ensue from church reform, and he summed them up in terms of characteristic power, and of a degree of coarseness not often met with in his speeches. He said, as a climax to his anticipations of good, that when these reforms should have been effected, "the bloated paunch of the unwieldly rector would no longer heave in holy magnitude beside the shrinking abdomen of the starving and miserably prolific curate."

Sometimes his sarcasm on individuals is really searing, sometimes playfully severe. We remember an amusing instance of the latter:—One day, at the Catholic Association, a volunteer patriot (a Mr. Addis, we believe) came forward and made a very strong speech, more remarkable for enthusiasm than prudence, in which he offered if necessary, to lay his head on the block in the cause of Ireland. His address was rather a dangerous one to those whom he professed to serve, as the crown lawyers were at that time more than usually on the alert. Mr. Sheil desired publicly to counteract the possible mischief; he rose, and, with his peculiar sarcastic emphasis, observed, "The honorable gentleman has just made us an oblation of his head; he has accompanied his offer with abundant evidence of the value of the sacrifice." Columns of abuse from Mr. O'Connell would not have proved half so effective as this quiet rebuke.

But we must draw these observations to a close. The characteristics and defects of his speeches have been more dwelt upon, because his eccentricities of delivery have been frequently and powerfully described. There is a striking correspondence between his personal peculiarities and the leading features of his speeches. He is unique as an orator. There is a harmony between the outer and inner man which you do not find in others—for instance, in Mr. Macaulay. Having read his speeches, if you see him, you are not surprised to find that it was from him that they proceeded. Small in stature, delicately formed, with a strongly marked countenance full of expression, he looks the man of genius, and betrays in every motion that impulsive temperament on which excitement acts like a whirlwind. He seems "of imagination all compact." You see the body, but you think of the mind. It is embodied passion, thought, fancy—not mere organized matter. "Look! what comes here?—a grave unto a soul, holding the eternal spirit against its will!" you are tempted to exclaim with the poet, who of all others could have appreciated such rare products of Nature's love-labor, such unusual blendings of the spiritual and the material. Yet there is nothing of the beautiful in a physical sense, little of that personal perfection or refinement which made a Byron or a Shelley so loved or worshiped by their intimates. The charm of Mr. Sheil's appearance consists in the striking and powerful development of intellect—in the quick reflex of thought in the features, the mobility of body, the firm grasp, as it were, which is taken by the mind of the corporeal frame, making it the ready and obedient slave of its slightest and most sudden will. Thoroughly masculine in moral strength, in the intensity of his feelings, and the strong power with which he impresses them on others, Mr. Sheil has also all the femineity which we attach to our idea of the poetical temperament, though it shows itself not in personal delicacy or symmetry so much as in a supreme and serene control over the body by the spirit. There is more of Edmund Kean than of Shelley in this transparency of the corporeal man to the intellectual light within. The present writer has elsewhere said, speaking of Mr. Sheil's personal appearance:

"Small in stature and make, like so many men of genius, he bears the marks of a delicate organization. The defects of a figure not disproportioned, and yet not strictly symmetrical, are overlooked in the play of the all-informing mind, which keeps the frame and limbs in rapid and harmonious motion when in action.

The body, though so small in itself, is surmounted by a head which lends it dignity—a head, though proportionately small in size, yet so full of intellectual development, so wide-browed, that, while it seems large in itself, it raises the apparent stature of the wiry frame on which it rests. The forehead is broad and prominent, but, at first sight, it rather contradicts the usual development of the intellectual; though really deep and high, it seems to overhang the brow. Under it gleams an eye, piercing and restless even in the repose of the mind, but indescribably bright and deep-meaning when excited. The mouth, small, sharp,—the lips chiseled fine, till, under the influence of passion, they are almost transparent like a shell—is a quick ally in giving point and meaning to the subtilest ideas of the ever active brain ; apt in its Kean-like expression, alike of the withering sarcasm, the delicate irony, or the overwhelming burst of sincere and passionate vehemence. The features, generally, are small, but, under the influence of ennobling emotion, they seem to expand, until, at times, they look grand, almost heroic. Yet when the baser passions obtain the mastery over this child of impulse—as they will, sometimes, over the best in the heat of party warfare—these features, so capable of giving expression to all that elevates our moral and intellectual nature, become contracted—the paleness of concentrated passion overspreads them. Instead of the eloquent earnestness of high-wrought feeling, you see (but this is rare indeed) the gloating hue of suppressed rage, the tremulous restraint of cautious spite. In place of the dilated eye, and features flushed with noble elevation of soul, or conscious pride of intellectual power, you have a keen, piercing, adder-like glance, withering, fascinating, but no longer beautiful. Yet the intellect, though for a time the slave of passion, is the intellect still."

His peculiar style of eloquence, his rapidity of utterance, variety and impressiveness of action, and harmonious tones of voice—now deep and richly melodious in the expression of solemn emotion, now loud and piercing in the excitement of passion—almost defy description. Imagine all the beauties of Kean's performance of Othello crowded into half-an-hour's highly sustained eloquence, and you have some tangible idea of what is the effect. While the impulse is upon him he seems as if possessed, his nature is stirred to its very depths, the fountains of his soul pour forth unceasingly the living waters. His head glows like a ball of fire, the soul struggles through every outlet of expression. His arms, now raised aloft, as if in imprecation, are, in a moment, extended downward, as if in supplication, the clenched fingers clasped like those of one in strong agony. Anon, and the small, thin, delicate, wiry hand is stretched forth, the face assumes an expression the very ideal of the sarcastic, and the finger of scorn is pointed toward the object of attack. A thousand varying expressions, each powerful and all-beautiful, are crowded into the brief time during which his excitement (which, like that of actors, though prepared, is genuine while it lasts) hurries him on to pour forth his whole soul in language of such elegance and force.

Mr. Sheil occupies a position different from that of most of his countrymen in Parliament. The Irish member who most approaches him in intellectual qualities, though not in actual eloquence, is Mr. Wyse. Like Mr. Wyse, he has associated himself with the Whig party, who chose him to be one of their ministers when they desired to fraternize with the Irish Catholics, because he was at once talented, moderate, and respectable. For joining them he was made the subject of virulent abuse by the extreme party in Ireland, but he has too much steadiness of purpose and good sense to be much affected by it. His position in the House is well earned, not merely by his eloquence, but also by the general amenity of his disposition, whether as a politician or a private individual. Were all the Irish members like Mr. Sheil, the Irish question might be speedily and satisfactorily settled.

LORD GEORGE BENTINCK.

Lord George Bentinck is quite a phenomenon in politics. Fifteen years ago, when he, as the phrase goes, "broke down" in the House of Commons, he was supposed to be extinguished as a public man. During the long interval between the year 1831 and the early part of the session of 1846, when he suddenly set lance in rest against Sir Robert Peel, he was so quiescent in the House of Commons as to be scarcely remembered except by those who industriously search the division-lists; nor was he ever heard of, save on one or two occasions when subjects connected with the laws on gaming came before parliament, until within the last few months. But the great crisis on the Corn-law question forced him, together with so many other earnest and high-minded men, out of his seclusion, and, perhaps, his native strength has only shown itself the more because it has been left to its own rough and natural development, not enervated by the habit of parliamentary training. If the simile be a stale one, it is not the less applicable, when we say that he is quite a phœnix, though no one would have predicted in 1831, or at any period since, that he would ever rise into eminence as a politician.

Lord George Bentinck belongs to the class of men who have greatness thrust upon them. It is probable, that up to within a week of his being chosen as the leader of the Protectionists in parliament, he had not the most remote idea of ever taking a prominent part in the debates on the Corn-bill, much less of being the head of a party, with a remote prospect of a place in the government of the country. His previous habits and pursuits, no less than the tendency of his mind, and his indifference to political passions and influences, had unfitted him for such a position. We will venture to say, that astonished as the whole House of Commons was when it was discovered that the mantle of leadership had fallen on him, no one wondered at it more than the noble lord himself. In their first bewilderment at the desertion of their acknowledged leaders, the Protectionist or country party knew not where to turn for substitutes. "Young England" offered itself; but good intentions unaccompanied by knowledge of mankind, and that "crooked wisdom" which weighs in politics, were not enough for a party in such sudden straits as the agriculturists were then in. Lord John Manners exhibited talents which promised to develop one day into a genius for philosophic statesmanship: but the subjects involved in the Corn-law struggle were uncongenial to his mind. Mr. Stafford O'Brien, till then only known as a sort of amiable pedant in politics, a *doctrinaire* of a somewhat dogmatic school, made one brilliant speech, for which Sir Robert Peel in vain endeavored to bribe him to his side by praise and flattery; but after that effort, although, tempted strongly to press forward, he declined to vault into the vacant saddle. Mr. Disraeli had long astonished the House by his powerful philippics, his concentrated sarcasms against the premier; all acknowledged his talent as a debater, and listened to his speeches with a keen interest and eager anticipation theretofore only accorded to the first men in parliament: but in his case it was felt that an intemperate and vindictive hostility to an individual was a bad guaranty for the expectant trustee of the interests of a party; that it was probable he would rather promote his own personal cause than that of his followers. He was admitted to be invaluable as an ally, but his claims to be a leader were set aside. At this crisis it was that Lord George Bentinck was suddenly chosen to head the opposition to Sir Robert Peel in the House of Commons. Position and talent combined to elevate him to this proud position. It was necessary that the man who was to be, for however brief a period, the leader of the landed aristocracy, or, at least, a great part of them, should have hereditary associations with the landed interest. Mere ability as a debater, or mere steadfastness and earnestness of character, would not alone qualify for the leadership. An unusual combination of those qualities, allied, moreover, to tact, sagacity, and knowledge of mankind, was required for the post; and that combination the different heads of the country party seemed by common consent to ascribe to Lord George Bentinck. His antecedents partly favored the belief, and partly contradicted it. He had been for many years in parliament, a silent observer of all political events, as far as the House of Commons was concerned, but privately mixed up as a partisan with the leading members of the Conservative party, who had many and frequent means of ascertaining and testing the sterling qualities of his character. He had also, as he has himself stated in parliament, been private secretary to Mr. Canning; and it was well known that that distinguished man held him in very high esteem, believing that he was capable of great distinction in the political world, if a constitutional indolence did not prevent him from exerting himself. On the other hand, his well known devotion to uncongenial pursuits, and the notoriety he had acquired in the sporting world, exposed him to some ridicule when he stepped forward as a leader, and made his chances of success appear to be so much the less. But he did not thrust himself forward; he was in a manner forced into the front rank

Having once accepted the honorable but onerous task, from that hour he devoted himself to it, body and mind. No exertion, no application was considered by him too great, if the result of it would be to render him more fit for his task.

Had the question in dispute been more of a mere party question—had it, for instance, been such a question as that of Emancipation, where appeals to a political honor and denunciations of ministerial treachery would have formed the staple of the speeches to be delivered, and when the tactics of management would be almost confined to mere resistance, the sudden acceptance of the leadership would not have involved so much mental responsibility. But in the case in question, the position of a new leader was quite different. The combined knowledge of the statesman and the political economist had to be brought to bear on a question abounding in statistics of the most varied kind, statistics changing with almost every week; and this in the face of watchful and able opponents on both sides of the House, as well those who had been engaged during their public life in assailing the positions to be taken up, as those who, having all along defended them, now suddenly abandoned them, and, knowing their weak points, turned that knowledge to advantage. To fill such a post, then, was no slight undertaking for a man like Lord George Bentinck, bred, as he says, a soldier, who was an active politician only in what he is pleased to call, in modesty of spirit, the "humblest office which a political man can fill," and who for so many years had turned almost his whole attention to other and less dignified pursuits.

His success was signal. The first speech of any importance he made on the Corn question appeared, on the face of the newspaper reports, to be a failure. In the House it was no such thing. The noble lord had an object in protracting his speech, and to accomplish that, he sacrificed some of its power and effect. He did not rise till a late hour, and then continued speaking for so long a time that the House grew impatient, and much confusion prevailed toward the close of his address. But in those parts of it which were heard, and which, in fact, contained the real pith of his argument, such a striking acquaintance with the complex and extensive facts, and such a power of argument, were exhibited, that the noble lord, prolix as he was, made a very deep impression on the House. His very next speech, made under more favorable circumstances, confirmed it; Lord George displayed so accurate and complete a knowledge of his subject, that even detraction was silent. Opponents were as ready as his own supporters to admire his displays. They knew from experience what an amount of application must have been given in order to enable him to obtain so thorough a mastery over so difficult a subject.

Lord George Bentinck, as may be supposed, has not attained, or even approximated to perfection as an orator. He was too much preoccupied with his subject to be able to strike out any new style of oratory for himself; it was enough to be able to deliver his speech with an average ability. So he trusted to old, time-honored forms in action, intonation, and delivery—forms long since abandoned by all but a few members of either House, and which, like cast-off habits, have traveled down through different classes, till they now dignify and embellish that kind of eloquence which one hears after dinner at the London Tavern. It is singular to notice how the infusion of the popular and mercantile element into the representative system has affected the oratory as well as the opinions and votes in parliament. Until within the last twenty years or so, gentlemen intended for public life were regularly trained for public speaking; a course under the elocution-master was deemed essential to an aspirant for honors. The consequence was, that the general characteristics of public speakers were very similar. A tediously slow delivery, extreme pomposity, verbosity, and monotony, action in what has been termed the "pump-handle" style, marked them all, and may still be found in great perfection in many whose old-fashioned oratory defies and survives innovation. The crowning virtue of this style in the eyes of its professors seems to be to end every sentence intended to be emphatic with a sudden jerk and a twang. Lord George Bentinck fell naturally into this style when he first began his recent opposition; but conflict and the influence of example have altered his style, even in this brief space of time. Yet to that which he gradually abandoned, his aristocratic bearing gave a kind of characteristic interest, well adapted to the subject-matter on which his speeches were delivered. Taken as a whole, bearing in mind the noble descent of the speaker, his whole aspect so essentially aristocratic, his speeches were emphatically a protest from the living representative of a past generation of statesmen, and of a code of political morality long since abandoned, against a new race of statesmen, untried for good, and suspected of evil. But for some time past, Lord George Bentinck has adapted his style much more to the modern tastes of the House of Commons. He speaks with more brevity and more to the point, and has got rid of an unpleasant drawling tone and a habit of hesitation. Fewer statistics and more argument characterize his politico-economic speeches, while his purely party or personal displays exhibit a power and vigor not shown in his earlier efforts. In his personal attacks on Sir Robert Peel, he allowed the warmth and sincerity of his feelings to carry him farther than has been usual in what Mr. Disraeli called these "mealy-mouthed" days; but then it should be remembered that he believes Sir Robert Peel to have acted, politically, with unfairness toward one for whom Lord George entertained the most ardent affection and respect, and that all men are not so constituted as to be able to treat politics as a mere game, in which only a kind of sham feeling is to be allowed to intermingle. Apart from the question of the propriety of these attacks, however, the energy and debating power they exhibited show that the noble lord can be, when aroused, a dangerous antagonist.

Lord George Bentinck's elevation was an accident of the Anti-Corn-law agitation. Certainly but for the effect of that agitation he would have continued a silent member in the House of Commons. It took much to arouse him from his retirement; but, having been once set in motion, we should be tempted to predict that he will hereafter take a distinguished position in political affairs.

MR. VILLIERS.

Advocacy of a repeal of the Corn-laws has been the one special political hobby of the Honorable Charles Pelham Villiers—a hobby he rode round the political arena with that degree of flourish which usually attends hobby-horsemanship, until the real men and horses of the Anti-Corn-law League came on the scene. Year after year he made his formal motion for repeal of the Corn-laws, and delivered almost the same speech—at least, the same arguments applied to new facts—with but little effect upon the House. Sometimes he was "counted out;" sometimes the matter was disposed of by a single speech from the government, or latterly from an agricultural member; but at all times the subject was regarded as a disagreeable one, not improved by the mode in which the honorable member handled it, and the House was always as thin as a decent respect for the proprieties would allow. Even after the League had begun to make a figure in the House, the annual motion of Mr. Villiers still was regarded as an annual bore; and when at last the out-of-doors agitation had invested the subject with a greater political interest, other and more powerful speakers commanded the attention of the House, and Mr. Villiers was, comparatively speaking, lost in the throng, although still allowed to retain his original position, as the parliamentary organ of the party.

The natural inference is, that a man who would so long persevere in the advocacy of any particular set of opinions, must be sincere in holding them. That, at least, is the obvious, as well as the most charitable interpretation. But it has long been the practice with ambitious men who desired to rise in the House of Commons, to connect themselves with some particular question, and to attract attention by the pertinacity with which they enforce their projects or their views annually on the House. A hundred instances force themselves on the mind immediately. Now, it did not require any very great degree of foresight in Mr. Villiers to see that the subject of the Corn-laws must one day or other, at no distant period, force itself on the legislature, and that an advocate on the popular side could not but in the long run have his reward. This may account for the singular perseverance of the honorable member in his difficult, and for a long time discouraging task.

Perseverance is the characteristic of Mr. Villiers. There is perseverance in his conduct as a member of parliament, perseverance in the unique perpetuation of his arguments during so many years, perseverance in the energetic monotony of his voice, perseverance, ay, in his very gait as he moves on, apparently so unmindful of what is passing around him, stooping more from weight of thought than physical weakness, his hands crossed behind him, with quick and plodding step. To this perseverance he mainly owes his public position. It was tantamount to proof that he was in earnest; and, as moral force prevails so much more than pure reason in modern politics, an earnest man will always become more or less an influential one.

The importance of Mr. Villiers as a speaker must be measured by the value of his arguments, for they derive no additional weight from his mode of delivering them. A man who, as far as politics are concerned, has devoted his whole energies to one subject, could scarcely fail to make himself master of it. This has been the case of Mr. Villiers. His one idea of free-trade assumed in his mind a prismatic variety of aspects. He turned and twisted it until it would have been almost impossible to place it in a new point of view. It is only just to him to say that he differs from most popular advocates, in this respect—that while he enforces his convictions vigorously, and with resolute determination, he does not merely deal in vague dogmatic assertions, or declamatory violence. He argues rather than affirms, and appeals rather than denounces. In his best speeches there has always been considerable logical force. In this respect, if not in general acquaintance with his subject, he equals, if sometimes he does not excel, Mr. Cobden. But all these advantages are neutralized by his mode of delivery, which is neither stimulating nor dignified. A hard, grinding, plodding, though forcible monotony of voice, with a pronunciation the (almost) vulgarity of which strikes one the more as coming from a man of noble birth, are not helped by his action and delivery, both of which are commonplace in the extreme. He never was nor ever will be a favorite as a speaker, whether in the House or at public meetings.

MR. T. MILNER GIBSON.

Mr Milner Gibson owed his elevation to office to his own unaided talents. He is a fresh and a striking instance of the practical liberality of our institutions (however aristocratic may be their superficial aspect), which makes it almost a matter of certainty that a man of talent will rise to high offices in the state, if he have the requisite conduct and perseverance. Mr. Gibson early displayed parliamentary talents of a high order, and although his elevation has been more sudden than could have been expected two or three years ago, it might have been confidently predicted that, if his ambition lay in the direction of office, it would, at no very distant period, be gratified.

But the public were scarcely prepared—Mr. Gibson himself could not have been—to expect that he would figure in the position of Vice-President of the Board of Trade under Whig auspices. In no invidious sense of the term, he may be said to have been an adventurer—a respectable and successful one, but still an adventurer. Looking back at his career, it does not seem that he has had any necessary or natural connection with the parties to which he has from time to time allied himself. He has traded on his talents, with an aptitude for observing the signs of the times, and an alacrity in profiting by his knowledge. He had read and seen enough to know, that even in the times of purely aristocratic parliaments a good ready speaker would always make a figure, and that since the infusion of more popular elements into the representation the chances of obtaining influence in debate, or over the public mind out of doors, were very much multiplied, if the aspirant was in every respect up to the popular mark. Now Mr. Gibson has always, even from his first appearance before the public, been able to make, at will, rattling, telling speeches; sometimes full of playful irony; sometimes of sound, powerful argument; sometimes of glowing clap-traps, such as captivate the vulgar. He has also that moral pliability, that happy knack of imitative enthusiasm, which enable the favorites of the multitude to throw themselves into any particular movement with well simulated fervor. Armed to the teeth with argument to suit any or every party, well provided with the small change of popular political knowledge, and having at his full command that sword of peaceful times, the orator's tongue, he saw in the world of party his "oyster," which he with that sword hath opened. Not quite a demagogue, he has been at all times the politician militant, and now he has won the prize, which was, to say the least, due more to his talents than his consistency. For his path has been a somewhat tortuous one; in his party alliances he has proved inconstant. In the blaze of his triumphs as a free-trader, the public were apt to forget that he started in the House of Commons as a Conservative, if not a Tory; that he had not been long in parliament, ere he exhibited in his proper person one of the most singular and startling instances of sudden "ratting" of which we have any record of late years, at least among men of no mark as politicians, no long cemented and well known character with which to play at nine-pins. For to subordinates it is not given to change long avowed opinions with audacious impunity—to display that sublime indifference to the law of political rectitude in which more powerful persons may indulge.

Mr. Gibson was a bold man to take the step he did He openly avowed his change, if not of opinions, at least of policy, and was too honorable, or too calculating, to play the part of traitor in the enemy's camp. It was at the time universally thought that his conversion was too sudden to be sincere; it was incomprehensible how a man, who had not even the plea of state necessity in his excuse, could, within the short space of a few months, be an active partisan on both sides of the question; and there was a dashing boldness in the address in which he communicated his intention of changing his side that altogether precluded the modesty of repentant conviction. One thing was at once achieved—notoriety. What he might say and do was ever after looked to with curiosity. This was a first step to ultimate success.

For some time his inconsistency placed him under a sort of ban. He was listened to, much as Mr. Disraeli is listened to, with a reservation of blame on personal grounds. In his own conduct he oscillated between Russellism and Radicalism, apparently uncertain which would prove the better card. All the while he was gradually effacing the memory of his inconsistency, and winning his way with the House by his light and playful style of speaking, he introduced occasionally displays of argumentative power which showed there was "stuff" in him. At length came his opportunity,—that which, it is said, is given to every man once in his life. The League began to show symptoms of its ultimate popularity and power, and Mr. Gibson, with his ready ability and popular style of speaking, alike effective in Parliament and with the public, was too desirable an acquisition to be otherwise than highly prized. With his usual facility he at once threw himself, with the requisite amount of ardor, into the struggle. He became one of the most influential of Mr. Cobden's allies, was important enough to be a sort of Tribune-

Associate in cases where the chief agitator could not be present, and now, at last, he is borne easily and triumphantly into office, when the object of the League has been obtained.

From what has already been said, it will be inferred that Mr. Milner Gibson is a very agreeable and able speaker. Whether he rises to make a mere party attack, or to deliver an argumentative speech, he is equally happy and effective. If he never does any thing positively brilliant, or that would bear to be remembered after the immediate excitement has passed away, he constantly treads on the very borders of first-rate excellence, and he rarely or never fails. One cause of the effectiveness of his speeches is, that looking at him you are not prepared to expect so much sterling talent and power; you do not expect wisdom from boys, or masculine vigor from women. The small, round, whiskerless face of Mr. Gibson, handsome even in features, and still more so in its vivacious expression, his brilliant eyes, and mouth round which a smile is ever playing lightly, do not indicate the qualities or the pursuits of a popular agitator, any more than does his delicate and feminine (not effeminate) organization. And the voice, low-toned but clear, harmonious, and modulated, until it is almost fluty in sound, matches singularly with the general aspect; his action while speaking, too, being of the most unassuming, but the most graceful kind. In the House, except on great and stirring occasions, he adopts a style which looks like trifling, but is fatally effective. The tiny arrows of his wit and humor come in quick volleys; they do not pierce very deep, but they are infinitely tantalizing. This youthful, gracious-looking, ladylike gentleman we have described will rise from among the rough, commonplace men who surround him, and, with a well assumed diffidence and air of drawing-room politeness, put a question to a minister (of course we speak of when he was in the opposition) that seems as if it would be of the most agreeable, harmless kind, to be answered with all the facility of a practiced official. But there runs through the statement which accompanies it a vein of tormenting banter, of sly, sarcastic humor, of assertion or of argument, couched in expostulation, that throws the House into suppressed titters, and is provoking in the extreme where the person questioned is personally mixed up, or where official necessity seals his lips and denies him the right of explanation. They are very hard blows, though they come from a very soft hand, and from a spirit that seems to breathe the very essence of bland gentleness. No fair-lady knight of Ariosto or Boiardo could couch the lance more gracefully, or direct its point with more keen and sure precision. And yet when you see Mr. Gibson at a public meeting, you lose sight of all these qualities, and find that for argument he is almost equal to Mr. Cobden himself, and that he can wield at will the passions of the multitude. Nor in the House is this playful vein his only, or even his ordinary, resource. In an argumentative speech he can prove himself a match for the best men; and he has thoroughly established himself as a good speaker in the opinion of that very critical body, the House of Commons. Like Lord Palmerston and Mr. Charles Buller, he combines great powers of argument with a happy use of ironical humor; if he be not quite equal to either, he strongly resembles both. It remains yet to be seen what sort of work he will make with the figures; but from his readiness and aptitude in so many different positions, there is little doubt that he will soon prove himself an effective minister.

MR. WAKLEY.

To Mr. Wakley belongs the honor of having been the artificer of his own fortunes. Unlike many more favored competitors in the race, he has had to make his tools as well as to perform his work. Comparing his position at the present time with what it was when he commenced life, the most prejudiced of his political opponents must admit that the task he has performed was one of no ordinary difficulty, and that no ordinary talents were required to accomplish it. Mr. Wakley's path to notoriety has, it is true, been both a rugged and a tortuous one. His life has been one continued battle with foes whom he has called into existence, expressly that he might have the honor of conquering them. Looking back to years now distant, we see him in the very infancy of his reputation, always even from the first, in a militant attitude toward those around him. We see him, as it were, in the position of the man, strong, perhaps, in mind and purpose, and determined to make his voice heard, who is, nevertheless, hemmed in at the extreme back of a crowd—struggling long in vain ere he can catch the ear of the multitude, and make himself heard above their roar. But, by pushing, and energy, and unscrupulous fighting—aided, too, by that lurking sympathy which a bold man always excites, even in his opponents, we see this same battling spirit gradually forcing his way through the mass, which, the farther he advances, opens the more to let him pass, until at last the unknown strong man is seen proudly taking his place on the platform among the notables of the hour, and pouring out his passionate declamation to the many-headed throng; ruling them now as powerfully by the pure influence of his mind, as he had but recently coerced them by his determination and physical energy. Such is a remote type of the public life of Mr. Wakley.

Mr. Wakley, even as a young man and a beginner in life, seems to have well studied the English character. He early perceived that for a man who has no precise standing—who is not put by Fortune into a groove and pushed on, with an easy momentum, to success—must, if he wish to rise in the world, begin by making himself notorious. This is an age of publicity. In proportion as the circle of intelligence in society has expanded, the quality of that intelligence has become depreciated. There is less discrimination in the public mind, and a lower order of talent will command success, than when every new comer on the public arena was subject to the severe criticism of trained minds and constituted authorities, and his place was assigned to him at once. This state of things holds out so great a temptation to quacks of all kinds, that they resort to every imaginable mode to impose their spurious mental wares upon mankind. Even real merit is no longer modest, but is forced, even against its will, into the same courses that disgrace its more shallow and pretending rivals. We are not going so far to insult Mr. Wakley as to impute to him modest merit. Modesty is not one of his distinguishing characteristics: merit, in the sense of strong thinking powers, sound judgment, tact, and devotion to the interests of the people, he certainly possesses. But he has never been disposed to hide his light under a bushel. To be talked about for any thing, provided it was not disgraceful, was, he knew, a good stepping-stone to something better and more respectable at a future time. Coming up to London from Devonshire (where, we may add, his family are respectable), with his profession chosen, and his way to make in the world, he seems to have had too much energy of mind to be content with the slow and plodding process by which a surgeon may, if he is lucky and does not get crushed at the outset, ultimately secure for himself a respectable maintenance. He rather sought a royal road to fame and profit. He seemed as though he had been born to be a reformer and grievance-hunter. No doubt, in the then state of the medical profession, there was great opening for an active-minded man to pull down many who were in the high places, and set up better men. Exclusiveness in the distribution of honors, degradation of a large class of the medical profession, who were daily growing in importance under the influence of altered habits in society,—these, together with individual cases of corruption and mismanagement, afforded a fine field for a thorough-going revolutionist. Accordingly, " The Lancet" was started. The boldness and vigorous venom of its articles soon attracted universal attention, not merely in the medical profession, but among the public at large. As a necessary consequence, its editor and proprietor became an object of interest. His purpose was gained—he was talked about; thenceforth, whatever he might do was sure to be made the subject of comment, and a basis was laid for future operations. In fact, " The Lancet" was so successful as to become the foundation, not only of his fame but of his fortune.

The restless and ever active mind of Mr. Wakley, however, could not long content itself with the comparatively confined sphere of action afforded by the castigation of medical offenders, or the agitation of medical reforms. Nature seemed almost to have designed him for a mob-orator: a very few attempts at public meetings gave him confidence in his own powers; for although some of his opinions might be unpalatable, there was a great attraction for the multitude in his popular mode of speaking, his boldness, and, above all, his humor. He seems early to have conceived the idea of attaining distinction in the political world, though to what object it was to lead, or in what way popularity with the multitude was to advance his fortunes, he does not appear, at this time, to have very clearly marked out for himself. Nay, even to this hour, and with the advantage of retrospection to guide one, it is utterly impossible to determine, with any certainty, the goal of his hopes. He rather seems to have been impelled forward by a natural energy and impulsive temperament, and we would, in all charity, give him credit for a sincere belief, that by persevering in the exposure of political abuses he might be of permanent service to his fellow-countrymen. Whatever his motives or his objects, certain it is, that he threw himself, with all the determined energy of the English character, into those questions which agitated the public mind immediately before and after the settlement of the Reform question. As is usual with adventurers who wait upon Providence to indicate the particular course they are to steer, he avowed himself a thorough Radical Reformer. Without being a Chartist, he pushed ultra-liberal opinions to their extreme verge. Such a man, possessed as he was, of shrewdness, tact, eloquence, and the command of the popular ear, was of great use to the more aristocratic agitators of that day, although they, in their cautious exclusiveness, affected to consider him a very dangerous person. But Mr. Wakley was not a man to be pooh-poohed or sneered into subservience. Such as his course was, it was of his own choosing; and he held his own. With such talents for mob-leadership, it was natural that in those days of political license, when even members of the aristocracy were tampering with questions which are now considered fraught with danger to the constitution, he should soon obtain a species of portable power in the shape of reputation and notoriety, which might be made subservient to designs upon some congenial constituency. Among other things, he started a newspaper advocating and called "The Ballot." When, soon afterward, he aspired to the honor of a seat in parliament, we can well remember the utter disdain and contempt with which his pretensions were, in the first instance, regarded. He was looked upon as a vulgar, noisy, troublesome demagogue, with a tainted character and a reputation none of the highest, who had made his position by wholesale calumnies on distinguished members of the medical profession, and had been more known, up to a recent period, as a defendant to actions for libel, than in any honorable career. The idea of his ever being able to take a respectable position in parliament, or even of his being endured in that aristocratic assembly, the House of Commons, except as a sort of coarse mountebank like Henry Hunt, was scouted as absurd. But after two failures in Finsbury (in 1832 and 1834), he came in triumphantly in 1835. Thus, by dint of perseverance, puffing, public speaking, and continual notoriety, did this active-minded man, without friends, without introduction, without fortune, and in spite of the prejudice against people who come from nobody knows where, raise himself from comparative insignificance into a position which, in theory at least, is one of which he may be honorably proud.

Mr. Wakley had not been long in parliament before he exhibited a demeanor totally the reverse of what was expected from him. He very agreeably disappointed even his friends, while his enemies, who had predicted a failure, were quite confounded. One of Mr. Wakley's chief characteristics is tact. If it was his real nature that exhibited itself when he was fighting his way, sword in hand, up to the front rank, so much the greater is his merit that he was able to tame and subdue it when he got into parliament. Now and then, to be sure, a dash of the old spirit would show itself in the heat of debate, or on some topics which roused the latent independence of his character. He would blurt out strange, unpalatable truths to ears attuned to courteous fictions. He would, once and again, forget that he was no longer addressing a Finsbury mob, and would use the cudgel where the broadsword or the rapier are the more customary weapons. But with such rare exceptions, it was singular to see how soon and how well he schooled his mind for its new duties. He studied his men, and adapted his conduct to the results of his observation. For a long time he was only tolerated. He seemed to be regarded much in the light of those wild animals, in which, although they are tamed, the savage nature is believed still to lurk. The respect which his debating talents command is mingled with a vague fear and a dislike still unconquered, because proceeding from a natural antagonism. But he has acquired a decided position.

Having thus brought Mr. Wakley to the highest point which an independent member of parliament can reach, the question naturally suggests itself, What are his motives and his objects in continuing a life of such mental and physical labor as he constantly undergoes? It has already been suggested, that in first pressing forward toward political distinction, he was stimulated by the irresistible impulse of an undefined ambition. His sagacity must very early have taught him that the political prizes within his grasp, even if he could with any consistency have accepted them, were utterly inadequate, in a pecuniary point of view, to meet the expenditure of a successful adventurer, while, in point of honor or distinction, they would never satisfy the cravings of his ambitious and restless mind. The question, Whether a public man, so situated, may, with honor, accept public employment? we conceive to have been set at rest. Mr. Wakley had a perfect right to accept any office which was offered him, or which, by fair exertion, he could obtain. The office of coroner for Middlesex having become vacant, Mr. Wakley offered himself for it. It cost him some trouble and expense to obtain it, but at length he was appointed after a severely contested election. The emoluments of the office are, it is said, sufficient to maintain its holder in the position of a gentleman: Mr. Wakley, with his usual energy and activity of mind, was not content with the proceeds as they were when he took the situation, but by a vigorous exercise of its functions, and an occasional stretching of almost obsolete rights, he has contrived, as it is understood, very materially to increase his emoluments. His proceedings, in his character of coroner, are a great study. He has constituted himself a sort of absolute Monarch of the Morgue, and with a kingly grasp he levies his indiscriminate taxes. He has as extraordinary a scent for an unfortunate catastrophe of the sort that comes within the range of his jurisdiction, as, in his political capacity, he has for an abuse. In the former case he has a stimulus, which in the latter is wanting. The more cases of mysterious death he can discover, the larger his fees of office. It is extraordinary what an incentive such a state of things sometimes is to public virtue. Mr. Wakley's activity is quite edifying. He is policeman, church-warden, Humane-Society officer, parish gossip, surgeon, public lecturer, spontaneous magistrate, and coroner, all in one. He "makes the meat he feeds on." He is a positive terror in all delinquent neighborhoods; and general practitioners, who have had an unlucky case, shudder when they think that some mysterious irregularity may be whispered in the Dionysius ear of this watchful functionary, and that "that fellow, Wakley," may come down among them with his writ, holding his inquiry, giving them the benefit of his judgment as a surgeon and the disadvantage of his speech-making as a magistrate, till, perhaps, they see, in the distance, an adverse verdict of an admiring jury, which blasts forever their professional reputation, and destroys their hope of fortune.

Power proverbially corrupts. We regret to have to say, that not even our honest-minded and liberal demagogue has been able to escape its influence. In his capacity as coroner, he belies his teachings as the advocate for freedom. In this court he is a dictator; that is, he would be if he could. Not even Field-Marshal the Duke of Wellington can have a more arrogant contempt for the press than has Our Great Coroner. He would fain have excluded the penny-a-liners from his court, but those gentlemen, like black beetles, are not to be supposed not present because they are not seen. Closed doors are not proof against their subtile and insinuating habits. In vain Mr. Wakley closed the portals of his traveling Temple of Justice to these, his Argus-eyed enemies. They were present in the spirit; and all his magisterial sayings and dictatorial doings were as faithfully reported to the public as if he had never issued his awful fiat. There is a strange mixture of the tyrant and the demagogue in his judicial proceedings. One moment he is all arbitrary power, and in the next he displays as great an avidity for the gossip of the neighborhood, and readiness to suppose every body—that is to say, surgeons, nurses, policemen, juries—in the wrong, all grossly neglecting their duties. His presence, nay, the very shadow of his bulky frame, causes as much terror as if he were a Grand Inquisitor.

These rigorous proceedings, however, are more fairly subjects of criticism by the medical profession, and those who are immediately affected by them, than in an article of this description. But the acceptance by Mr. Wakley of the office of coroner, and his indefatigable attention to its duties, bear, to a certain extent, upon his political character. It is of great consequence to the public to be able to determine with some degree of accuracy the amount of dependence they can place on those who stand forward in parliament as the reformers of abuses. We are not going to claim for Mr. Wakley the praise of immaculate purity. We do not believe that ambition has had any the less influence in stimulating him to action than in the case of more confessed adventurers. On the contrary, his whole life has been a series of bold pushings. But we do claim for this gentleman, as covering a multitude of minor imperfections, the merit of sincerity. Looking at him only as a politician, he is the sort of man we should wish to deal with. There can be little doubt that he believes in the existence of very great abuses in the constitution, the law, and the administration. He thinks, too, that the best guaranty for the sure correction of such abuses would be to admit, to a greater extent, into the constituencies, the classes upon whom the consequences of those abuses press the most heavily. In these matters, his theory is the reflexion of his convictions, formed upon a long and close observation of his fellow-countrymen, particularly of the industrious classes, whom he has had peculiar opportunities of studying. He is essentially a practical man; and provided the objects which he seeks to attain can be accomplished through the existing machinery of government, he would not be the advocate of rash or speculative change. It is probable that recent events have very materially modified the democratic tendency of Mr. Wakley's opinions. He perceives that the aristocracy are no longer, as he once thought they were, leagued together for the conservation of abuses. He sees them, in different fields of action, taking a friendly and earnest interest in the affairs of the people. He sees such men as Lord Ashley in one sphere, Lord

John Manners in another, and Sir Robert Peel in another, establishing the principle that the social welfare of the unprotected classes must be made the basis of all legislation; and the angry feeling, the constitutional jealousy, in which, against the good-humored bent of his nature, he once indulged, has become supplanted by more really liberal views, and a greater amount of confidence in those who are in power under the existing order of things. There could not be a better specific for taming and civilizing a furious democrat.

If we turn to Mr. Wakley's exertions as a social reformer, we shall find the same earnestness and sincerity animating all his speeches and actions. He will take up the cause of the poor because his heart is really in them, and his indignation is aroused as an Englishman at any thing that savors of tyranny and oppression. He has never been a heartless trader in popular grievances; he has been loud in proclaiming them, it is true, but it has been with motives superior to those of ordinary demagogues. It is a singular fact, that Mr. Wakley has been more active and energetic in the exercise of his voluntary duties, on behalf of the unprotected classes, since he has been coroner than he ever was before. Night after night he has bestowed unremitting attention on his parliamentary duties, serving by day, too, on committees, and going through all the labor of investigation and preparation necessary in bringing forward cases of individual misconduct or of public mismanagement, when the government officials are always on the watch for the slightest errors. All this voluntary service from one who has reached the highest point in the way of pecuniary reward is, at least, *primâ facie* evidence of the absence of selfishness, and of any desire to trade upon philanthropy.

There is decided character about Mr. Wakley as a platform-speaker. Although any violence of tone which there may at one time have been in his speeches has been softened down, he is still, in his physical and even in his mental peculiarities, a type, and a very striking one, of the demagogue. Nay, his broad, burly frame, his powerful voice, his careless, unstudied action, and his blunt, off-hand mode of address, may have contributed, even more than his actual conduct, or the sentiments he has from time to time expressed, to gain for him his former political reputation. He is just the man to sway a mob; nothing daunts him; no man dare attempt to put him down. Not even O'Connell himself can wield with such a perfect will the rude elements of democracy. He stands amid the storm and shock of a public meeting like a rock or a tower, immovable, uninfluenced, even by its utmost fury. An absolute command of temper, yet a determined spirit to put down opposition, a watchful eye, a shrewd perception, and a ready touch of humor to catch the current of feeling as it turns, give him a power over a miscellaneous multitude such as could not be wielded by men of, perhaps, much greater intellect, but not the same amount of determination, patience, tact, and knowledge of the weak side of human nature; for in a crowd the weak side shows most prominently: the best men shrink from publicity.

Mr. Wakley, as a speaker in the House of Commons, is more distinguished for shrewdness and common sense than for any of the higher accomplishments of the orator. A plain, simple, blunt, downright style disarms suspicion and bespeaks confidence, even at the outset of his address. A manly frankness, both in his bearing and delivery, precludes the idea of any preparation, or of any design to entrap by means of the ordinary tricks and contrivances of the practiced debater. He has a brief, conversational manner, as though his thoughts were quite spontaneous, and not the result of preparation. He seems to be thinking what he shall say next, as if the subject came quite fresh to his mind, and he were, by a sort of compulsion, drawing as much truth out of it as he could. This gives both freshness and vigor to his speeches. By his singular shrewdness and common sense, his perfect command of temper, his good-humored irony, and store of information, available at the moment on almost all subjects, he has acquired an amount of influence in the House disproportioned to the demands of his position. He has inspired much confidence in his judgment, and by an original, because an unfettered, turn of thinking, he contrives to strike out new views of the subjects before the House, and to supply materials for thinking or for debating out of what seem to be threadbare themes. This is the consequence of the original turn of his mind and the independence of his position. He has no party ties; he has received no training; he has no class prejudices, such as obtain influence in the House of Commons, but has been a shrewd and constant observer of human nature in all grades, and is not burdened with an overpowering sense of the immaculate purity of public men. Still you never hear from him those coarse charges of personal corruption against individuals which will often fall from Mr. Duncombe, notwithstanding his gentlemanly manners and superficial refinement. Broad as his insinuations sometimes are, there is a degree of delicacy in the phraseology in which they are clothed; and though he often indulges in a sarcastic humor, it seldom or never carries a venomous sting. Although a very honest and uncompromising popular advocate, determined in his exposure of public abuses, and still more in his championship of the neglected poor, he shows a gentlemanly respect for the forms and restraints which experience has rendered necessary in debate, and a forbearance to press charges to useless extremities of personality. Many a highly educated aristocrat in the House of

Commons might take a lesson, in this respect, from this self-taught and self-trained politician. Mr. Wakley loses nothing in personal influence by this sensible self-restraint. If he has not quite conquered the prejudices entertained toward ultra-Radical intruders by men of birth and station, he has at least made them feel his intellectual power and acknowledge his moral equality. In this respect he has done more to advance the interests of the millions, by making their advocacy respectable, than have many more flashy and showy popular leaders. His style of speaking is the most simple and unaffected. He has been too busily engaged in the hard work of life to have had much time to bestow on oratory. He has the appearance of a provincial, and has also the accent of one. The associations thus excited still further negative the idea of polish or preparation. You might fancy, but for the knowledge of passing events, not less than of subjects of higher order, which his speeches display, that he was some country farmer suddenly smitten with a passion for speech-making. The structure of his speeches is quite inartificial, and the language usually the most simple and colloquial of everyday life. It is plain, even homely, without being inelegant: a manliness of sentiment, and a quiet self-possession in the speaker, impart a kind of dignity to the most ordinary expressions. There is breadth and force in his argument and declamation, and a rough pathos in his descriptions of pauper suffering is often far more stirring and affecting than the most accomplished eloquence of more finished speakers. Mr. Wakley does not so much make speeches, as deliver the thoughts which burden his mind on any given subject, with frankness and sincerity. Even hard words do not come offensively from him, such is his good-humor and the amenity of his disposition. He constantly displays great shrewdness of perception, unmasking the motives of opponents with a masterly power, and, at the same time, with an avoidance of coarse imputation. Yet he can be sarcastic when he chooses; but his sarcasm is more in the hint conveyed, and in the knowing look of face and tone of voice, than in any positively cutting expressions. He handles the scalpel with delicacy and skill, never cutting deeper than is absolutely necessary. Some of his "points" have, from time to time, told remarkably well; such, for instance, as that in which he described the Whig ministry as being made of "squeezable" materials. That one expression contributed considerably toward gaining for him the position he holds in the estimation of the House of Commons.

Mr. Wakley has extraordinary energy, both physical and mental. To see him bringing up his portly, bulky frame along the floor of the House of Commons, with swinging arms, and rolling, almost rollicking gait, his broad, fair face inspired with good-humor, and his massive forehead set off by light, almost flaxen hair, flowing in wavy freedom backward around his head, and the careless ease of his manly yet half-boyish air, as though he had no thought or care beyond the impression or impulse of the moment; to watch the frank, hearty good-will with which he greets his personal friends as he throws himself heedlessly into his seat, and interchanges a joke or an anecdote, or perhaps some stern remark on the passing scene, with those around; then, in a few minutes afterward, rising to make, perhaps, some important motion, laying bare some gross case of pauper oppression, or taking up the cause of the medical practitioners with all the zeal of one still of the craft; to witness the freshness and vigor with which he throws himself into the business before him, you would little guess the amount of wearying labor and excitement he has already gone through during the day: yet he has perhaps been afoot from the earliest hour, has perchance presided at more than one inquest during the morning, listening with a conscientious patience to the evidence, or taking part with an earnest partisanship in the case; then off, as fast as horses could carry him, down to the committee-rooms of the House of Commons, there to exhibit the same restless activity of mind, the same persevering acuteness, the same zeal and energy, in sifting the foul intricacies of an Andover Union inquiry; and, after hours, perhaps, spent in this laborious duty, rendered still more irksome by a heated atmosphere and the intrigues of baffling opponents, returning home to accumulate the facts necessary for the exposure of some glaring abuse in the Post-office or the Poor-law Commission, to manage the multifarious correspondence which his manifold public duties compel him to embark in. Yet such is often the daily life of this hard-working man: he is absolutely indefatigable; nothing daunts, nothing seems to tire him. He may be an impostor, a political quack, a dangerous fomentor of discord: but, at least, he does not get much reward for his exertions, and not even the prime minister goes through more active labor. The comfortable, apathetic officials of the government, ever anxious to shirk trouble or to shrink from exposure, often find him a disagreeable opponent in consequence of his perseverance.

With Mr. Wakley, grievance-hunting is a very serious business: it is the occupation of his life. As his time is very valuable, he might do better with it than bestow it on the public; yet he works away harder than ever. He certainly makes greater sacrifices than Mr. Duncombe, if he does not win quite as much ephemeral applause, or obtain it quite as easily. It may be urged that his patriotism is all prospective; at least, however, he pays down a heavy deposit. Upon the whole, too, he has done much good, if, in the course of his career, he has also caused some evil. The errors of "The Lancet," and the occasional violences of an enterprising demagogue determined to rise in the world, may be forgiven in the man who has done so much to unmask the minor tyrannies which oppress the pauper population of the country.

DR. BOWRING.

If much talking could make an orator, or much writing a philosopher, Dr. Bowring is the man to accomplish the miracle. He has talked and written enough in his time to fill an Encyclopedia, or to set up with a stock in trade all the Radicals in the House of Commons, and all the Political Economists of the press. Dr. Bowring is the least agreeable legacy left by Jeremy Bentham to the political world. All the vigor of that remarkable thinker comes to us diluted in the pages and the speeches of the learned doctor. He is a political economist, and conceives himself to be a statesman. He has been, moreover, a traveler in various parts of the world, and has a sort of speaking acquaintance with many of the great men of foreign countries, who, no doubt, encouraged for their own amusement the loquacious propensities of this singular variety of the genus Philosopher. The personage of whose friendship he seems to be most proud is Mehemet Ali. He has tried to establish an Ali worship in England, by an uncompromising laudation of every thing done, in his short-sighted energy, by what the learned doctor calls the great ruler of Egypt. A wager might safely be laid that Dr. Bowring would never let a speech of his come to a close without lugging in, in some way or other, his inimitable Pacha.

Unless it be from the circumstance of his having been the executor of Jeremy Bentham, and the appointed editor of his woıks, we have never been able to understand how Dr. Bowring acquired any standing or influence with his party. It is true that he edited "The Westminster Review," and that he performed the same office for the works of Jeremy Bentham after his death. But in his own person he appears to have neither the mental claims nor the attractive qualities which could account for his being made in the slightest degree prominent by common consent. Perhaps if the Liberal party had a more generally recognized and more powerful head, a public man like Dr. Bowring might sooner find his level—might speedily have some position assigned to him, in which his laborious disposition and his accumulation of facts might be rendered serviceable to his country. But in the general scramble he stands as good a chance as the best.

At present he has mistaken his vocation. He does not possess a single qualification which could render him useful—at least, in proportion to his own idea of his pretensions—in the House of Commons. He wants that most essential requisite, tact, in an eminent degree. There is nothing a popular assembly dreads more than a bore. They know they must listen, but they hate the tormentor. They take their revenge by laughing at his suggestions, confounding even the good with the bad. Thus it is with Dr. Bowring. He does not know that nature has not fitted him for an orator, and that a rigid economy in his displays would be generally acceptable. With the best possible intentions, he is always saying good things at wrong times, and has, therefore, never succeeded in winning the ear of the House. He is too didactic. Too much learning hath bewildered him. He knows not when to pour out his stores and when to restrain himself; out it all comes in the most crude state, possibly because it has never been properly digested. The best speakers do not overcrowd their speeches with either thoughts or facts, knowing that a multitude is not like a single mind, and can not well be fixed to the reception of a train of thinking; they rather fix on a few leading ideas, and spend their art in dressing them up. Not so Dr. Bowring. He does not understand the *ad captandum;* with him it must be all or nothing. He carries no small change of knowledge, but brings to the market large masses of bullion, which, however valuable, will not pass current.

Add to this a most unfortunate mode of delivery and not the most dignified or commanding personal appearance, and it may be supposed that Dr. Bowring, whatever may be his personal worth, his public services, or his intrinsic value as a perambulating dictionary of commerce, is no great favorite in an assembly like the House of Commons, impatient of even the most praiseworthy mediocrity, and singularly alive to a keen sense of the ridiculous. Dr. Bowring has a most disappointing physiognomy. At first sight he seems to have a fine intellectual forehead, but a second glance shows that it wants some of the noblest characteristics, and that it is considerably indebted for its seeming depth to the baldness of the head. A dogmatic severity monopolizes the expression of the countenance, the complexion is cadaverously pale, and he has the sharpest of Scottish noses, with a pair of twinkling eyes, more expressive of cunning than habits of deep thinking. He usually speaks in a large pair of silver spectacles, which, as he has a continual stoop, appear as if each minute they would fall off, more especially as he has an absurd habit of wagging his head and shaking his finger while speaking, like an aged pedagogue trying to awe a very naughty boy. From his mind being overburdened with ideas and facts, he pours them out in a confused jumble, without order or arrangement, in intricate and imperfect sentences, and without any thing like a connected chain of thinking. All this crude mass of words, too, comes forth in a tone of voice so wearying from its grating monotony as only to be likened to the grinding of a hurdy-gurdy or the sounding of the key-note while tuning a violoncello. With all these disadvantages, it may well be imagined that frequent exhibitions of his oratorical powers, when the learned doctor is so firmly convinced that mankind are in want of knowledge, and that he has a mission to impart it, might become a very serious infliction.

It is more than probable that Dr. Bowring seriously and sincerely desires to make himself useful to the public. He is a very patriotic, laborious, and learned man, and has devoted much time to the accumulation of facts illustrative of the state of the trade and commerce of this country. Could he be spirited away from parliament, and put into some appropriate administrative office, all parties, himself included, would be gainers.

MR. T. S. DUNCOMBE.

Mr. T. S. Duncombe is the most gentlemanlike demagogue of whom we have any recollection. Of course we speak of the exterior man alone, not desiring to go the length of assuming that other men, of perhaps more ardent patriotism, but of manners more rough, may not possess quite as many of the real qualities of the gentleman—those who are independent of conventional customs, habits, and dress. In those externals, however, let their worth be what they may, Mr. Duncombe is certainly distinguished from the members generally of the House of Commons; so much so, that a stranger entering the assembly would naturally observe the singular elegance and finish of his attire, as distinguishing him even in a place where well dressed men are rather the rule than the exception. We have been almost tempted to think, too, that in proportion as his Tribunitian displays grow more bold, and his principles more democratic, he has become more and more anxious to preserve his old character as one of the most fashionable men about town—thus, as it were, drawing the personal distinction more and more strongly, the more he approximated toward the principles of the working classes. Strange as it may seem, the most able parliamentary advocate of the "great unwashed" is himself a perfect model of every thing that is *recherché* in dress, manners, and carriage—nay, he has even been called the

"Dandy Demagogue." One thing, at least, is certain, that he is, to look at, almost the very last man from whom you would expect such powerful, nervous, and humorous speeches as he has made during the last few years, or the bold and clever tactics, followed out under every disadvantage and against overwhelming odds, with which he has puzzled and sometimes discomfited the most distinguished masters in the petty strategies of party politics.

It is well that we should get over our surprise at this contrast between the man and his doings, because we shall then be better able impartially to estimate the value of those doings, and to examine the machinery with which he has obtained his unquestionable influence in the debates of the House of Commons, beside exciting a certain degree of interest in the public mind on behalf of whatever subjects he may choose to bring before parliament; otherwise we should be continually puzzled with practical contradictions. Not in his careful attention to dress alone does he so differ from his colleagues in Radicalism; the contrast extends to his physical and mental organization, his whole bearing and demeanor. There is not one of them, however honest may be his intentions, or respectable his conduct, who does not prepossess a casual observer unfavorably rather than favorably. They have all some physical defect to overcome, or some want of mental training, or some jaundiced, distorted view of things, grating on the feelings of a lazy public, and creating a predisposition not to attend to their representations. But Mr. Duncombe has every natural advantage in his favor. Whatever disapprobation he may at times excite by the license he occasionally gives himself when making his personal attacks, it is a difficult thing for him to destroy the prestige at first created on his behalf. Tall and very well proportioned, there is a striking air of elegance in his whole figure, which is rendered still more pleasing by the absence of all affectation; which is, in fact, precluded by a peculiarly frank and manly deportment, and a captivating openness of manner, almost amounting to familiarity. A handsome face, singularly expressive of the humorous, a remarkably intelligent eye, and a voice at once sonorous and harmonious, complete the attractions of this fortunate and favored candidate for popularity.

Still, it was some time before Mr. Duncombe was able to take his present prominent position in the House of Commons. Apparently, he paused long ere he could make up his mind to take the decisive plunge into Chartism. His early efforts in parliament, not only in the Unreformed House, but also for some time after the passing of the Reform-bill, were of a much more mild and less ambitious nature. His antecedents had not been favorable to parliamentary success. The day of the men of pleasure was passing away: the House of Commons was beginning to grow ashamed even of the memory of the race of statesmen who left the gaming-table, or bacchanalian orgies, for the discharge of their senatorial duties. The time was near at hand when the practical men were to be in the ascendant. As Mr. Duncombe had a wide-spread reputation as a man of pleasure, with a strong dash of the fashionable *roué*, it is needless to say that in this state of things some very desperate stroke of policy was necessary in order to give him a chance of rising to distinction. It will always appear uncharitable to doubt the sincerity of any man's avowal of opinion; nor, indeed, except by way of guess or inference, has one any right to do so. It is in that spirit alone that we are tempted to express a doubt whether Mr. Duncombe, in his own secret mind, is prepared to go the length of his declarations in the House of Commons, or that he really entertains those ultra-democratic opinions which he professes, but which meet with such a practical contradiction in every particular of his idiosyncrasy. There have not been wanting, in the history of revolutionary movements, or of popular assemblies, instances of young aristocrats, who, from some cause, have lost the prospect of legitimate distinction in their own sphere, suddenly being struck with a passion for reforming the world, and putting themselves forward as the leaders of the populace, thus supplying a dangerous amount of mental ingenuity and energy to what would otherwise be an inert physical mass. Such, modified by circumstances, is the explanation we have heard given of Mr. Duncombe's intensity of Radicalism; and for ourselves, we must say, confessing as we do to a lurking liking for him, which nothing will ever conquer in our mind, that the more we see and hear him, the more we study his conduct and sift his motives, the more the conviction is forced upon us that this earnest advocate of the wrongs of the people is only playing at politics for the advancement of private objects and purposes, a keen foresight having long since told him that the millions by whose labor the whole fabric of society is maintained, increasing as they are in intelligence and information, at least, if they are not in wisdom, will not much longer be satisfied with an exclusion from political power, not justified by the theory of the constitution. The honorable member for Finsbury feels that he is perfectly safe in agitating for such a cause; and that there is every chance, in the long run, of his obtaining some of those honorable rewards which are always within the grasp of those who play the winning game in politics.

This easy adoption of the principles which seem most likely to tell, explains much of Mr. Duncombe's mode of proceeding in parliament, which might otherwise seem unintelligible. It also explains the apparent contradiction between his education, appearance, and social connections, and his political associations. The truth is, that politics always appear, in Mr. Duncombe's mode of handling them, as if they were capital pastime—a provision by which well educated men with nothing to do may at one and the same time drive away *ennui* and satisfy their ambition. He never succeeds in convincing you that he is in earnest, though he strives very hard, indeed, to do so, and will use very strong language in order the more surely to satisfy you of his sincerity. It is his political profession to find out grievances, and to represent them to the House of Commons. In this pursuit he displays a most praiseworthy alacrity.

Were his motives above suspicion, England might well be proud of a patriot possessed of so much virtue and public spirit. There are, however, a few peculiarities in his manner of proceeding which occasionally suggest suspicion. For instance, Mr. Duncombe seldom or never urges a grievance for its own sake. Obscure cases of oppression he leaves to obscure advocates. Those in which he most delights are cases in which some great public principle is involved, some hereditary legacy of former demagogues, and upon which there is an easy appeal to the constitutional prejudices of the British people. Mr. Duncombe is careful to be always on the popular, and, therefore, for him, the winning side. He never throws away his patriotism, nor wastes it on objects either undeserving or unfruitful. In whatever he does he has an eye to the electors of Finsbury, looking upon them as a sort of barometer of public opinion. If he can please them he feels confident that he will also stand well in the opinion of the public at large.

It is in the last degree amusing to witness one of his attacks on a government; for, be it known, it is one of the first principles of such a politician always to have some bone of contention with the ministry of the day.

Mr. Duncombe apparently proceeds upon the convenient assumption that there is something radically wrong or corrupt in every administration, that it is only a matter of accident which iniquity is laid bare first, or how long they may be able to conceal their misdeeds from the jealous guardians of the public interest. Another invariable rule is, to assume that every government official is prevaricating and mystifying, having no object whatever but to withhold as much information as possible from the public. This gives scope for much stereotyped abuse. It is observable, also, that Mr. Duncombe's patriotism is particularly active at the commencement and close of every session, just at those periods when, in the first case, public men are more the object of general attention, and in the last, when they may have to come in contact with their constituents. Should there be symptoms of a dissolution of parliament, then his patriotism absolutely knows no bounds—there is no restraining the ardor with which at that time he is determined to serve his fellow-countrymen. A ministry, however strong it may seem, should begin to suspect a decay of popularity if they find Mr. Duncombe attacking them; the decay, they may depend upon it, has commenced, even though they may not themselves be aware of it. Or, if there be one member of a ministry weaker than another, he will soon be reminded of his deficiency by an attack from Mr. Duncombe. Ordinarily, however, one or two displays serve the honorable member for the stock in trade of a whole session. A bad case under the Poor-law, or (still more fortunate!) a letter-opening case, with an unpopular home secretary to badger night after night, these are of incalculable value.

There can be no doubt that, in a moral point of view, all this theatrical patriotism stands very low indeed; that all thinking men repudiate a plan of tactics which makes politics a mere pastime, if not a trade, and prostitutes to the purposes of a temporary ambition or personal convenience some of the noblest privileges enjoyed by the citizens of a free country. It is true, also, that only the foolish people out of doors are taken in by it, and of them not even the whole; while the wise ones look on, some amused, others irritated, at such a perversion of the functions of the legislator. The secret of Mr. Duncombe's influence within the walls of parliament seems to be the imperturbable good-humor with which he conducts a case, the ease and nonchalance with which he will deliver the most violent diatribes, the cool assurance with which he will advance to the attack, and work up what shall seem to be a most overwhelming case out of very slender materials. There is always a waggish glance of the eye, and a smile lurking about the lip, which seem to say, "Of course, *you* know that this is all acting: but I am not talking to you, except to show my own smartness. I am taking in the people out-of-doors, who, when they read the reports to-morrow, will believe all these charges as so much gospel." And strange to say, it is this levity which makes the House endure with complacency what would otherwise be sometimes extremely offensive; for, in the course of these clap-trap speeches, Mr. Duncombe will often go great lengths, will make charges and use language scarcely permissible in any society of honorable men, but will urge them with so provoking an impudence, such a half-jocular semblance of earnestness and indignation, that an indefinite sense of amusement will take the place of what would otherwise be sometimes very like disgust. One or two hardy speakers, confident in their own powers, and, above all, in their own innocence, have at times essayed to unmask this assumed public virtue, have met the honorable member in his own vein, treating the whole affair as a got-up exhibition for electioneering purposes. But they found they had a dangerous customer to deal with—that Mr. Duncombe would only be jocular when it suited himself; and they have been suddenly astonished to find themselves put out of court by a well feigned semblance of indignation that the wrongs of the people should be treated with such disrespect,—and this, too, from the man whose whole public life has been a practical mockery of the functions of a representative!

Mr. Duncombe deserves the credit of displaying great ability as a speaker. As a mere debater, he is one of the best in the House. There are few speakers who can so soon and so thoroughly grasp the points of a case, or who have so happy a mode of so putting them as to make their full force and effect apparent. He is also extremely powerful in reply, another evidence of great ability as a debater. He has a most agreeable delivery, free, graceful, and unaffected, except when acting a part, and altogether, a most winning manner as a speaker. He has also great powers of humor, especially in a bantering style, which is very annoying to officials, who fret and smart under inuendoes and aspersions which they are precluded from directly noticing. He seldom says any decidedly witty thing which will bear quotation, but by odd contrasts and groupings of ideas, and a way he has of hammering incessantly at the ridiculous side of any question, he contrives usually to keep the House in a state of continual risibility while he is on his legs.

From these remarks it will be seen that we are no great believers in the sincerity of Mr. Duncombe's devotion to the public good. We are disposed to compliment him on his talents at the expense of his integrity. Still, such men are not without their use in the political world. Whatever may be their motives in ferreting out abuses, they sometimes do good by exposing them, and public men are held in restraint by the fear of having their misdeeds paraded. These grievance-mongers are like the licensed jesters. For the few good things which they sometimes say or do they are tolerated in many errors and offenses.

R

MR. WYSE.

When the Melbourne government had determined on adopting a "conciliatory" policy toward Ireland, it followed almost as a necessary consequence that they saw the importance of including some of the Irish Liberal members in their government; such an official amalgamation being the outward and visible sign of compacts of the kind then entered into, adopted then with regard to the Irish Liberals, and since again resorted to on the occasion of the alliance with the Free-traders. In choosing the individual members who were to join the government, they naturally looked out for those who were most respectable and least objectionable in the eyes of the English public, always more or less prejudiced on the subject of Ireland. Among others, they fixed on Mr. Thomas Wyse, the member for Waterford, a gentleman who had been conspicuous in the struggle for Roman Catholic emancipation, and whose opinions, although in the highest degree patriotic and national, were at the same time moderate and not characterized by hatred of the English name and institutions.

There were several concurrent causes which tended to the selection of Mr. Wyse. The government of that day, taunted as they were by their opponents in England, wished, however ineffectually, to remove from their proceedings with regard to Ireland the imputation of being under mob influence. They shrunk at that time from the charge of being leagued with Mr.

O'Connell, to which they strove by every possible means to give an indirect contradiction. Now Mr. Wyse had on more than one occasion resisted successfully the dictation of Mr. O'Connell, and was known to be a man prepared to make any sacrifice rather than agree to total repeal of the union. He was also a member of a very old family, which at one time sat for Waterford, either the county or the city, during many generations, and so far from being a nominee of Mr. O'Connell, he had been at the Waterford elections in direct collision with him. On the other hand, the public spirit of Mr. Wyse, and his devotion to the cause of his country, were beyond question; so that, in making the selection they did, the government effected a double object. It is to be inferred that their choice was deemed a good one, not merely in England, but in Ireland also, for, notwithstanding that Mr. Wyse had been denounced by Mr. O'Connell because he will not agree to absolute repeal of the union, he has still kept his seat for Waterford, and seems likely to do so as long as it suits him to remain in parliament.

His politics embrace all the opinions and views of the Liberal party in Ireland, short of repeal of the union, to which he is decidedly opposed; but he is a most important and useful member of parliament in other respects, more especially from his active and energetic promotion of every measure of a practical nature that can be of service to his country. In such pursuits he is indefatigable, and he is always the first to raise his voice in favor of such plans from whatever party in the state they may come, for his mind is too really liberal to be bounded by the narrow views and objects of faction.

Mr. Wyse is essentially catholic in his mind, which is expansive enough to embrace any and every proposition which is calculated to elevate, intellectually and morally, the human character. His whole life has been devoted to the ardent pursuit of such objects, in parliament by his speeches, and also various contributions to cotemporary literature. To secure some grand and comprehensive scheme of education for the people is the one absorbing idea of his life, conceiving as he does, that if the intellectual standard of a people be raised, other beneficial consequences follow as a matter of course. He has either originated or promoted with ardor most of the efforts that have been made to prepare the public mind on this question. He has written upon it with great power and perseverance; and his plans combine the practical and the critical in an eminent degree. One large work of his on education is a complete treatise on the subject, with an elaborate plan of action, followed out into its minutest details. It would be impossible to estimate the amount of labor which the fervor and zeal of Mr. Wyse have led him to bestow on the snbject; to him will belong a great part of the merit of having saturated the public mind with the idea of the necessity of a system of public education. He did not join the government of Lord Melbourne until he had received a pledge that a plan of education should be proposed to parliament—a pledge the fulfillment of which circumstances prevented. It is more than probable that he will be intrusted with an active share in the proposal and execution of whatever measure Lord John Russell, in pursuance of his promise, may bring forward on the subject of national education.

Mr. Wyse is also an ardent and active promoter of the fine arts. He has labored zealously and effectually to infuse into artists a more æsthetical spirit; and whenever the interests of art require in any way legislative interference or protection, Mr. Wyse is always at hand to afford an earnest and hearty coöperation. He is not a mere *dilettante*. From his earliest youth the pursuit of art has been a passion with him; his personal associations have all conduced toward this end; and, indeed, we have heard that he is himself a painter of no mean order, though he says but little on the subject. Mr. Wyse's well known devotion to such subjects led to his being named one of the royal commission for superintending the building of the new houses of parliament. It must have been a source of no slight gratification to him thus to have aided in the triumph of Mr. Barry, the associate of his youth, with whom he had studied the principles of architecture from the finest works extant, when they were both young men, in Greece, Asia Minor, Syria, and Egypt.

Mr. Wyse is recognized in the House of Commons for his devotion to the different objects we have mentioned. He is untiring in the perseverance with which he follows them up, and some of the most excellent speeches made in parliament on the duty of the state to do the utmost to promote education and art have come from him. His enthusiasm seems to acquire fresh fuel from the apathy of the legislature, and his energy is undaunted by successive failures. But although it is so difficult to stimulate parliament to active exertion on subjects so surrounded with difficulties, and where the excitement of political strife is wanting to give a zest to discussion, such repeated efforts as his are not without their result, and it may be seen in the improved state of public feeling, more especially as regards the national encouragement of art.

Mr. Wyse is an enthusiast on his favorite themes, and his eloquence partakes of the prevailing character of his mind. The matter of his speeches, the ideas and language, are such as to place him in a very high rank; and did he pay more attention to the arts and graces of delivery, he would stand still higher. In the ardor of his own pursuit he does not observe that those around him are not animated by the same passion for the good and the beautiful; he is too intent in pouring out his own soul to take measure of the capacities of his hearers, whom he inundates with ideas. Thought follows thought, illustration is heaped on illustration, till the mind becomes almost wearied with the effort to receive and retain so much, and it would gladly take refuge in some more prosaic speech—something that would be more suggestive. Mr. Wyse's utterance is much too rapid for effect. The sentences follow each other too quickly, not, as in the case of Mr. Sheil's eloquence, where frequent pauses and the most delicate and careful emphasis temper a delivery which would otherwise be of lightning-like rapidity. But with all these faults—which are so often to be found in the orations of the most eloquent of his compatriots—Mr. Wyse's speeches are of remarkable power and richness of illustration. Out of the House of Commons, when addressing some meeting of artists, or on any occasion where his audience feel a ready sympathy with the subject of his discourse, he becomes powerfully effective, and rouses his hearers to his own high pitch of enthusiasm.

The presence of Mr. Wyse at the deliberations of a Whig government will be of essential service to his country. For while he is decidedly liberal in his views, he is a man of the most moderate and temperate turn of mind, one who would rather realize a practical good than lay down an impracticable political theory; and his demeanor in the House has been such, and the character of his mind as developed in his speeches is so much more constructive than destructive, and he has so much respect for the opinions of others, even though differing most widely from them, that he is not looked on with suspicion even by the most jealous Protestant. His political conduct is felt to be the natural and legitimate consequence of his principles and inherited faith; and, as well for his own sake as by contrast with some of his more violent countrymen in the House of Commons, he is treated with universal respect.

MR. HAWES.

People have been accustomed to make merry with the name of Mr. Benjamin Hawes, irreverently abbreviating the patriarchal part, and prefixing thereto an adjective indicating the fact that he is not the tallest of men. He entered parliament at an unpropitious period, when the aristocratic part of the representatives of the people were still sore at the introduction of the *bourgeoisie;* and he unfortunately took a more active part in the public business than either his position or his experience appeared to warrant. His peculiar pursuit or trade, too,—that of soap-boiling—was an additional enormity in the eyes of amateur or gentlemen-legislators, and of those writers in the press who prefer to echo the prejudices or the dislikes of their patrons. And his position was not mended when it was discovered that he was disposed to take a lead in furthering Radical or semi-Radical objects. On the whole, he has been the object of more ridicule and obloquy than any other member of the class of representatives to which he belongs, and the abuse and condemnation have been, as usual, in an inverse ratio to his deserts. At all events, other men who deserved it much more have received it more sparingly. For although it is the misfortune of Mr. Hawes, as of another member of the legislature, to be saddled with the weight of that Judaical prefix, and to be in height rather below than above the heroic standard of humanity—although for many years he was in the habit of interfering, to a troublesome extent, in all sorts of affairs, whether he understood them or not, and while his Lambeth honors were yet in their first bloom and blush, was the busybody of the House of Commons—although he might have been obstinately guilty of coming down to the House to his legislatorial labors in full evening-dress, with straw-colored kids, and was as fussy and talkative as any *parvenu* in parliament could possibly be, still, for a long time past, he has been gradually getting rid of these little pretensions, has applied himself steadily and soberly to subjects coming properly and naturally within his ken, has abandoned his habit of meddling with questions too important to be handled by any but first-rate men, modestly taking his place in the ranks of the regulars, instead of striving to be the officer of a little rebel troop of his own; and as state necessity compelled Lord John Russell to include in his new administration one, at least, of the pets of the ten-pound householders, why, we don't know that he could have fixed upon a more sensible, able, well informed person, or one who has profited more by his parliamentary experience, than Mr. Hawes. As the police-reporters say of their favorite inspectors, he will, no doubt, prove an "active officer." He has been long enough in training, and has received sufficiently hard rubs in his career to be content with the position of a subordinate, at all events for some time to come; while his being the representative of a metropolitan borough, and his known identity of opinion with a portion of the "progress" party, gave him that political weight, and his appointment to office that significance, which are essential to Lord John Russell's purpose in the present state of political parties. In the choice the noble lord made of the place he assigned him, he rather consulted some ministerial convenience than his personal fitness; for general opinion, considering the class of subjects to which he has given his attention in parliament, would rather have assigned him the Home-office as his sphere of action. Be that as it may, Mr. Hawes will prove a laborious and useful ally in any office.

The oratorical powers of Mr. Hawes are not of a very high order, but they are considerably above mediocrity. He stands about midway between those who may almost be termed professional orators—men who rely on their eloquence mainly for their political standing, and those purely practical men who have no ambition to shine as speakers, but who merely deliver themselves of the opinion which they think their duty to their constituents calls for in the most simple and plain language. Mr. Hawes is essentially a man to work hard; that is his ambition, and he succeeds. As we have said, he was not always what he is now; he was once only a very "busy" man, now he is a very good man of business. He deals with the subjects that come before him in a plain, practical, pains-taking way, and eschews all attempts to play the orator, except on very particular occasions, when important public measures are discussed, and when, as a metropolitan member, it is almost his duty to speak. He will then rise sometimes to a higher order of language, and throw himself with greater earnestness into the subject; but he has lost the pretension which once made his efforts ridiculous, and when he speaks with the most ability he is to all appearance unconscious of his own comparative excellence. Nature has not fitted him for displays of the kind. He has neither personal nor mental qualifications entitling him to enter into competition with first-rate men; but his position in the scale of representatives entitles him to record his opinion. His style is (now) unpretending, his language simple but well chosen, his reasoning clear, and his views as comprehensive as it is possible for a man in his social and political position to hold. He has long since been growing in the good opinion of the House; the fact of his selection by so astute and cautious a statesman shows this. He has applied himself indefatigably to the study of the great questions of the day, and is extremely well informed upon most of them. He has also acquired an intimate personal acquaintance with the wants and wishes of the people; and, if the possession of office does not have at once the effect of contracting his views and blunting his sympathies, we may look to his being an effective and useful member of the government, not alone in the department to which he is specially attached, but more particularly in the preparation and discussion of those measures which the new premier has promised, the object of which is to promote and extend the improvement of the physical and moral condition of the unprotected classes. We have here purposely leaned a little to the favorable side in noticing Mr. Hawes, because he has been hitherto rather hardly dealt by, and because he appears of late years to have taken very considerable pains to render himself more and more useful as a member of parliament, and more fit to hold some administrative office. Lord John Russell has shown discrimination in choosing him, under the circumstances; but he had long been looked on in the House of Commons as a man likely to be adopted by the Whigs whenever (to use a phrase of Mr. Duncombe's) "the old Whig dodge" would answer no longer, and they were compelled to join hands with the representatives of the middle classes.

MR. WARD

In appointing Mr. Ward to a post, however subordinate in his administration, Lord John Russell gave the best possible guaranty of his desire to make it representative of the opinions of his followers in the House of Commons. This gentleman has long been considered as one of the most distinguished among the rising members of the Liberal party, and he has so blended the undoubted Radicalism of some of his opinions with that practical good sense and knowledge of statesmanship which are essential in a minister, that, even with his extreme opinions staring the world in the face, they have been more disposed to regard him as a Whig a little in advance of his party, than as a downright, unadulterated Radical,—which, however, he can scarcely in fairness be called. For a considerable time he acted as a kind of parliamentary fugleman to the extreme section of the Liberal party, but as the Whigs approached more and more to the opinions of that section, so he became less and less ardent, until, at last, Lord John Russell was able to incorporate him in his administration. He has the materials of an excellent minister.

There are some men of that restless activity and energy of mind, that they will make themselves in some way or other prominent among their cotemporaries in spite of all adverse obstacles, till they stamp their own individuality, and come to be counted among the notabilities of the world. Such a man is Mr. Ward. Placed wherever he might be, he would have more or less distinguished himself from those around him. His parliamentary reputation has been entirely of his own making. When he first entered the House of Commons he was but little known, except as the son of the author of "Tremaine," and as having held some diplomatic employment in South America. Amid the general multitude of members at that time professing Liberal opinions, bidding against each other for popular favor, these would have been but slight qualifications; and Mr. Ward might have gone on for many a year making clever speeches, and being regarded as a shrewd, active-minded politician, without ever rising to the point of having his proceedings watched as indicative of probable changes in public opinion, or seeing his opinions and propositions analyzed with jealous fear by the most distinguished men of the day. But Mr. Ward struck out a new path, opened wholly new ground. With a sagacity and foresight for which he has never received due credit, he detected the tendency of the policy of the Liberals, and determined to anticipate it. He orginated the famous principle of "Appropriation," which afterward occupied so much of the time of the House of Commons, and ultimately led to such serious results. It is needless to say that the government of the day were defeated on Mr. Ward's motion, or to add that from that moment he became a marked man. Such success was, perhaps, almost too sudden to be followed by others in a ratio of increase; but Mr. Ward, although he, of course, did not continue quite so prominent for some time after as at the time of his successful motion, yet gradually acquired considerable influence in the House, both as an apt and ready speaker, and because of the general shrewdness and soundness of his views. Beside, once a conqueror, always a conqueror. He had achieved one singular triumph in party warfare, and that was always borne in mind.

Perhaps the chief characteristic of Mr. Ward's mind is the sagacity with which he estimates the importance of party movements, their probable tendency, and calculates their effect on cotemporary politics. In this he is like Mr. Duncombe, but with more honesty of purpose. There are few men of his party who better understand the public mind, or are able so well to feel the pulse of the public. Although he has fixed views and opinions on particular subjects from which he has never swerved during his career, he looks at politics as a practical man, knowing that the movements of individuals are often of more moment than the intrinsic truth of principles; and although he has been consistent in his own conduct, he fully admits the value of "expediency" in determining the course of policy of a government. His mind has always harmonized with those of the leading men of the day in this disposition to take a practical view of things, and to make every allowance for the necessities of statesmanship. He treated all public questions in a ministerial spirit long before he could ever have dreamed of being a minister himself. He watches public opinion with great care, and avails himself of all indications of mutation with skill: the results of his observations and cogitations come out in his speeches, which often contain admirable sketches of public men and sagacious prophecies of their future proceedings. Nor should it be omitted that, despite a certain vivacity of manner which almost looks like levity, he is a man of decided caliber, and that he carries ballast. He has had extensive opportunities of observing mankind, of which his keen and lively intellect has much profited. He has also read much, and has acquired a very general and comprehensive knowledge of public affairs.

As a speaker he is agreeable, and in many respects original. There is a freshness and raciness in his speeches that make them highly entertaining, while at the same time they almost invariably carry heavy metal. It follows, from the habits of observation we have ascribed to Mr. Ward, that he is a great tactician. He never wearies the House with a repetition of arguments they have already had *ad nauseam*, but starts from the real debatable point, taking certain things for granted, admitting certain conditions, and then starting fair in the fight. A speech from Mr. Ward always gives an impetus to the debate; he is sure to strike out some new views, introduce some happy illustrations, and at least to throw out something that serves as a bone of contention. He presents you with a happy combination of argument, humor, and fact. His speeches are open to critical objections. His humor at times descends to something very like levity, and that, too, of a clumsy kind. He is too verbose, and tantalizes his audience by perpetually traveling out of the straight road of his argument in pursuit of some illustration which a more artistical speaker would have interwoven naturally with the theme. An excessive volubility of speech, a trivial and effeminate manner, and a redundancy of action, still further weaken the effect which speeches, possessing so much intrinsic merit, and which are at once so sound and so lively, would otherwise produce. Where so much excellence is attained with so little apparent effort, it seems a pity that Mr. Ward will not bestow that amount of attention on his delivery which would speedily place him on a level with the chief speakers in the House of Commons.

MR. ROEBUCK.

Of all the lawyers whose first appearance in the House of Commons is within our recollection, we can remember none, with the single exception of Sir William Follett (who at once achieved a signal triumph), to whom so favorable a reception was accorded as that given to Mr. Roebuck. Rumor had heralded his approach. It was said that he had already, in other fields of action, developed oratorical powers of a striking character, and that there was a boldness and vigor in his proceedings which indicated an original turn of mind. It was known, also, that he was the paid parliamentary advocate of the Legislative Assembly of Lower Canada; and it was inferred that his appointment to such a post was itself a guaranty of some intellectual distinction. When Mr. Roebuck made his appearance in the House, it was seen from his aspect that he was a man possessing no ordinary mental power, although Nature had not been to him as liberal as to others in the gift of those personal advantages which are so great a help to the orator. The ardor, and at the same time the ease, with which he plunged into the political disputes of the hour, showed him to be of a bold nature and not to be daunted by the novelty of his position, or that paralyzing modesty of nature which makes men, even of a high order of mind, the slaves of conventionalities. The consequence was, that in a very brief space of time Mr. Roebuck acquired considerable notoriety, and no small amount of favor, in the

House; and although, as we shall presently see, there was much in both his words and his actions to draw down reprehension, still the mental vigor and determination of purpose displayed in his speeches procured for him that amount of attention, and even of deference, which tact might, in the course of time, have fostered into permanent influence. It is true, he was feared more than he was liked; but to make yourself feared is to gain a strong position in a popular assembly. We are now speaking of the years 1833 and 1834; and we do not hesitate to say that at the close of the latter year, when Mr. Roebuck had been scarcely two sessions in parliament, he had already laid the foundation of a future reputation which might long before the present time have enabled him, through the usual channels of honorable promotion, at once to have served his country, which his talents would have qualified him to do, and to have advanced his own interests, for which his political position was at that time singularly favorable. But, by a strange fatality or infatuation, for which we must endeavor to account, he has willfully thrown away all that position, and all that growing influence, until, from having been one of the remarkable and rising men in the state, he has dwindled down into a mere excrescence of the Liberal party, his weight in the House yearly decreasing in proportion to his despairing efforts to add to it. Brought into a position of influence by his talents, he has destroyed its advantages by his intemperance and want of tact. Self-raised, he is also self-destroyed. Let us look a little into his public life, that we may the better understand this wanton eccentricity in his personal character.

When, in the year 1827–28, the House of Assembly of Lower Canada determined on having an agent to represent their interests in England, Mr. Roebuck, who had already drawn favorable notice on himself, and who was, moreover, a connection of Papineau, was selected as the most fit person to fill the newly constituted office. It would have been difficult to provide a young man with a more advantageous passport into the political world. It was a lever which, with skill, might be made a powerful auxiliary in clearing the pathway to power, for it supplied at the same time an honorable position and pecuniary means, not in itself sufficient to establish its owner; and in 1832 Mr. Roebuck was returned for Bath. On the opening of the session of 1833, he made his first speech in the House of Commons: it was in every respect characteristic of the man who made it, containing as it did the germ of his future parliamentary proceedings. As a mere piece of declamation, it was singularly successful. It is seldom, indeed, that a first attempt, in any assembly, possesses the vigor and force which marked the speech. It was seen at once, as well from the thoughts and language, as from the stern manners and abrupt delivery of the speaker, that a new element was to be introduced into parliamentary discussion; that strong language, plain speaking, and downright hard hitting, were thenceforth to take the place of those oily courtesies and ingenious circumlocutory modes of offense and defense in which legislatorial spleen had hitherto indulged. It was evident, too, that the new member had very great confidence in himself; that whatever might be the extent of his powers, he, at least, would not let them rust for want of being tried. There was an air of arrogance and self-sufficiency which would have been easily mistaken for an exaggerated and an unfounded self-conceit, had it not been that, however offensive it might be in itself, it was, to a certain extent, justified by the amount of ability displayed. There was also a familiar tone in Mr. Roebuck's address which augured ill for his modesty. Had he been twenty years a member of parliament instead of only a few weeks, he could not have more entirely forgotten what is due from one who comes for the first time into the presence of any number of his fellow-men; that enter what place you may, courtesy, at least, if not policy, demands an obeisance at the threshold. The speech itself, we repeat, was strikingly illustrative of Mr. Roebuck's character as it afterward developed itself. With the exception of some protestations of devotion to the public, which we have no doubt were sincere, and some declarations of fundamental principles, to which we are bound to say Mr. Roebuck has throughout his career consistently adhered, this first effort of one till then unknown in parliament,—of a mere school-boy in politics compared with those around him,—consisted of an attack grossly personal in its nature, upon a man as much his superior in knowledge and eloquence as in position, but whom this aspirant no doubt thought to be but an equal match for himself. Happily for the tranquillity and good order of the legislature, the practice of dragging forth individuals as the targets for political passion to aim at has become less and less necessary as the amenities of life have found their way into the debates of the legislature; and by common consent, except in very extreme cases, personality is avoided. A man with more delicacy and tact than Mr. Roebuck possesses would at once have seen that, if such attacks were objectionable in themselves, they came with a still worse grace from such a mere tyro in parliament as himself; but this gentleman seemed from the first to suppose that the mere fact of his having been elected for Bath at once placed him on a footing of equality with even the most distinguished members of the House of Commons. He had evidently no idea of those gradations which are created by a natural deference for superior talents and abilities. He rushed into the arena at once, and flung his gauntlet at the first or the most prominent antagonist he could discover.

Some parliamentary adventurers think it good policy to create a disturbance on their first appearance, and afterward to subside into decent respectability. Not so Mr. Roebuck. His first essay was mildness itself compared with his subsequent displays. During the first session of his appearance in parliament, his language became so violent that he was called to order publicly in the House. He was charged with having virtually preached open rebellion.

His combative disposition was destined to be still further displayed. In the early part of the year 1835, we find him taking Sir Robert Peel to task for having challenged Mr. Hume; but in the course of a very few weeks the censor himself assumes an attitude which renders it imperative on several public men to challenge him. Mr. Roebuck, it should be observed, had early placed himself in hostility to the Stamp Duty on newspapers, against which a vigorous agitation was going on. In order to disseminate his opinions more readily, and at the same time to test a disputed point in the law, he himself became the proprietor and editor of an unstamped publication. This appeared during a portion of the year 1835, and was entitled "Pamphlets for the People." While they were in a course of publication, Mr. Roebuck happened to make a short speech in parliament, in the course of which he made some very strong observations upon the corruption of the stamped press and its conductors. For these remarks he was assailed in "The Times," "The Morning Chronicle," "The Examiner," and other papers. Their remarks were not, as may be supposed, in the highest degree flattering. They stung Mr. Roebuck's too irritable temperament; and he retaliated in his pamphlet by attacking, personally and by name, the gentlemen whom he believed to be the editors of certain newspapers. On referring to those attacks, it is difficult to conceive how any man, unless in a frenzy of ungovernable spite, could have allowed himself to make them. They were such as no provocation whatever could have justified, still less the remarks which drew them forth. The natural consequence was, that these gentlemen, thus dragged from a retirement in which they had a right to shroud themselves, sent messages to Mr. Roebuck. In the cases of Mr. Sterling and Mr. Fonblanque, matters were accommodated, and Mr. Roebuck conditionally retracted. But Mr. Black's case was much more serious. That gentleman had been charged with tergiversation and abandonment of principle so gross as to make any explanation almost impossible. A challenge was the consequence.

Mr. Roebuck had charged Mr. Black with conduct base and utterly disagraceful in the management of "The Morning Chronicle;" and as he would not retract these words the parties met, and two shots were fired without effect. Mr. Black's second then withdrew him, and there was an end of the affair as far as the duel was concerned. We have only referred to it because it illustrates Mr. Roebuck's character. We have no doubt he sincerely believed that he was vindicating a principle of great public utility, in exposing the corruption which the use of the anonymous in newspaper writing affords scope for. We do not believe that in making his original charge he was actuated by feelings of personal vindictiveness; on the contrary, some of the gentlemen attacked were his personal friends. But it is Mr. Roebuck's misfortune that he never can assert public principles without the exasperation of personal feeling. As we proceed with his career, we shall find instances of this multiply upon us. From his first effort in parliament, up to the last month of the last session, it may with truth be said of him,—

"His life is one long war with self-sought foes."

To return, however, to our review of Mr. Roebuck's public life. By the middle of 1836, his unbridled declarations of democratic principles, and unceasing strife with all who crossed his path, whether they were friends or foes, had made him so formidable or so obnoxious to some parties in parliament, that a strong, and, as it proved, a desperate effort was made to get rid of him. The pretext resorted to was the incompatibility of his being at one and the same time the paid agent of the Lower Canadians and the representative of a British constituency. Sir John Hanmer moved a resolution to this effect, which, although couched in general terms, was confessedly aimed at Mr. Roebuck; and a long debate ensued, which resulted in the defeat of the motion, and, so far, in the triumph of Mr. Roebuck, who, it must be confessed, showed an unwonted temper and forbearance under these very provoking circumstances. The motion, however, was not so ill-timed or so purposeless as it appeared; for already Canadian affairs had begun to assume a most serious aspect, and the peculiar connection of Mr. Roebuck with the popular party in the colony made it very necessary that he, as the agent of the anti-British party, should not derive any factitious importance from his position at home. In 1837, the wisdom of this precaution was made apparent; for on the Canadian question coming formally before parliament, Mr. Roebuck expressed himself in terms of such violence, that his language could only be excused on the plea of his being but an advocate making an *ex-parte* statement on behalf of his clients, and not a member of the British legislature, bound by his honor, not less than by his oath, not to use his legislative functions in any way that could impair or destroy the integrity of the empire. His speeches at this period required that every allowance on these grounds should be made for them. Several of them were of the most incendiary character, amounting almost to the preaching of open rebellion. A very natural consequence of all these violent diatribes, and of the awkward scrapes into which Mr. Roebuck's testiness and ill temper had brought him, led to his being rejected by the constituency of Bath at the general election, which soon after took place. Behold him, then, for four years out of the House of Commons.

Looking back at this, the first portion of Mr. Roebuck's public career, we find that he had by his boldness, his straightforwardness, and a certain originality which characterized his earlier speeches, created a strong prestige in his favor; but that, by a continued indulgence in splenetic virulence, an unrestrained license of speech on political subjects, and a constant appeal, for the most trivial objects, to sacred privileges reserved by the constitution to the people as a last resort in extreme cases, he had gradually weakened whatever influence he had possessed, until he was no longer looked upon as a person of note or importance—no longer appealed to as one of the thinking minds whose decisions might be indicative of the course taken by others,—but merely regarded as a clever speaker, possessed of more talent than temper, out of whom it would be utterly impossible to take the conceit which was the ban of his mind; so as to make him fit for service in any way, either in some ministerial capacity or as a member of an organized opposition.

At the general election of 1841, Mr. Roebuck was again returned to the House of Commons as member for Bath. Some curiosity was evinced to know whether time and retirement had produced any favorable change in his disposition—whether his temper had become less sour, and his judgment more matured. Certainly, his first speech on his return favored the supposition that a change had indeed come over him.

Physically, he appeared to possess much less energy than before: he seemed even to be afflicted with chronic illness; and sympathy was felt for him on this score, because it was known that by the exercise of his talents alone it was that he could hope to rise in the world. But although his speech on the Address (to which we refer) breathed the same hostility, on public grounds, to the Whig ministry that had been the theme of his first speech in 1833; and although there was firmness and vigor in his denunciation of their treachery toward the people by abandoning their avowed principles of 1831, still the speech was so much more temperate and statesmanlike than those with which he had extinguished himself in 1837, that very sincere hopes were entertained of his confirmed restoration from a distempered state of mind, and of his being destined to become, at some time or other, an ornament to the legislature.

But these hopes were destined to be only too speedily disappointed. The tone of his political declarations was softened; but it seemed that his personal irritability had augmented in more than a proportionate ratio. Whether it was an excitability produced by physical causes, or only the result of chagrin at having been left so long in unnoticed obscurity, it is certain, that from this period Mr. Roebuck's temper displayed itself in a more unamiable light than ever, until it required all the proverbial indulgence of the House of Commons to bear with his eccentricities. Scarcely had the House entered on general public business, when an outbreak of this gentleman's ill-temper took place, such as we do not remember ever to have seen equaled in either House of Parliament. His return to parliament was the signal for the appearance in "The Times" of an article directed against Mr. Roebuck, in which he was spoken of in a tone of playful contempt, not at all suited to his own ideas of his own importance.

Vituperative men are proverbially thin-skinned. Mr. Roebuck, who had so often attacked others with sarcasm much less refined than that used by the newspaper, ought not to have objected to being paid off in his own coin. But his self-love was wounded : he was furious. Without thought, without plan, he rushed down to the House, the paper in his hand, and commenced an incoherent appeal on the ground of breach of privilege. The exhibition he made utterly destroyed the reputation which he had begun to recover with his political cotemporaries. Those who have not seen Mr. Roebuck speak under excitement, can have no idea of the incoherent fury of his gestures, the utter incongruity between the breathless solemnity of his exordium, and the ridiculous insignificance of his charges, the total abandonment of his mental and physical powers to the accomplishment of a wild and undefined revenge. On this occasion he excelled himself in passionate feebleness, in inconclusive invective. Forgetting what, as a lawyer, he ought to have made his first consideration, namely, that he had no distinct case on which to ground his charge of breach of privilege, he commenced a violent attack on the conductors of "The Times," some idea of the coarseness of which may be conceived, from his assuming that the registered proprietor might, as a matter of course, be found in prison for libel, while he recommended those who were aggrieved by the paper not to resort to legal means of securing reparation, but at once to horsewhip a gentleman whom he chose to designate as the proprietor—a gentleman whose years and character alone ought to have protected him from so rude and unmanly a recommendation, if even there had not been another reason in the fact, that he had but recently ceased to be a member of the House. It is painful, even at this distance of time, to recall the exhibition Mr. Roebuck then made—painful to reflect, that not even the talents which he unquestionably possesses could save him from this ebullition of an engrossing egotism and an inflated conceit. Imagine this man of magniloquent speech but diminutive form, standing up on the floor of the House, arresting the progress of business, to claim his right of speaking on a point of privilege, and courting the attention and the sympathy of more than five hundred gentlemen, who have assembled at the most inconvenient season for the transaction of important affairs of state—imagine him solemnly declaring, that he is about to expose to them a case for their interference to protect a member of their body from public outrage. Pale, even livid, with suppressed rage, and trembling from finger to foot with passion, he opens in a voice now choking with swelling emotions, now dwindling into the whisper of physical weakness, an attack upon his private antagonists in the journal in question, against whom he conjures the House to act in his behalf; and makes the extraordinary recommendation to inflict personal chastisement instead of resorting to that civil authority to which he now himself appeals. When he has proceeded so far in his diatribe as to weary, if not to disgust the greater portion of his hearers, he is called upon to read the article of which he complains. He hands the newspaper to the clerk at the table, who reads it in his monotonous stammer to the House. They see in the remarks of the writer a singular aptitude to the case of the individual before them; that, had he possessed the gift of prophecy, he could not more surely have anticipated the scene that was being enacted before them. The more they listen, the more they see how groundless is the complaint,—how apt and pointed must have been the character drawn in the article, to have thus stung and exasperated the complainant. They laugh; then impatient, they murmur: they wish the farce to be brought to a close. Mr. Roebuck, who has grown paler and more passionate as his discomfiture grows more imminent, calls on the House, first, to declare the article a breach of privilege, and then to bring the printer to the bar, that he may, "on his knees" (mark the low tyranny of your democrat!) "beg pardon of the complainant for the offense." But not one of those five hundred members can be induced even to second the proposition. The charge drops for want of a single supporter, and with it he who preferred it also falls below zero in the esteem of his contemporaries. He has extinguished himself, for a time, at least, as effectually as if all the wit or all the scorn to be found in that assembly had been poured upon him. And he has not even the consciousness, the pride of martyrdom. He knows that to his own folly, his own intemperate passion, his downfall alone is owing. Will it operate as a warning? We shall see.

How different is the position of this same man a year after, when, instead of being the intemperate advocate of his own private wrongs, he stands forward as the champion of a great public cause! In the month of May following the September in which the scene we have just described occurred, Mr. Roebuck drew upon himself the attention—we might almost say the admiration of his countrymen, by the courage, temper, and self-possession, with which he exposed before the world, by the confessions of the parties themselves, that system of election compromises by which, although the most gross bribery might have been committed, the ends of justice were defeated, and the constituencies deprived of their constitutional rights. Then, Mr. Roebuck stood in a proud position. No longer the impotent executioner of his own revenge on antagonists whom he could not touch, he boldly and manfully asserted one of his first privileges as a member of parliament, and, strong in the justice of his cause, defying conventional arrangements, and looking corruption in the face, he made those who had trafficked with the privileges of the people—not those only whom he attacked by name, but many more who were touched by the electric shock of conscience, tremble before him, single-handed as he was, and till then oppressed with the ridicule of his former failures. When the affair was finally concluded, the effect was to repair the very serious inroads on his reputation which the past events have caused; and he stood before the public in the position of a man who, single-handed, and by the sole force of his own will, contrary to the expectation and the advice of his political associates, asserted some of the most valuable privileges conferred by the constitution on the House of Commons—privileges which, until he rescued them from abeyance, had fallen into almost total disuse.

Mr. Roebuck's infirmity of temper is such as to neutralize all expectations that he will act like ordinary men. The least check offered to his arrogant assumption of infallibility for his principles—the least hint, conveyed in however courteous terms, that he is in the habit of overstepping the bounds of fair discussion in his speeches, is sufficient to drive him furious with blind, purposeless resentment. He is as eccentric and uncertain in his modes of retaliation, as he is prone to resort to them. On another occasion we find him (this was in 1844) making some remarks on Mr. Smythe, so openly personal and insulting as to provoke a challenge from that gentleman. Mr. Smythe was justified in supposing that Mr. Roebuck, having given him offense, would also give him "satisfaction." But by this time a change had come over Mr. Roebuck. The wind of his caprice had set in another quarter. Since his triumph in the Election-compromises case, he had been preaching up the supreme fitness of the House of Commons to decide upon all questions whatever, be their relation to its business however remote. From a man of hard words and blows, he had become a man of hard words and peace. He claimed the privilege of saying what he chose, and of throwing upon the House the *onus* both of judgment and of punishment. According to his new theory, he flung the code of honor overboard at once, and laid the letter of Mr. Smythe before the House in a sanctimonious harangue, professing so intense an admiration of peaceful and legal modes of settling differences, as to seem quite oblivious of those other modes which society has been forced to adopt in order to restrain undue license of speech. It is fair to say, that Mr. Roebuck's speech on this occasion was much more mild and dignified than is usual with him where his personal feelings are mixed up. He adopted quite a moral and didactic tone in speaking of the impropriety of Mr. Smythe's proceeding. To have heard him, you would have supposed that fighting had never been recognized by his hearers as a means of reconciling differences which words would not heal; and certainly you would not have suspected that Mr. John Arthur Roebuck had ever placed himself in the attitude militant. By persevering, with an austere indifference to remonstrance, in his affectation of extreme parliamentary morality, he succeeded in placing Mr. Smythe in a false position, and compelling him to apologize for having sent the challenge. But it will be, perhaps, unnecessary to apprise the reader, that although the House felt it necessary to enforce its rules, the sympathies of the members ran very much in favor of the gentleman who was thus put *hors-de-combat.*

We pass over many minor instances in which Mr. Roebuck, by his petulance and arrogant demeanor, placed himself in a hostile attitude with the House, believing that the reader must be sufficiently wearied by these details of perverseness and splenetic humor. But an instance of the kind occurred during the last session too amusing to be altogether passed over. On this occasion, Mr. Roebuck's self-chosen antagonist was Mr. Disraeli. That gentleman had, we need scarcely say, made himself conspicuous by the great and unexpected talent that he had displayed as a speaker. Unfortunately, he had beat Mr. Roebuck hollow in his own peculiar line—that of personality and sarcastic vituperation. The cool, polished, searching irony of Mr. Disraeli was as superior to the wild abuse adopted of late by Mr. Roebuck, as intellect is to passion. It had, no doubt, been galling in the extreme to the member for Bath to see the intense expectation excited by the promise of a speech from Mr. Disraeli, and the uproar of cheering which his well aimed hits drew forth, and to compare with his rival's success his own decreasing influence, the averted looks, and the scarcely disguised weariness, with which the House received his galvanic attempts to produce a sensation. He saw Mr. Disraeli achieve the most triumphant effects with, apparently, the slightest effort; while his own most labored sarcasms, though charged with all the venom with which a vindictive spirit could arm a disappointed man, fall still-born on his audience. In the absence of any more direct provocation, it is only in this way that we can account for Mr. Roebuck's otherwise unprovoked personal attack on Mr. Disraeli. His speech had all the appearance of having been prepared for the occasion. The extreme confidence, the chuckling self-gratulation which accompanied the speech, showed that he anticipated a signal triumph. He had miscalculated both his own powers of attack and his rival's means of retaliation. Incoherent inconclusiveness, wild, pointless aspersion, and personal jealousy, ludicrously betrayed, were but poor weapons against so collected and self-possessed a master of fence as Mr. Disraeli. His reply covered Mr. Roebuck with ridicule. With that provoking frigidity of manner and affected indifference which were calculated to be especially annoying to so vain a person as Mr. Roebuck, he parried that gentleman's random blows with inimitable skill. Nor was he content with merely foiling his foe. Some remarks of Mr. Roebuck on his mode of delivery justified him in retaliation; and he took ample revenge. Mr. Roebuck's style of speaking, his wild gestures, his violent efforts to produce dramatic effect, and the ridiculous feebleness of his envenomed but pointless sarcasms, were all sketched by Mr. Disraeli with the hand of a master in satire; and when he wound up, he convulsed the House by the happy terms in which he described Mr. Roebuck's pompous vagaries in language and action, as "Sadler's Wells sarcasms" and "melodramatic malignity." The truth of the picture was instantly recognized, and Mr. Roebuck, though he has received many a setting down during his brief but turbulent career, was never so utterly at a discount in the opinion of his cotemporaries as after the delivery of that speech.

It may be considered, however, as extraordinary, that a man who has willfully made so many enemies, and has so often rendered himself troublesome to the House, should ever have possessed influence there. But we have presented the worst side of the picture. Had Mr. Roebuck only exhibited himself in this unamiable light, he would long since have been put down. But his early speeches satisfied the House and the public that he really had the qualifications of a valuable member of parliament. It is his intemperance alone that has clouded his fair fame. From the first hour of his entrance into the House of Commons, his public career has been characterized by an independence of spirit, stern even to obstinacy, an indifference to personal consequences, rarely, indeed, to be met with in an assembly where class interests and aristocratic influence combine to paralyze moral energy, and to divert the minds of public men from the course of political rectitude. We have watched his conduct from first to last, and are prepared to affirm that it has exhibited a rare and unique consistency; that it has even been a fault in Mr. Roebuck to have pertinaciously refused to join in those party combinations by which great measures have usually been carried; that having set up for himself a standard of right, he has inflexibly adhered to it, striving against all obstacles to reach his appointed goal. His whole life in parliament has been one certificate of sincerity. He is, however mistaken may be his views, a true friend and advocate of the interests of the poor, a hater of political cant, and a determined opponent of all class legislation on unjust principles. He has stood up, time after time, under a storm of disapprobation, to assert principles which he holds to be true, and which, if only for the sake of truth, ought to be argued, although their advocacy was certain to render him unpopular in the House of Commons. His very first speech stamped him as a man of superior talent as a debater, and secured for him a hearing at all times; of which he availed himself to advocate the cause of the people in their many social sufferings. He gave full fling to the democratic tendency of his mind, while at the same time he infused a species of philanthropy into his exertions. It is to his honor that he does not, as some of his compatriots do, wait till a subject is popular before he takes it up. A natural restiveness of temper, and an unconquerable love of justice, which he would secure even at the peril of social convulsion, urge him with an irresistible impulse to act upon what he conceives to be the abstract merits of the case, with which he will not allow expediency to interfere. Of course, this spirit sometimes carries him into extremes, and betrays him into wild defiance of constituted authority; but those who would be the most likely to shrink from these extravagances of an earnest mind, can not refuse to respect the uprightness which sustains Mr. Roebuck against unconquerable prepossessions in the minds of certain classes, and renders him, in respect of many subjects, a model of that very scarce character—an independent member of parliament.

In accounting, as we have done, for the kind of influence which Mr. Roebuck's uprightness and consistency early secured for him, we should not omit to state, that during a long period of time his speeches were such as to command the attention of all parties. It was not only that he asserted his principles boldly, but his arguments were well put, and even where, to the eye of reason, they might be deficient in cogency, the perseverance and earnestness of the speaker gave them a kind of force. The constant reiteration of propositions, however dogmatic, will secure for them a degree of credence, even when unsupported by proof. One thing Mr. Roebuck's audience were almost sure to hear from him: a lucid exposition of the real question at issue, stripped of all the factitious embellishments with which the sophistry or the party prejudices of previous speakers might have invested it. This made his speeches abstractedly useful to those who followed him, while the clearance which he made of the arguments on both sides was sure to please either one party or the other. That Mr. Roebuck should have voluntarily flung away the influence which these various causes had obtained for him, is matter for regret. That he has done so, there can be no doubt. His constant indulgence in an irritability which seems uncontrollable, his reckless imputations on the character of opponents, his profuse scattering of personal insults on all around him, friends and enemies alike, and his wanton trials of the patience of the House—have certainly undermined the reputation which he had acquired; and it will almost be as difficult for him to regain the position he formerly held, as it would be for a man of less talent and moral energy originally to attain it. It is not easy to account for so ill-advised a perseverance by Mr. Roebuck in a course of conduct which would bring even the most favorite member of the House into disrepute. It is the more surprising that his talents should have taken this sinister direction, because he evidently is under the sway of an ambition of no ordinary kind, and would spare no exertions to advance himself to power, either through direct popular influence or in the regular channels of promotion. The only solution of the difficulty we can offer is, that Mr. Roebuck is a disappointed man. His excessive egotism and high opinion of his own powers led him to expect that he would have received from the great men of the day, not only a more rapid but also a more substantial acknowledgment. He evidently did not understand the constitution of the House of Commons, or what a mountain of inert prejudice the adventurer has to cut through in order to clear the road to power. He did not see that there, as elsewhere, an apprenticeship must be served —that he who would fain command must first learn to obey. Mr. Roebuck overlooked these conditions of success, and neglected to avail himself of the very favorable impression his first efforts created. He thought to take the citadel by storm, but having rushed to the assault with inadequate means, he failed to make an impression, and has only fallen back in the trenches. Not seeing how much his own arrogance, petulance, and splenetic indulgence in personality, have really caused his non-success, his mind has become imbittered as well against individual antagonists as against the members generally, who, he conceives, have not sufficiently acknowledged his merits. As his mind has become more jaundiced, he has grown more bitter and more personal. His speeches have gradually become the reverse of what they used to be—their faults more glaring, their merits more rare. They now abound in assumption and egotism, only occasionally redeemed by vigor, and pointed language and thought. It is more than probable that Mr. Roebuck entered parliament with hopes and objects that were not confined to mere personal advancement. A charitable construction of his conduct will lead us to admit that he looked on his mission as representative of the people in an exalted light—that he saw in it the means of working out great, and as he believed, necessary changes in the political and social condition of the country. His exaggerated opinion of his own powers led him to choose a line of action that was not likely to lead to a success commensurate with his desires. But the censure which he ought to attach to his own mismanagement, he visits on those whom he assumes to be in a kind of conspiracy against the people; and we are therefore disposed to attribute much of the splenetic humor he displays, not to mere wounded vanity, stinted in its allowance of admiration, but also to a conviction of the moral unworthiness of those whom he insults by his arrogant impertinence—a conviction, mistaken perhaps, but still sincere. Certain it is, however, that the longer he has been in parliament, and the more the disappointment of his ambition has been brought home to him, the more his harangues have increased in virulence, while they have proportionately decreased in power.

The more closely we look at Mr. Roebuck's oratory in detail, the more cause we see to find fault with it—the more reason to regret that a want of modesty of spirit should have prevented Mr. Roebuck from submitting himself, humbly and patiently, to that training which is necessary to success in any department of mental exertion, but more especially in the art of public speaking, perfection in which depends so much upon minor accessories. Mr. Roebuck is a very disappointing speaker. His eloquence depends for its force more upon his earnestness, and a bold repudiation of conventional modes of address and molds of expression, than upon any intrinsic value in the thoughts or polish of the language. He trusts much to the impulse of the moment, and, to all appearance, does not give his speeches that preparation which even the first orators of the day find to be necessary. His mind is not so well stored with information, nor his oratorical powers so well trained and disciplined, as to make this a safe course. As he is an intemperate man, liable to be drawn, by the slightest interruption, away from his main theme into personal altercations, he is still more open to the risk of not being able to preserve that self-possession which is absolutely required by an accomplished orator. An almost necessary consequence of this reliance on resources which are not always at command, is, that Mr. Roebuck, however well informed he may be upon a subject, or however strongly he may feel upon it, is just as likely to break down as to achieve a success. We have known him to rise at the most critical and exciting period of a great debate, when he had intruded himself on the attention of the House, to the displacement of the heads of either party, when there was, perhaps, a general feeling that he was presuming too much thus to stand in the way of a political manifesto or of a division. But still an indulgence has been extended to him because of his original position. He has availed himself of the opportunity thus afforded him to commence a speech, in which he has, perhaps, dashed with a bold and vigorous hand into the very core of the subject, holding the real question at issue up, for the first time, to the attention of his audience, cleared of all the fallacies infused into it by previous speakers. To all appearance, he is carrying the House with him. Repeated cheers hail his terse and well pointed propositions, and his presumption is forgotten in the able exposition he makes of his case. But, suddenly, he says something which provokes an ironical cheer, or a sneer, from some opponent. This stings his *amour propre*, and off he starts, on the instant, into personality, sometimes uttering, without adequate provocation, unendurable insults and aspersions on character. From that moment, his speech, so auspiciously commenced, becomes a failure. His infirmity of temper once touched, he becomes an altered man. There is no longer vigor, sense, argument, or even coherency, in what he pours forth. Yet he has not the discretion to stop, but makes a long, rambling speech, full of feeble repetitions of what he has so forcibly put, or of offensive personalities, or outrageous defiance of the growing disapprobation of his hearers, until, at last, he fairly tires out their patience, and his display, which at his commencement had brought him honor and respect, ends by his being covered with ridicule and contempt.

The same causes produce an effect very similar in the *matériel* of the speeches themselves. For want of a little care his sentences are almost always imperfect. Aiming constantly at an antithetical style, he foils himself, and provokes comparisons, by not having trained his mind into the channels of thought which alone will produce that style with effect. It is not so much a slovenliness, the result of an indifference, as a gross failure, after a deliberate attempt. He is thus a very provoking speaker. Even in his best moments, when you are led on from point to point, in the expectation that the next will be something superlatively good, you are mortified on reflection to find to what little purpose your attention has been occupied, and what a small amount of that tedious and ambitious harangue is worth remembering. Mr. Roebuck has a didactic style of speaking, which also beguiles his hearers, until too late they find that this teacher of men has really little to teach. He seems ever on the very brink of success. At each portentous pause, when he appears to have gathered up his strength, you expect to hear some aphorism, some great political truth; but as often you are disappointed, cheated with some pompous but feeble piece of commonplace, ridiculously small as compared with the reflection or the premises which usher it in. The head may be of gold, but the feet are of clay. In like manner, there is a want of coherency and sustentation in his explanations of political principles or theories. A little care, a little modest pupilage to experience, would make that clear and strong which is now confused, vague, and feeble. You see that the mind of the speaker has not been really brought to bear upon it. It is clear that he wants to be a philosopher, but has not the enduring patience necessary to constitute him one. He is also too ready to grapple with every subject that comes before him, whether he understands it or not. This leads him to talk on so many questions, that he can not render himself perfect on any. There is an affectation of simplicity in his reasoning; but as his mind is by no means fertile, he constantly reproduces the same views; and this reiteration, which is intended to simplify and to impress more strongly the mind of the hearer, leads to an involvement which brings about quite the contrary result. Among the vices of his style of speaking is a habit of dogmatic assertion, persevered in without modesty, either of mind or manner. A constant egotism destroys the symmetry of his speeches, by displacing abstract reasoning on the question at issue, or declamation which might influence the feelings; and the irritable temperament we have already described still further distorts and deforms the products of his mind. For a man so ready to attack, it is wonderful how impotent he is in defense. Blind with rage, he strikes about him, right and left, and is unable to defend himself, because, in his fury, he does not see his own vulnerable points. His hot, intemperate passion runs away with his judgment. You see that he has got hold of a capital idea, which a master-mind, or even an inferior capacity, cool and collected, would work into a powerful sarcasm or a happy retort; but he is so distempered with vindictive feeling, is in such haste to wreak his vengeance on his adversary, that he applies the match too soon, and the explosion harms himself more than any one else. In this respect Mr. Disraeli is far his superior. With the same disposition to attack, the same love of personality, the same oblivious inclination to gratify private animosity through the medium of public debate, he has the advantage of Mr. Roebuck in his imperturbable self-possession. However excited may be his feelings, or however bitter his resentments, he never loses his temper. He utters his sarcasms at white heat.

Mr. Roebuck's manner of speaking is unique and original, without being agreeable. He is earnest and violent, without being impressive. He labors under great natural disadvantages. His appearance is not prepossessing, nor has he any of that fascination which invests some public men with an irresistible attraction, and propitiates favor even before they open their lips. Mr. Roebuck is small, even diminutive, in stature, and he has not those symmetrical proportions which, in some little men, supply the want of height. Continual ill health adds to an appearance of feebleness, which not even his mental energy and activity are sufficient to neutralize. His voice is also feeble. It has a harsh, sharp sound, like that which you will often hear from persons of confirmed ill temper. His face bears a soured expression, and if a smile ever finds its way to his mouth, it is the smile, not of good-humor, but of irony or sarcasm. A livid paleness of complexion may be the result of ill health, but it is more likely to be the consequence of habitually indulging a splenetic disposition.

His exhibitions in parliament, even his most successful ones of late years, present a melancholy spectacle of diseased vanity and overrated powers. Conceive the sort of person we have described always ill attired, sometimes culpably slovenly, sometimes extravagantly overdressed, taking up a prominent place in the House, from which he continually lays down the law to his Radical associates around him, who usually repay his arrogant interference with contemptuous smiles; conceive him keeping up a running commentary of ironical cheers, supercilious smiles, and theatrical gestures, on what is going forward in the House, and attracting attention, which does not always take the shape of pity, toward the absurd attitudes and contortions into which he puts his diminutive person; conceive him, after having thus, by involuntary pantomime, let out the conceit and self-sufficiency of his disposition, rising to address the House, with a full conviction stamped on his countenance that he alone, of all men there, can grapple with the subject before them—that he alone can extract truth and wisdom from it. Remembering all that we have said about his arrogance, his petulance, his needless repetitions and his outbreaks of passionate violence, imagine him confronting the House, his head, while he is standing, scarcely reaching above the level of those of others who are sitting around him, his arms swinging about with convulsive energy, now raised aloft in the air, now stretched downward toward the floor, and now pointing horizontally across the House, his voice elevated to the highest pitch of its little capacity, and now lowered to so feeble and inarticulate a whisper as to be scarcely audible even to his next neighbor; imagine, too, the conceited air of invincibility, the impotent attempts to express scorn, while rage alone is uppermost in the mind, the sarcasm enfeebled by spite, the irony arrested by chuckling self-approval, the mysterious threatenings, the awful enunciations of nothing, and puerile denunciations of every one, the waspish, snarling recognitions of the slightest interruptions, even though of the most friendly character ;—and you have some idea of the applicability of the epithets so aptly applied to his oratory by Mr. Disraeli, when he twitted him with his "Sadler's Wells sarcasms" and "meldramatic malignity." The longer Mr. Roebuck continues in parliament, the worse he seems to grow. Once, these exhibitions were rare exceptions, occasioned, and even justified, by provocation, and the main body of his speeches was such as to repay his hearers for the trouble of listening, while they reflected credit on himself. But now all his errors are multiplied, while the qualities which once redeemed them are becoming more and more obliterated. If we look back to his latest displays, we shall find his faults exhibiting themselves in an increasing ratio. In the face of such a steady and progressive decline, there does not seem to be any sound reason to hope for better things in future. But, on the other hand, we freely give him credit for moral integrity, and for an exalted sense of his political duties : it is impossible to say what may not yet emanate from such rare and sterling qualities of mind.

SIR THOMAS WILDE.

Sir Thomas Wilde is one of the most remarkable living instances of the facility with which men of talent and perseverance can rise to the highest posts in this country. He had, at the very outset of his life, social barriers to surmount, even before he could rise to the position of an attorney—barriers presenting to the young man of humble origin a much more obstructive and threatening front than any political difficulties offer to an aspirant who starts from a more favorable position. But even in his character of barrister, Sir Thomas Wilde was opposed by no ordinary obstacles. He was not called to the bar until he was five-and-thirty years old—a time of life at which those who profess to be acquainted with the subject will tell you it is utterly hopeless for any one to attempt success in so arduous a profession, where even the most decided talent must have the sanction of time in many years spent as a silent member of the bar, before it can hope for an opportunity of displaying itself. Sir Thomas Wilde's difficulties, however, did not stop here. Circumstances of a private nature, upon which some prejudice was created against him in the profession, would, it was said, preclude the possibility of his ever rising to great eminence; and he had, from the very first, to struggle, not only against that mass of inert opposition which is one of the greatest discouragements to those who choose the bar as a profession, but also against active prejudices, which jealous rivals were not slow to improve to their own advantage.

Talent, however, and perseverance, will overcome still greater obstacles than these. Great as his disadvantages were, they only make his subsequent successes more signal and wonderful. Less than thirty years of active professional and political life, in the course of which, not the most malignant enemy could impute to Sir Thomas Wilde any conduct such as would justify or corroborate early adverse impressions, present the obscure practitioner, who, in 1816, was scarcely deemed eligible to be admitted to the bar, in the exalted position of Lord Chief-Justice of the Common Pleas—a position which he does not hold by political manœuvering, but to which he was long since nominated, as being the most fit person to fill it, by the unanimous voice of the legal profession. Nor is his social position less remarkable than his high professional rank. Neither his origin nor his rank in society justified him in expecting to form a high alliance. Yet we find him the husband of a lady who, if not by the law of succession, at least by every moral law, is one of the nearest relatives of her majesty—a lady whose choice, if rumor be true, was made under circumstances of romance rarely associated with the dry and austere pursuits of the law, and who thus added a sanction, at once the most prized and the most graceful, to the privileges which, in this free country, successful talent can command.

In thus dwelling upon the success of Sir Thomas Wilde, it should be remembered that, during the interval between his first distinction at the bar and his first appointment to office, he met with some obstructions. At the bar his distinction was early recognized, and his advance rapid. He became a sergeant in 1824, and was made a king's sergeant in 1827. Nor was it long before he was recognized as being one of the first advocates of the day. The promotion of Sir James Scarlet, in fact, left him almost without a rival, and he might, in one sense, be said to have had the Court of Common Pleas at his absolute disposal. He also entered parliament as early as the year 1831, and was not undistinguished as a speaker, though he never attained any very high eminence. Yet although opportunities were frequently occurring of offering him that promotion to which, according to the customs of parliament, he was entitled, it was not till 1839 that the Whigs made him solicitor-general. In 1841, he was made attorney-general, but did not reap the profits or even the honors of that office, as the administration went out only a few weeks after his nomination. But fortune, which had so slighted him on this occasion, made him ample amends on the sudden return of the Whigs to power in 1846, for he had scarcely been reappointed attorney-general, and had not, in fact, been reëlected to parliament, when the late Chief-Justice Tindal died, and he was at once raised to the bench at the head of the Court of Common Pleas. But it will be obvious to the reader, that some powerful reason must have influenced the Whig government to withhold from him during so many years that official promotion for which he was so eligible. Whatever may have been their reason, his exclusion continued so long as almost to take, in the eyes of the public, the shape of persecution. They did not forget how a spirit of aristocratic exclusiveness had too often regulated their proceedings in the selection of members of the government; and when, at last, Mr. Sergeant Wilde was appointed solicitor-general, the effect of his having apparently been placed under a ban was to obliterate in the public mind the unfavorable impressions which rumor had circulated as to some events in his earlier career.

Of Sir Thomas Wilde's powers as a speaker, his continuous and triumphant success in the Court of Common Pleas is a sufficient proof. In estimating the quality of his mind, that success should not be allowed too much influence. His forensic triumphs were won rather by extraordinary ingenuity in the management of his case, and an overpowering physical energy and vehemence in addressing a jury, than by the display of the higher attributes of the orator. If he had had a more able competitor in the Court of Common Pleas, it is questionable whether he would so quickly have attained so unrivaled an eminence. Or if, for instance, he had been brought into close and constant competition with a man like the late Sir William Follett, he would at once have provoked comparison, and have suffered from it. Occasionally, the influence of a great cause would, for a time, elevate his mind, and draw from him passages which looked very like lofty eloquence. But these effects were transient only, and his ordinary style was one which rather dragged down his subject to the level of an extremely vigorous, but still only a practical mind, and precluded the possibility of his adding any to those monuments of forensic eloquence which have been left on record by some of his illustrious predecessors. Not that we would, for an instant, undervalue Sir Thomas Wilde's abilities as an advocate; on the contrary, they were such as to inspire absolute confidence on the part of his clients. You felt, when you had intrusted your cause to him, that he would not merely exercise upon it the ordinary ingenuity of a lawyer, but that he would also identify himself with your interests, and imbue himself with your feelings, so that you should readily admit that he had fulfilled all your wishes better than, even with the same talents, you could have done it yourself.

As a speaker in parliament, Sir Thomas Wilde did not, except on one occasion, take a very high rank. He always acquitted himself with ability, and never even approached to what might be termed a failure, by the exhibition of want of vigor, or of inability to cope with the argument of the question before him. But he brought the habits acquired at the bar, of redundancy, repetition, and constant appeals to the feelings, with too much carelessness, into a place where the audience are accustomed to have their intellectual palates catered for, even by an inferior class of speakers, and who look for something more than a mere straightforward expression of opinion. There was always plenty of power in his speeches, but it was rough and undirected, and his style was loose and wanting in emphasis. He made one great speech, however, which gave him immediately a strong position, by showing of what he was capable when a great occasion called his powers into full play. His speech on the privilege case of *Stockdale* versus *Hansard* was a masterly effort; but it was no proof of parliamentary talent, because it was an argument on law, not on politics. It was one of Sir Thomas Wilde's faults, as a speaker, that he took too much time to explain himself. He had no idea of compression, or of so disposing his argument as to avoid repetition. He would bestow upon an ordinary political speech almost as much time as he did in his great privilege speech. In the one case this diffusiveness was admitted to be necessary; in the other it became insufferably tedious. It was, probably, advantageous to Sir Thomas Wilde's reputation that he was not retained in the House of Commons long enough for him to exhibit his comparative inferiority as the legal advocate of the government on political topics, and that he has been elevated to a sphere of which, to all appearance, he is destined to render himself an ornament.

LORD SANDON.

THOSE who frequently obtain admission to hear the debates in the House of Commons, or who are in the habit of attending the meetings at Exeter Hall, will be surprised to find Lord Sandon thus included among the orators of the age. Strictly speaking, he has no title to be thus selected from among the great mass of members of parliament, who, from time to time, express their opinions in the House without aiming at any oratorical distinction. Neither in the intellectual quality of his speeches, nor in the manner of their delivery, is there any thing to distinguish him from the hundreds of members of parliament who are looked upon with confidence and respect by their constituents and the public at large. We have, however, at the very outset of this volume, stated that the scheme of the work does not confine it merely to those public men who acquire distinction by the arts and graces of oratory, but is extended to embrace those who, by the exposition of their opinions and their general conduct as public men, succeed in securing influence over large classes of their fellow-countrymen. Lord Sandon is one of these; and his position, whether in parliament or out of doors, is so important, that we are induced here to notice him in preference to many other men much more prominent and notorious, whose qualifications may be much more showy and pretensious than his, while they are far less useful.

Lord Sandon's claims as an orator may be very

summarily disposed of; they do not constitute his greatest merit. Considering his weight in the House, he is one of the least pleasing or prepossessing speakers there. Being a man of sound common sense, highly educated, and with very extensive information, the matter of his speeches is generally of a superior order, and on questions of a higher interest than the ordinary political topics of the day he displays an earnestness, at once religious and philosophical, which elevates the tone of his language, and invests his ideas with more weight and importance than would be attained by the specific value of his ideas or propositions. But it requires some patience and observation to detect these merits under a perpetual hesitation of speech, and an apparent confusion of utterance, which at first produce unfavorable impressions. But a little consideration satisfies you that these defects are of physical origin only—that the mind is right, although the organ of speech does not immediately perform its wonted duty. You see that there is a high tone of moral feeling, combined with great practical knowledge, and that the noble lord has a highly cultivated and well regulated mind, which has been well and assiduously applied to the elucidation and management of even the most minute details of public business. On subjects which have a religious bearing, such as Education, or matters connected with the Church, he is earnest and impressive, animated by the most exalted views for the welfare of mankind, and sustained by principles which he will not compromise, although ready to yield the most liberal acceptation to the views of opponents. On questions of practical legislation, involving the social welfare of the people, he distinguishes himself by a mode of handling them which is at once manlike and philanthropic — holding, with much uprightness and ability, a middle course between the harsh dogmas of some political economists, on the one hand, and the rash, sympathetic ardor of some political philanthropists on the other. With mild manners and benevolent purposes he has a manly spirit, which will not suffer itself either to be led away by delusive hopes of legislative perfectibility, or to be quelled by the threatening influence of congregated opinion. At the same time, although on the more vital principles of government, as connected with religion and morals, he displays an unyielding spirit, he is fully alive to the importance of party combinations, and to the necessity of occasional compromises in political affairs. His high character preserves his motive on such occasions from suspicion. The most striking sacrifice he made to expediency, within a recent period, was on the Sugar question. It will be remembered how his motion on the subject of the Sugar duties jeopardized the Melbourne administration: it might naturally have been supposed that, having taken so prominent and decisive a part on that question, he would have felt it necessary to adhere to a consistent course—to have been indifferent altogether to party considerations. Yet the result did not justify this expectation. Lord Sandon having given a steady support to the great measures of Sir Robert Peel's administration of 1841, did not choose to peril the existence of the government, as far as his example could have affected it, by opposing the new premier on the Sugar question. Yet, when we remember what were the grounds on which his motion in the first instance proceeded, we shall see that there was gross inconsistency in such a course. On the other hand, it should be remembered that Lord Sandon steadily refused to accept office from Sir Robert Peel, although, from his having been a member of his former government, he could have done so without impropriety or suspicion.

Lord Sandon's chief value and influence as a member of the House of Commons, however, rest on a ground wholly irrespective of politics. There are in that assembly, as almost everywhere else, two classes of men —the ornamental and the useful. The ornamental members, your Macaulays, Sheils, and a host of less distinguished men, make very fine speeches, and occasionally strike out grand ideas of policy and legislation. But there is also a large portion of work to be done in parliament, for which, with all their talents, they are unfit; and this is performed by those whom, for distinction's sake, we have designated as the "useful" members. The public have but little acquaintance with the laborious nature of the duties they have to perform. A glance at the mass of bills, public and private, which every session pass the House, to say nothing of those which are arrested in their progress, will show that not a small amount of time and attention must be bestowed on their details. Every measure is fully canvassed in all its bearings, and the most minute inquiry and discussion instituted into the probable effects of every clause. These matters are entertained and disposed of by delegated bodies of members who are called "Select Committees," and "Committees on Private Bills;" and of these Lord Sandon is a frequent and most valuable member. As the limits of time and convenience forbid these measures being discussed in detail in the House itself, great reliance is of course placed on the report of the Committee, and an influential member of such committees, like Lord Sandon, incurs constantly a serious moral responsibility. His integrity of character, the cheerful alacrity with which he thus gives up his time to this the most laborious and the least attractive part of the duties of a member of parliament, and his very general information and correct judgment, occasion his being constantly selected as a member of those committees. The amount of service thus rendered to the public, without praise or reward, is incalculable.

As a platform speaker, at meetings of a religious and philanthropic character, Lord Sandon is very influential. He is heard to much more advantage as a speaker in this sphere than in the House of Commons, where there is always something to embarrass even the most confident and accomplished orators. Here, too, his personal appearance propitiates—his intelligent countenance, radiant with amability and benevolence. Here he is always found to be one of the foremost in the earnest and persevering advocacy of every association, or of every plan that can possibly be anticipated to be beneficial to the human race. And his support is the more valuable, because it is not the mere ebullition of an enthusiast (who is often gratifying his own love of activity as disinterestedly working for his fellow-men), but the deliberate and steady determination of a practical and sensible man of the world, who will seldom patronize or aid in the promotion of any thing that he does not perceive to contain within itself the elements of permanent success. Upon the whole, according to his position and powers, we do out know a more estimable, disinterested, or useful public man, whether as a politician, a philanthropist, or a man of business, than Lord Sandon.

THE REV. HUGH M'NEILE.

In the foregoing pages it has been the object of the author not merely to illustrate and portray the characteristics of distinguished living orators, but also to show by many bright examples the extraordinary influence which the power of public speaking exercises in the advancement of those who have to carve out their fortune in the world. It has been seen that the possession of this power, allied, of course, to other valuable faculties, has sufficed to raise unknown lawyers to the highest social and political rank; to draw from obscurity literary men, and bear them onward until they have taken the most distinguished places in the councils of the nation; and that in the case of individuals to whom high birth has given more chance of success in the political world, the art of oratory has been necessary not only to enable them to compete with their less favored rivals, but also to secure them ascendency and distinction among their own compeers. If the limits of this volume had allowed, instances of the same powerful influence might have been drawn from various ranks and conditions of life; for every hustings and every platform has seen such triumphs, though neither the sphere of action nor the rewards of successful talent have been so magnificent. But, to take even a single instance from philanthropists, would have required so much space as to have prevented a due notice of more prominent and remarkable, if not always more able, public men. One exception, however, we must make, partly because the individual stands out in such bold relief from his cotemporaries both for his talent and his success, and partly because while the sphere of his action has been a legitimate one, his career illustrates in a remarkable degree a growing disposition in the public mind to bring the influence of religion more directly to bear than it did in a lax age upon the actual business of life—to restore something of its old power and efficacy to the office of THE PREACHER. The Rev. Hugh M'Neile has been now for many years in various ways before the public. His name is familiar to all; but a more intimate acquaintance with his talents and qualities of mind is possessed by, comparatively speaking, but a few. Without pretending to enter into any thing like a close or critical analysis of his character, we propose to supply a few of the leading traits and characteristics of this, in many respects, remarkable man, chiefly with the view to show how, in the church as well as at the bar, or in the senate, eloquence will raise even a humble and unknown man to fame and fortune.

Mr. M'Neile's elevation is almost solely to be ascribed to his ability as a preacher and public speaker. Born of respectable parents residing at Ballycastle in the neighborhood of Belfast, his early destination was to a career very different from that which he afterward chose for himself—one in which his fine natural qualifications and the higher faculties of his mind would have been wholly obscured. It would have been really a loss to his fellow-countrymen had the talents of M'Neile been allowed to rust in an attorney's office. Yet for that branch of the legal profession he was intended; nay, he was for a portion of his early life in an attorney's office. But either his own consciousness that he was fit for a more exalted sphere of activity, or the friendly counsels of some good genius, persuaded him to break from the growing trammels of the law, and betake himself to a study more congenial to the habits of his mind. He resolved to devote himself to the Church, and commenced the study of divinity, taking his degree of M.A. at Trinity College, Dublin. In the mean while, he had the good fortune to be selected by the Archbishop of Dublin (Dr. M'Gee) as tutor in his family; and here those attractions and superior qualities of mind and person which afterward rendered him so influential with a large portion of his countrymen, won him a reward which must indeed have been to him a prestige of future success. Mrs. M'Neile is the daughter of the archbishop, and their attachment was formed while the young student of divinity still held his post of tutor in the family. Their subsequent union was with the consent of Dr. M'Gee.

It can not be doubted that this was, in his then position, a most fortunate, even a splendid alliance. It gave him not merely what he no doubt prized above all worldly distinctions, but it also gave him that position and that introduction into public life, the want of which is always the greatest obstacle to one who has to rise by his own talents, however great they may be. He was not long in availing himself of the opportunity thus afforded him. He was immediately successful as a preacher. Nature had been lavish in her favor toward him. At his present age he would be accounted one of the finest-looking men even among his juniors by twenty years. But at the period to which we refer, when still very youthful, he was one of the most splendid-looking men of his day, with a commanding and dignified person, a face strikingly handsome, even in mere features, but far more noble from its highly intellectual expression; and a voice so magnificent as to realize all one's conception of the perfection of voice as an organ at once of majesty and harmony. There is but one orator of the day whose voice even approaches that of Mr. M'Neile, in its extraordinary volume, capability of modulation, and sonorous tone. In Lord Denman's best days it was as positive a pleasure to listen to the tones of his voice, as to listen to the most perfect vocalist. But the voice of Mr. M'Neile, exalted in all its chief charms, with the addition of much greater power and capacity for inspiring awe. With such qualifications as these it was not surprising that he should soon attract large and admiring congregations, more especially of those who, more than our own sex, are susceptible to spiritual influences. But his public displays were not confined to the pulpit. His strong political feelings, and his intense hatred, as an Orangeman, of the Roman Catholics, made him an eager and vehement speaker at the Rotunda meetings in Dublin, and it can easily be conceived how his spirit-stirring tones would stimulate those excitable audiences, when he spoke on a theme in which his passions were so propitiously sanctioned by his religious principles. The influence of the archbishop was of course very serviceable to him in this career, *his* exalted position in the Church lending a sanction to even the most violent diatribes against popery.

Mr. M'Neile having for some time been one of the most prominent characters, both as a preacher and a political speaker in Dublin, resolved to change his sphere of action, and, like all men of high ambition, he determined at once to bring his powers to the test of the critical opinion of the metropolis. Most of our readers will not require to be reminded of this period of his life. During the thirteen years in which he was located in or near London, he was distinguished as a preacher, and also occasionally as a writer. He did not, however, take a standing so high as he had held in Dublin, nor did he attain an equal influence. With a small, but highly respectable and influential class of churchmen, he was all in all. But the public opinion of the metropolis is, fortunately, not so readily agitated as that of Dublin, by the breath of party passion, and the consequence was that while the talents of Mr. M'Neile were universally admitted, they were considered to be partially obscured by the extreme virulence of his anti-Catholic opinions. The termination of his metropolitan mission was not exactly flattering to his spiritual pride. He had a rival to contend against, whose attraction, at least, though not, perhaps, his sterling value, exceeded his own. Edward Irving out-Heroded Herod in the exciting stimulants he offered to the spiritual appetite, and the malicious will have it that on one fine day, congregation, trustees, sexton, and all, left the exhortation of Mr. McNeile to throw themselves at the feet of his erratic but brilliant antagonist. Of the truth of this statement the parties themselves can be only judges.

From the metropolis Mr. M'Neile was invited to Liverpool, where he has preached (at St Jude's Church) now for twelve years. The causes which militated against his success in London gave him at Liverpool an immediate ascendency. Political and religious passions ran as high, at that time, in Liverpool, as they had done in Dublin, and as the nature of Mr. M'Neile's mind led him immediately to ally himself with the Tory and Anti-Popish party there, it is not surprising that with his extraordinary talents, energy, and enthusiasm in the cause, he should immediately have achieved a great triumph. He took a leading position in Liverpool from the first day of his appearance there. Those who have not been accustomed to study the provincial mind can have no conception of either the nature or the extent of the influence Mr. M'Neile wields in Liverpool. Whatever may be the differences of opinion as to the truth or the fairness of his politico-religious doctrines, all must admit that an influence which has been attended solely by the exertion of extraordinary talents, allied to an unimpeachable moral character, is at least a legitimate one; and if the public mind of Liverpool allows itself to be swayed by the will of this spiritual dictator, why, the public mind of any other part of the kingdom has no right to complain. It appears from recent circumstances as though even the authorities of the town were, mechanically speaking, under his thumb.

The corporation have many times shown themselves his dutiful agents, and he is said to be as entirely mayor-maker for the good people of Liverpool, as ever the great Warwick was maker of kings. That his influence is of no ordinary kind, over his congregation at least, was proved shortly after the visit of Prince Albert to Liverpool some time since. He preached a sermon upon that event, which was afterward printed at the request of his congregation. It required no small amount of that absolute reliance, amounting almost to adoration, with which he has inspired the people of Liverpool to make them complacently endure a discourse with such a title as this:—"Every eye shall see him; or Prince Albert's visit to Liverpool, used in illustration of the second coming of Christ." Without, however, caviling at any extravagances which the earnest spirit of Mr. M'Neile may lead him into, it is just to him to say that he is a most active and useful member of the community to which he belongs. He is always sure to be the foremost man in any local movement. Not a meeting but boasts his presence, not an audience but is familiar with his manly, soul-stirring eloquence. He takes the lead in all agitations for social improvement. He would fain attach to all such movements a religious sanction. He is not, however, content with this, but in the enthusiastic severity of his opinions, he always intermingles political feeling, even with his philanthropic exertions, and by so much he impairs his own usefulness. Of course this successful career has not been unaccompanied with more solid acquisitions. Last year he was made a canon of Chester Cathedral by the bishop of that diocese, who respects his usefulness or fears his talents. In worldly wealth Mr. M'Neile is rich.

Mr. M'Neile's eloquence is more distinguished for its power, energy, and declamatory vehemence, than for the more refined and graceful, though not, perhaps, the higher qualities of oratory. His natural advantages have influenced his style. His commanding, even majestic presence, and magnificently sonorous voice, pointed out to him his true sphere of excellence. But it must not be understood that Mr. M'Neile would therefore have been disqualified to shine in a different sphere. Had he schooled his mind and trained his faculties for more deliberate and artificial display, he possesses that natural ability and superiority which would have enabled him to achieve a success as powerful as any he has yet attained either in the pulpit or on the platform. But as it is, his language is more forcible than choice; his imagination is too prone to that luxuriance which is the common fault of his countrymen; and that torrent-like enthusiasm which, unfortunately, is too often allied to political passions and sectarian hatred, carries him on as if by an irresistible impulse, in a heat of declamatory vehemence, till he forgets to observe those nicer graces of style and language which form one chief charm in the master-pieces of more cool, collected, and self-restrained orators. But, on the other hand, it is this abandonment of the mental powers to his absorbing ideas, this ready yielding to ungovernable impulses of deep feeling, that gives to the eloquence of Mr. M'Neile its originality, its grandeur, and its irresistible power.

THE END.

www.ingramcontent.com/pod-product-compliance
Lightning Source LLC
LaVergne TN
LVHW020234110826
845151LV00003B/921

* 9 7 8 1 4 2 5 5 3 1 0 1 0 *